Angola in the Frontline

Michael Wolfers and
Jane Bergerol

Other Books by Michael Wolfers

Black Man's Burden Revisited (Allison & Busby, 1974)
Politics in the Organization of African Unity (Methuen Studies in African History 13, 1976)

Translations

J. Luandino Vieira *The Real Life of Domingos Xavier* (Heinemann, 1978)
Michael Wolfers (Editor) *Poems from Angola* (Heinemann, 1979)
Amilcar Cabral *Unity and Struggle* (Monthly Review Press, New York, 1979 and Heinemann, London, 1980)

Angola in the Frontline

Michael Wolfers and Jane Bergerol

Zed Books Ltd., 57 Caledonian Road, London N1 9BU

Angola in the Frontline was first published by Zed Press,
57 Caledonian Road, London N1 9BU in 1983.

Copyedited by Anna Gourlay
Proofread by Rosamund Howe
Cover photo courtesy of Angola Information
Cover design by Jacque Solomons
Maps by Margaret Mellor
Typeset by K.M. Phototypesetting
Printed by The Pitman Press, Bath, U.K.

British Library Cataloguing in Publication Data

Wolfers, Michael
Angola in the frontline.
1. Angola–History
I. Title II. Bergerol, Jane
967'.304 DT611.5

ISBN 0-86232-106-9
ISBN 0-86232-107-7 Pbk

First Reprint, 1985

US Distributor
Biblio Distribution Center, 81 Adams Drive,
Totowa, New Jersey 07512

Contents

Abbreviations

AFL-CIO	American Federation of Labour-Congress of Industrial Organizations
AFV	Armoured Fighting Vehicle
ANC	African National Congress of South Africa
CAC	Amilcar Cabral Committee
CIA	Central Intelligence Agency (of United States)
CIR	Centre for Revolutionary Instruction
Comecon	Council for Mutual Economic Assistance
COMIRA	Military Resistance Committee of Angola
CPB	People's Neighbourhood Committee
DISA	Directorate of Information and Security of Angola
DOM	Department of Organization of the Masses (of MPLA)
EEC	European Economic Community
ELP	Portuguese Liberation Army
FAPLA	People's Armed Forces for the Liberation of Angola
FAR	Revolutionary Armed Forces (of Cuba)
FLEC	Front for the Liberation of the Enclave of Cabinda
FLN	National Liberation Front (of Algeria)
FLNC	Congo National Liberation Front
FNLA	National Front for the Liberation of Angola
FRELIMO	Mozambique Liberation Front
ICFTU	International Confederation of Free Trade Unions
IMF	International Monetary Fund
JMPLA	MPLA Youth
MFA	Armed Forces' Movement (of Portugal)
MPLA	People's Movement for the Liberation of Angola
NATO	North Atlantic Treaty Organization
OAU	Organization of African Unity
OCA	Communist Organization of Angola
ODP	People's Defence Organization
OMA	Organization of the Angolan Women
PAIGC	African Party for the Independence of Guinea Bissau and Cape Verde

PDA	Democratic Party of Angola
PDCI	Democratic Party of Ivory Coast
PIDE	International Police for the Defence of the State (of colonial Portugal)
SADF	South African Defence Force
SDECE	Service for External Documentation and Counter-Espionage (of France)
SWAPO	South West Africa People's Organization (of Namibia)
UNITA	National Union for the Total Independence of Angola
UNTA	National Union of Angolan Workers
UPA	Union of the Peoples of Angola
UPNA	Union of the Peoples of Northern Angola

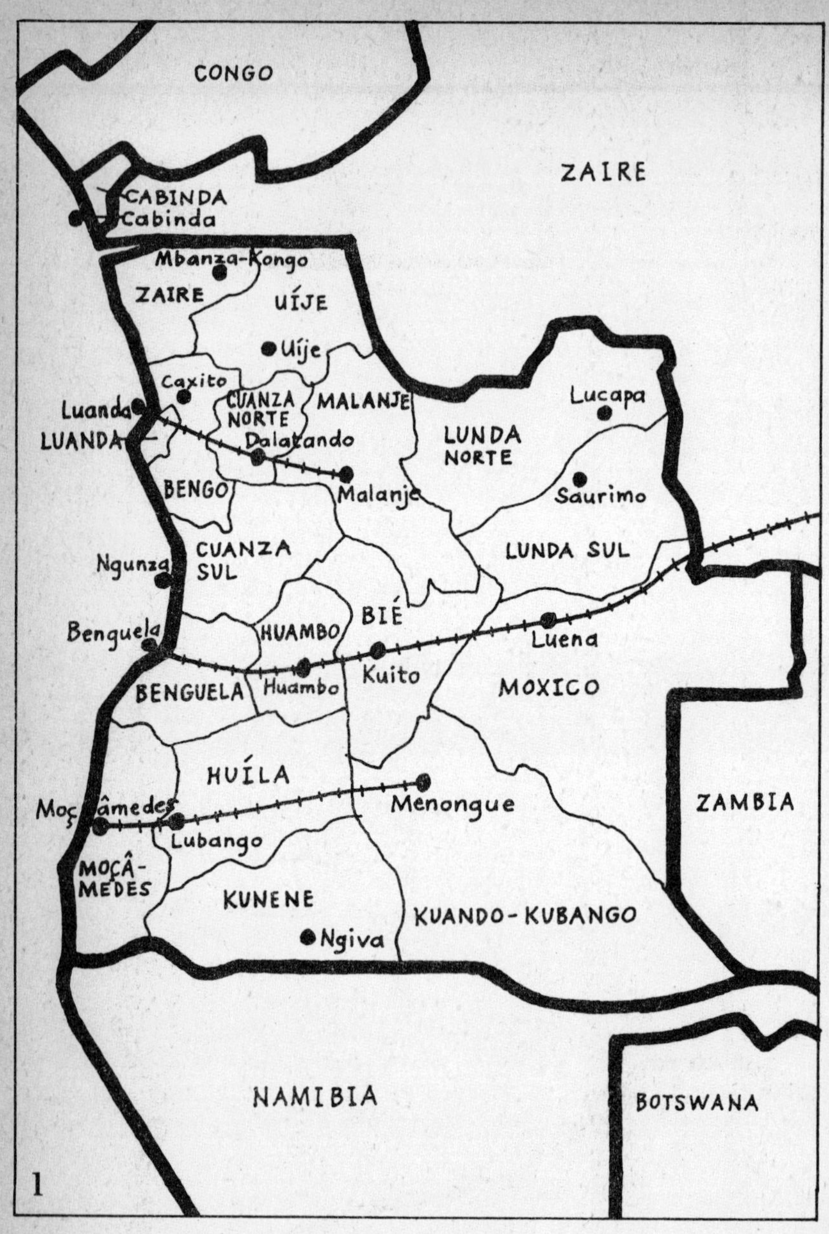

Map 1: Angola's Provinces and Their Capitals

Map 2: The Centre-Southern Front, 1975–76

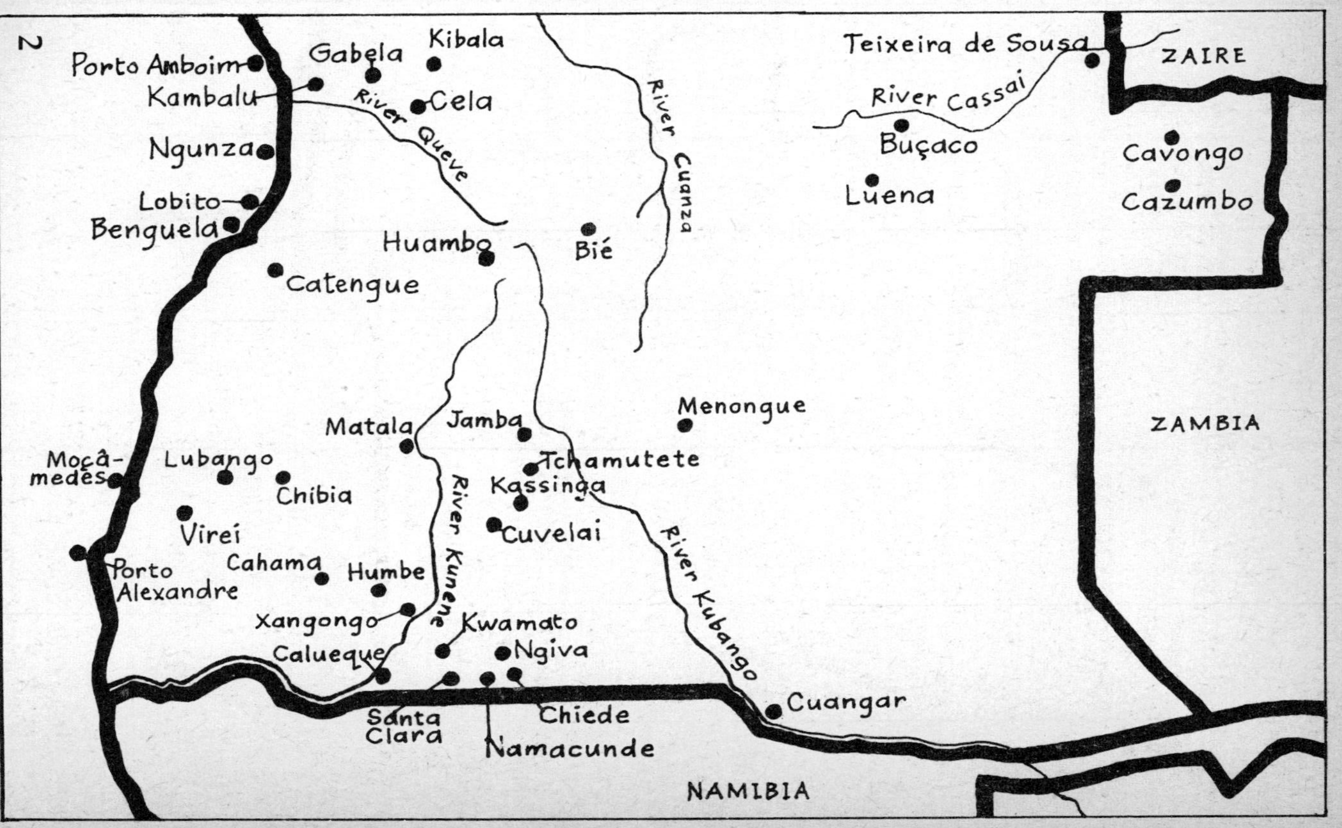
2
Porto Amboim
Kambalu
Gabela
Kibala
Cela
River Queve
Ngunza
Lobito
Benguela
Huambo
Catengue
River Cuanza
Bié
Teixeira de Sousa
ZAIRE
River Cassai
Buçaco
Luena
Cavongo
Cazumbo
ZAMBIA
Menongue
Matala
Jamba
Tchamutete
Kassinga
Cuvelai
River Kunene
River Kubango
Moçâ-medes
Lubango
Chibia
Virei
Cahama
Humbe
Porto Alexandre
Xangongo
Kwamato
Ngiva
Calueque
Santa Clara
Chiede
Namacunde
Cuangar
NAMIBIA

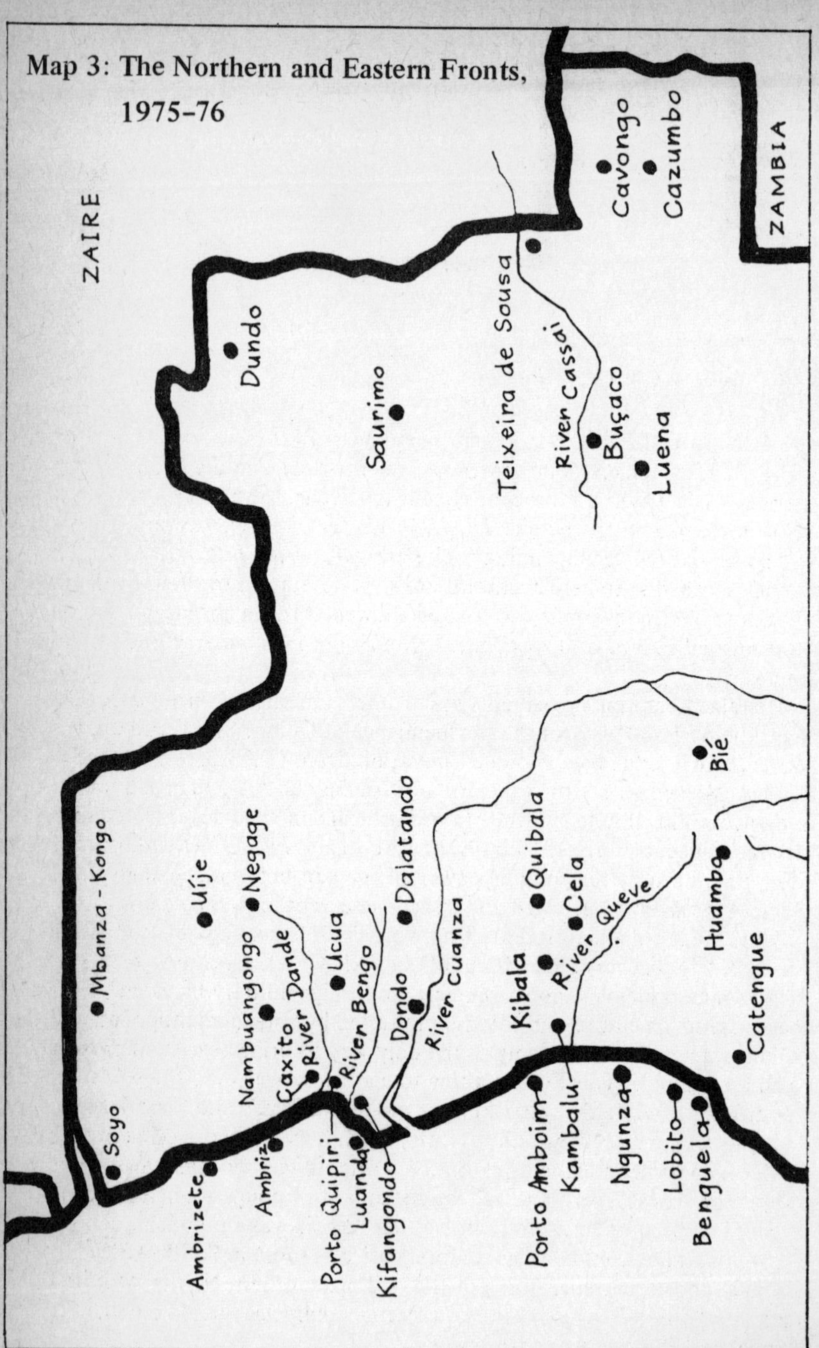

Map 3: The Northern and Eastern Fronts, 1975–76

1. Introduction

Why the West Intervened

When the Armed Forces' Movement swept away Portugal's fascists on 25 April 1974, Africans understood there must be some change in the colonies. But independence was not a foregone conclusion. General Antonio Spinola, placed in the leadership of the Armed Forces' Movement (MFA), was opposed to it, he had set out his strategy in his book *Portugal and the Future.* The West would be called in to help backward Portugal develop its overseas territories; a measure of self-government would be allowed. African advancement would be permitted so long as it was limited enough not to threaten white capitalist interests.

Genuine liberation movements in Portugal's colonies at once opposed the plan: the African Party for the Independence of Guinea Bissau and Cape Verde (PAIGC), the Mozambique Liberation Front (FRELIMO) and the People's Movement for the Liberation of Angola (MPLA), all called for total and unconditional independence from Portugal and a handover to the organized resistance. By July 1975 both the PAIGC and FRELIMO had officially been recognized by the colonial power as rulers of fully independent states. Yet in Angola, civil war raged and outside intervention was escalating.

What made Angola different? Why was MPLA less acceptable to Portugal and its NATO backers than FRELIMO or PAIGC? All three movements stood for the same principles: non-alignment, no foreign military bases on their soil, social justice, an end to unbridled exploitation by foreign monopolies, and the building of a socialist economy as the only way to bring peace and prosperity to all their people. There was nothing to choose between the three. Yet Angola was different from either Mozambique or Guinea Bissau and Cape Verde.

It was an immensely wealthy country; with huge off-shore oil reserves by 1975 which earned it a mention on CIA world oil reserve charts, even though production was still very low by world standards. Enough foreign mining surveys had been undertaken to prove that Angola was a promising source of a range of strategic minerals as comprehensive as those in South Africa: uranium, cobalt, chrome, fusing quartz and many others. Neither Mozambique nor Guinea Bissau and the Cape Verde archipelago could compete. Angola was 'Portugal's African Jewel'.

A second long-term factor worrying NATO was the strategic domination by the West of the South Atlantic. The Indian Ocean was covered. Diego Garcia, Kenya and South Africa were all available for NATO fleets, but the South Atlantic was becoming a problem. Zaire, politically dependable, had no coastline to speak of, Walvis Bay in Namibia was already an international issue at the United Nations. The Angolan ports of Luanda and Lobito had to be secured so that US navy vessels could continue to call there. By 1973 the US was heading a NATO special group dedicated to building a South Atlantic Treaty Organization involving countries of the southern cone of Latin America (Argentina, Brazil, Uruguay were seen as the most important), with a secret option of a South African contribution, as well as direct participation by the NATO powers themselves. 'Angola for the Americans is the Atlantic' Admiral Leonel Cardoso told British and US correspondents in Luanda on the eve of independence. 'I give the Americans three years to win it.' The Admiral was in a good position to assess the American attitude: not only was he a leading officer in Portugal's NATO navy, he was Portugal's last High Commissioner in Angola.

Angola presented further problems for Western interests. Unlike Mozambique, its economy was strong and completely independent of South Africa. Under an independent government, Angola's enviable resources could finance a no-strings-attached development policy. It could also finance other liberation movements fighting apartheid, colonialism and Western exploitation in Zimbabwe, Namibia and South Africa.

Namibia, in particular, must gain independence from illegal South African occupation. The United Nations was already legally involved. To some extent Angola would determine what kind of independence Namibia would have by its support (or lack of), for the guerrillas of the South West Africa People's Organization, SWAPO.

The Western powers were blocking African revolution, which slowly but surely was gathering strength under the leadership of the liberation movements. FRELIMO was no less revolutionary than MPLA, but the West felt that its hands would be satisfactorily tied by dependence on South Africa for foreign exchange, trade, transport and investments. Besides which, Pretoria's troops only had to penetrate a few miles from their common border with Mozambique to strike at the capital, Maputo.

So Angola, more than Mozambique, came to be seen as the main, immediate threat to continuing Western domination of southern Africa.

Western Action Against MPLA

The roots of Western intervention in Angola's independence struggle were put down at the time of the Congo crisis. While the US bloodily intervened in Africa, for the first time directly committing its troops on the continent to stave off Lumumba's revolutionary forces, the Angolans to the south launched their armed struggle. Angola at once became part of a Central African arena under strategists' observation. The People's Movement for the Liberation of Angola – the first Angolan nationalist organization to be formed – was founded in December 1956. By 1961, many of its underground militants had been arrested and leaders were locked up in Luanda's political prison. On 4 February 1961 activists stormed the prison and tried to release their comrades. Armed only with cutlasses and stones they were easily beaten off by well armed fascist police, but the settlers panicked. Their worst fears were apparently confirmed when in March a general peasant uprising took place across the north, fuelled by members of a tribally-based underground, the Union of the Peoples of Angola (UPA), founded by Holden Roberto in 1958.

By April, the MPLA was organizing for guerrilla war; the first columns of MPLA guerrillas entered Angola from Zaire in mid 1961. On 9 October a squadron of 21 MPLA guerrillas led by Tomas Ferreira was killed by UPA inside Angola. According to a former UPA Secretary General, Jonas Savimbi, in 1961 Holden had been engaged by the Americans to act for them. These murders were UPA's first actions against the MPLA. Later, Savimbi would split from Holden, form his UNITA, and by 1972 be involved in similar anti-MPLA tasks, this time on behalf of the Portuguese. The US gave UPA enough concrete support to build up a liberation front that was plausible at the OAU, but posed no real threat to Washington's NATO ally, Portugal. UPA was led by a small group of corrupt and tribally exclusive Angolans from around Holden's birthplace in north-western Angola. Holden himself had been brought up in Zaire where he now lived, and his relationship with General Joseph Mobutu, a CIA fund recipient since 1960, and then President of the country, soon blossomed. Although there were 300,000 exiled Angolans in Zaire who had fled Portuguese rule and settler atrocities, UPA did not win their mass support.

UPA was the least popular of the three political organizations active amongst exiled Angolans: MPLA had a substantial following, based on its demand for total independence and its active community welfare self-help programme. So, too, did the smaller Angolan Democratic Party (PDA), built around north-eastern exiles from Uije who disliked Holden's corruption and tried to model their work on MPLA community style meetings and projects. After MPLA opened its first northern guerrilla front, Zaire forced MPLA to close its external headquarters and its offices in the country. UPA's orders were to train fighters to exterminate MPLA guerrillas whenever these could be found. A faithful account of UPA's anti-MPLA campaign has been given by a leading UPA officer, Margoso, who rebelled against the leadership and took part in an attempt to overthrow Holden. (The coup was overcome by Mobutu's Zaire paratroopers and Margoso fled to Brazzaville where he joined MPLA.) Portuguese army officers also frequently reported UPA's warfare against MPLA.

MPLA now set up its external headquarters in Congo-Brazzaville. From 1963 onwards, MPLA's access to northern Angola was through openly hostile Zaire, and it had to run the gauntlet of UPA anti-MPLA squads. Undeterred, it launched a Cabinda front from Congo-Brazzaville in January 1964.

Meanwhile, UPA's failure to gather support was causing concern. It was encouraged to seek an alliance with the PDA, and in March 1962 together they formed FNLA, the National Front for the Liberation of Angola. Had the front ever been a genuine joint organization it could have kept PDA grass-roots support and might have developed into a genuine liberation movement. But UPA insisted on maintaining the upper hand, PDA officials were either kept out of the leadership or given fringe positions – its secretary-general was appointed to head Social Affairs and then not given any means to carry out a social policy. FNLA was the same as UPA and so lost the exile community's support.

UPA's fierce tribalism, its lack of a mass following, and Holden's firm grip on the organization soon alienated another interest group in its ranks: the southerners, led by Jonas Savimbi. The roots of the UNITA organization he founded will be examined in more detail later.

But although Savimbi may have originally set up his own organization as a genuine break-away from UPA, by 1972 documentary evidence from the files of Portugal's political police, PIDE, show that his UNITA was Portugal's firm ally. Its task was to break MPLA's eastern military and political front, launched in 1966 from bases in Zambia. Savimbi was corresponding with senior Portuguese officers and receiving weapons, supplies and medical treatment from the Portuguese army.

So what kept three rival Angolan 'liberation movements' alive for the conflict that followed the Armed Forces' Movement coup in 1974 was not mass popular support. Before 1974 this had been reserved for the MPLA alone. It was counter-revolution that provided for FNLA and UNITA, and that physically kept them going. And the counter-revolution was being waged by the United States, Portugal, Britain and France, against the MPLA.

The NATO contribution to Portugal's wars against MPLA has been documented elsewhere; so has South Africa's military assistance. In 1966 this began with South African military and helicopter patrols in the south-east, directed at SWAPO guerrillas crossing into Namibia from Zambia. But it soon embraced the eastern front where MPLA influence was spreading among the peasants and proving too much for the Portuguese army to control.

Nixon's 1970 Tarbaby Option, giving full support to white racism in southern Africa, further indicated NATO intervention on Portugal's side against the Africans. Chemical and biological warfare against MPLA liberated zones – not against areas where either UPA or UNITA were present – was carried out with US toxic agents.

Rumblings of revolt in the Portuguese army, and Spinola's book, alerted NATO and South Africa to the possibilities of sudden and probably violent change in Portugal, sometime before the April 1974 coup. By September 1973, the CIA was financing a major recruiting drive for the FNLA army in Kinshasa. Angolan exiles on their way to work were arrested by Zaire police and para-military units and taken off to FNLA's Kinkuzu base for military training. They were kept in readiness there for months, and there was no suggestion that they join the maquis. It is interesting that the forced recruiting programme coincides with one of the most critical points in MPLA's history. In 1973 the movement was deeply divided, struggling with internal political factions – especially Daniel Chipenda's 'Eastern Revolt' – suffering from heavy Portuguese military action in the east, and with its armed struggle at an all-time low ebb. As a result of its many problems, it was receiving less Soviet support in weapons than at any other time, before or since. Earlier, it had also declined substantial offers of Cuban military aid for training its guerrillas, preferring Angolan to foreign instructors.

In March 1974, a month before the coup, Nathaniel Davis was appointed US Assistant Secretary of State for African Affairs. Davis had a record in Chile and earlier in Guatemala, during a US conceived 'pacification program' against left forces. The OAU responded to the appointment with an unprecedented formal protest that it 'most vehemently condemns any move to import into Africa the odious practice of political destabilization'. A series of similar appointments followed. A former member of the Chilean 'Operation Centaur 1973' team, Deane Hinton, was made US Ambassador to Kinshasa. William Bowdler, involved in the Cuban Bay of Pigs campaign, was sent as US Ambassador to Pretoria. South Africa publicly welcomed these appointments as 'a clear indication of Washington's attitude towards us'. Some well informed journalists sensed the reinforced South African connection, and articles such as Tad Szulc's 'Why are we in Johannesburg?' in *Esquire* magazine, queried what was going on behind the scenes.

From the April 1974 coup onwards, the Portuguese military and intelligence establishment, with the exception of an almost insignificant handful of committed progressive officers, backed FNLA and UNITA for power. Many felt that Savimbi represented the most pliable ruler for a neo-colonial Angola where Portuguese could continue to milk Angola's profits, and Portugal would be saved from sliding alone into oblivion, deprived of its overseas glories. FNLA was to provide the strong-arm tactics and the bully boys.

The US was already firmly committed to FNLA; now it launched a covert operation to get its cyphers into power. John Stockwell, head of the CIA task force on Angola, says:

> The objective of the Angola program was to impede and interfere with the Soviet program in Angola. In April 1974 the Portuguese coup indicated that they would give up their colonies. In May the Chinese went in with 112 advisors and then followed with 450 tons of arms (to FNLA). In July the CIA began funding Holden Roberto of the FNLA modest amounts of money, more than you pay to buy information, but not what would be required to buy arms and airplanes. The Soviets came in the next month, August, and announced that they considered the MPLA to be the representative of the Angolan people.

At this stage, Stockwell states, Soviet arms had not been shipped in to reinforce the light arms and 122mm rockets the guerrillas had been using against the Portuguese army. Later, he says 'they began a trickle of arms to the MPLA, but that was very modest'.

After the coup, only the MPLA demanded full and complete independence from colonial rule. Both Holden Roberto and Jonas Savimbi, heading FNLA and UNITA, declared publicly on several occasions – and their statements were widely carried in the press – that Angolans were not ready for independence and that some form of gradual transition would be appropriate. Savimbi signed a formal 'cease-fire' with Portugal at this stage, within six weeks of the coup, at a time when peaceful demonstrations in Luanda were still being violently dispersed by club-wielding fascist, white police. FNLA followed. MPLA did not sign its cease-fire and emerge from underground until November. By that time Spinola and his supporters of continuing colonial rule had been overthrown and a new government in Lisbon was pledged to grant full independence to the colonies.

Spinola had gone too far. Originally appointed to head the government as a figure for national reconciliation, by officers far more left-wing than himself, he had discarded the Armed Forces' Movement's principles and begun to seek a personal mandate to swing the country to the right. His foreign policy was to ignore the genuine liberation movements and seek out pliable Africans to build into a third force in alliance with the settlers. In Guinea he started the FLING. For Angola, he summoned a secret meeting on the island of Sal, Cape Verde, in September 1974. Those who attended included Holden Roberto, Jonas Savimbi, Daniel Chipenda (heading the MPLA breakaway faction the 'Eastern Revolt', that was trying to oust the leadership) and the President of Zaire, General Mobutu. Under the Sal accord, which has never been published, Portugal would begin immediate withdrawal of its troops stationed along the Zaire border, and of its frontier patrols, so that FNLA and Zairean troops and weapons could flow freely into Angola. Training of UNITA troops would continue in the UNITA area, already carved out under the colonial agreement. Portugal would hand over weapons to the UNITA, which would then claim to have captured them in the guerrilla war. Spinolist officers and civil servants would be appointed to key posts in Angola.

After Spinola's overthrow at the end of September 1974, serious efforts were made to solve the Angola problem, resulting in the November cease-fire with MPLA, and the January 1975 Alvor all-party independence conference at which all three organizations were placed on an equal footing. (The Spinola Sal plan eliminated MPLA but sought to conceal this by including Chipenda and his small breakaway faction.) Admiral Rosa Coutinho was sent as Governor and finally undermined white secession plans by ordering whites to join the black organization of their choice and abandon thoughts of apartheid politics. But he was powerless to rule Angola effectively. Only a handful of Armed Forces' Movement officers were scattered in the huge country: army, police, and even fascist secret police of the PIDE still carried on almost as usual. The Sal plan went ahead, the army withdrew from the north, and FNLA and Zaire's troops poured in.

John Stockwell says:

> In late Spring 1975 Zairean troops went in with the FNLA . . . You had

> Zairean combat advisors with armor and recoilless rifles and mortars. But in mid September we put in Zairean battalions, air commando battalions flown in in C-130s fighting as foreign units, if you will, in the conflict . . . . What our propaganda was churning out was that the Soviets intervened with massive arms shipments and the Cubans went in with their regular army units . . . . Each major escalation was initiated by our side, by the United States and our allies.

In March 1975, the fighting began with the FNLA murdering 50 unarmed MPLA recruits on their way to an MPLA camp near Kifangondo, north of Luanda. It was the start of nearly four months of FNLA-Zaire terror against the people of Luanda. Meanwhile UNITA was training thousands of young Ovimbundu it called east to Luso to 'defend the tribe'. The training was rudimentary, there were no politics, just basic instruction on how to handle a gun. When these recruits were ready, UNITA also began to attack MPLA, with the help of PIDE and Portuguese army officers usually wearing FNLA uniforms. In July, Luanda threw out FNLA and UNITA. FNLA had already balkanized the north, UNITA now seized control of the centre. MPLA still held firm in the far south and the east. By August 1975 it was clear that the disciplined and politicized men of MPLA's small fighting force were running rings around the disorganized and recent recruits of FNLA and UNITA.

All the country's cadres, including those whites who felt themselves to be Angolans, had joined the MPLA. Workers had identified with a movement that called for decent wages, literacy, health care and education for all and honestly spelled out the hard work that would be involved in building a new state free of exploitation. Figures as different as Tom Killoran, US Consul General in Luanda, and left-wing Admiral Coutinho, openly stated the MPLA was the only organization capable of governing the country. The transition government ministers of FNLA and UNITA had proved to be disastrous, interested only in feathering their nests, or enjoying their privileges.

Much greater outside support would be needed if these Western-backed groups were to gain power. And so the South Africans came in from Namibia, and US, French, and British mercenaries were organized in the north, while the US army co-operated with the South African army to boost the Zairean and FNLA troops' fighting capacity. MPLA was desperate for help. Portuguese officers were continuing to block any open arms shipments the MPLA tried to bring into the country from its Tanzanian bases, planes were turned back and ships ordered out of the harbour without unloading. It resorted to underground arms running. The amounts were pitifully small: a Peugeot van with rifles under piles of clothing, headloads as in the guerrilla days, small craft plying the coast unloading a Yugoslav freighter lying out to sea, municipal council workers leaving their jobs and spending the night unloading dinghies and going to work next morning as usual. Later, after the South African invasion, more ships turned up off the coast and were unloaded in the same way.

What went wrong with the Western plan? If, as Stockwell, the CIA task force chief claims, the US initiated every major escalation, why did it not win the war? The problem was that by 1975 neither the US, fresh from its Vietnam defeat, nor Britain nor France felt able to involve their own armed forces directly in Angola. FNLA and UNITA were no match for the guerrilla forces of MPLA. This left the West with two alternatives: mercenaries and racist South Africa, which was impatient to start, having recently passed legislation empowering its army to intervene 'anywhere south of the equator' if its interests were at risk.

The mercenaries, who had begun to lose their reputation as invincibles were found useful in the last resort. The South Africans ought to have been 100% reliable: armed with the latest NATO weapons, their officers and technicians trained in the West's military academies, and their politicians and intelligence organization in close contact with Western governments and high finance. So the South Africans were given the go-ahead. On this secret accord, Senator Barry Goldwater said 'There is no question but that the CIA told the South Africans to move into Angola and that we would help with military equipment.' The South African Defence Minister, Pieter Botha (later Premier) said his country intervened with the foreknowledge and encouragement of the US. Vorster's tongue at the time was tied.

All the major Western powers were deeply involved with FNLA and UNITA. Britain and France provided mercenaries, weapons, and military communications as well as extensive diplomatic and financial support. Third World countries from Africa to the Caribbean were put under heavy pressure by the West not to assist MPLA. Yet MPLA defeated the imperialist military intervention.

The magnificent, rocky, rushing river Queve, halted the South African Defence Force just long enough for MPLA to call upon socialist Cuba for fighting support. So Cuba's volunteers, fighting alongside Angolans, held off apartheid's crack units. Around Luanda, Angolans alone defeated the combined FNLA-Zairean-mercenary offensive. But as the weeks dragged on, it was world opinion that contributed to the West's defeat: in 1976 people would not stand by and accept apartheid in alliance with Western capitalism as a liberating force. They pushed for recognition of the MPLA; and by 1982 the USA is the only UN member not to have done so.

PART 1
War

2. South Africa Invades

Looking South

The first signs of outside interest in the future of Angola after the coup came in southern Kunene province, on the Namibia border. Initiated by UNITA and South Africans inside Namibia, talk spread of a 'greater Ovambo' state, straddling the frontier.

In June 1974, shortly after its 'cease-fire' with Portugal, UNITA opened an office in Ngiva, capital of Kunene province. and only 12 miles from the border. The same month, South African forces launched a fierce campaign against SWAPO in northern Namibia, and hundreds of young people fled into Angola. Under the nose of the Portuguese fascist and military authorities in Ngiva (no replacements had yet been made despite the April coup), the Namibians flocked into the UNITA office, the only legal black organization. They were directed north to Luso and the UNITA offices there. By July 1974, the people of Luso were puzzled by the wave of young Namibians flooding into the town. 'We Angolans of MPLA were still underground. The Namibians went to the UNITA office and were taken off to Zambia. The Portuguese let it go on, as it was all part of the links they were trying to build between UNITA and SWAPO. SWAPO itself of course didn't have an office.'

The UNITA office in Kunene, and the activists sent there, began spreading talk of 'Ovambo unity'. The colonial border between Angola and Namibia cut through the Ovambo-Kwanyama tribe. Older people could still aspire to tribal unity, and peasants who had lost their land to settlers might also see it as leading to land reform.

South African propaganda in Namibia echoed the UNITA talk, calling for a 'greater Ovambo bantustan' to embrace the Angolan Kwanyamas. Otherwise, Pretoria seemed unconcerned with events and continued with its detente politics. There was a sharp change when MPLA opened its Ngiva office early in 1975, after signing the Alvor Independence Agreement.

In April, Pretoria made its first move, calling for a meeting with the MPLA and FNLA Kunene delegates. MPLA's John Hailonda and its FAPLA Regional Commander Pedro Domingos attended with three FNLA officials. On the South African side was SADF Namibia Commander-in-Chief Jannie de Wet and the BOSS Namibia officer Piet Ferreira. A number of other white officials from the Ovamboland bantustan made up the South African team. It was to be the first in a series of unpublicized meetings on the border, in which the South Africans made repeated attempts to provoke the MPLA. This first time, they complained about UNITA recruiting Namibians and voiced concern about the Kunene River Scheme. It was strange, in view of their complaints, that the South Africans had not asked to meet the UNITA delegate. As for the Kunene Scheme, this was to provide the main pretext for the war.

Portugal's Third Development Plan for 1968-73 had belatedly included a 'white barricade' project to obstruct the nationalists with massive new arrivals of settlers. Costly integrated development schemes at Cabora Bassa in Mozambique and on the Kunene River in Angola were to provide irrigation for the white farmers and cheap hydro-electric power to South Africa and Western mining companies in the Republic and Namibia. By April 1975 Pretoria had invested over Rand 600 million in Kunene. Dams at Gove near Huambo, and Calueque and Ruacana in Kunene were more or less finished, and in Namibia the first generating station was ready to go on stream less than a mile from the border. Britain had a substantial but indirect interest in Kunene; by mid-1976 it was due to supply most of the electricity required by Rio Tinto Zinc at its Rossing uranium mines.

Later in April the South Africans again called a meeting, this time raising questions over the Ruacana dam. In May, South African sources warned the Portuguese District Governor of Kunene of a possible SADF attack against Ngiva. Horrified, he warned the MPLA, FNLA and UNITA and called for a meeting with the South African officials. At the meeting the Boers made every attempt to provoke an admission from the MPLA that they favoured Namibia's armed struggle and SWAPO. They failed.

Pretoria, however, needed a concrete pretext for putting its forces into the south. It seemed that since the 'communists' were not easily baited, aimed provocation had to be organized. A South African engineer working on the Calueque dam inside Angola was attacked, robbed and beaten up by a bunch of UNITA soldiers in July. This was the signal for South African army units to enter Angola. They headed straight for the dam and the village where all three Angolan nationalist groups had offices. FNLA and UNITA were disarmed. MPLA prisoners were taken, the MPLA office sacked and the SADF made off with every paper and document they could find.

Shortly afterwards, on 9 August the SADF moved permanently on to the Calueque dam site with a force of over 1,000 regular soldiers, armoured cars and helicopters. Twelve and a half kilometres inside Angola, Calueque straddles a strategic dirt road running west-east along the border, then turning north parallel to the only tarmac highway. It was a road the army was to use in its major invasion in October. Now the SADF also occupied Ruacana.

Two companies of Portuguese troops were still stationed in Kunene and their Commanding Officer requested explanations from Pretoria. On the day of the meeting, FNLA and UNITA declined to attend, so accompanied only by MPLA the Portuguese proceeded to the South African camp at Calueque. But the Angolans were not allowed in; guns were trained on the small group of MPLA cadres and soldiers. After some time, the Portuguese re-emerged escorted by two South African Panhard armoured cars. The Portuguese captain explained that the South Africans said they had been 'provoked' into taking 'operational action' but would stay only a certain time 'to protect the dam'. Some weeks later, pressed by angry reporters, the Portuguese Ministry of Foreign Affairs released a long overdue communiqué that appeared in the Lisbon press on 5 September: a month after the South African action. It said:

> A squadron of some 30 soldiers [according to Pretoria] [had been] removed to the dam site as necessary protection of South African workers. This was necessary to guarantee – in conformity with the agreements in force between Portugal and South Africa – the maintenance of water supplies vital to the subsistence of the Ovambo population in the area.

Not only was this characteristic of South African propaganda, deliberately understating the size of its force and implying that its intervention was actuated by concern for the Ovambo peasants' water source, which was in no way affected by the dam – it also indicated which way the Portuguese wind was blowing. Portugal, despite a progressive government, was to remain inactive and silent as increasing evidence of South African military intervention mounted up in southern Angola. There is little doubt that President Costa Gomes and later Pinheiro de Azevedo had been silenced by the NATO powers. In the Lisbon Presidency the military positions of the MPLA, FNLA and UNITA were marked with coloured pins on a wall map. By the end of August white pins (South African?) were beginning to spread across the southern part of the map. But they were never reported in the abundant communiqués on the Angolan situation from mid 1975 on.

There was a sharp escalation in South Africa's attacks at the end of August. On 21 August the SADF came across the border at Santa Clara – the main crossing point on the tarmac highway – in armoured cars (AFVs), firing mortars and bazookas. They fired on the nearby FAPLA base, on the supermarket which they then looted, and after writing 'MPLA USELESS' on the walls of the immigration control point returned to Namibia. On 25 August UNITA was forced out of Ngiva after attacking the MPLA, leaving FAPLA in full control. The 26 August saw immediate retaliation by the SADF. Penetrating 10 kms up the highway as far as Namacunde, where MPLA had a Centre for Revolutionary Instruction (military and political training centre), the SADF came into the dusty roadside village with three helicopter gunships, a force of more than 30 AFVs and Unimog troop transports, attacked the MPLA installations, which, thanks to good advance scouting procedures were empty, and then moved on to Chiede, eastwards on a track road. These were to be main entry points for the South African 'Zulu' column two months later.

The MPLA delegate, John Hailonda, and the FAPLA commander went with a white flag to the Santa Clara border post to demand a meeting.

> When we got there the South African troops all came up at once,

> pointing guns at us. We began to laugh. I called for their commanding officer. Eventually he came but refused to comment on their attacks. The next day, 27 August, I left Ngiva at dawn and stayed away till after mid-day. As I turned back towards the town about 50 kms north, we met people fleeing. They said the South Africans had attacked Ngiva and there were many dead. They had been looking for troops. They had come in with 30 AFVs, many troop transports and helicopters. Many people were killed – one helicopter gunner killed six civilians and FAPLA standing together in one group – and others were taken away in sacks.

A SWAPO eyewitness reported:

> The events of 27 August were a well calculated move which came after UNITA was forced to abandon Ngiva on the 25th. It was launched at about 11 am and we found out later from our people in Namibia that it had started from Grootfontein and Ochikango. 30 AFVs, 18 helicopters, 28 troop carriers and a spotter plane were mobilized for the Ngiva attack.
>
> They first encircled the town with armoured cars before they went in with helicopters attacking key positions and bombing installations such as the electricity generator. Most of the people in the town were unarmed civilians simply not in a position to defend themselves. Those who were not killed or maimed by bullets were wounded with petrol bombs thrown to devastate the buildings during the attack. Because of work by missionaries to bury the unknown victims, it is difficult to give an exact number of people killed in this invasion. One week afterwards 80 bodies were still lying unattended. The following morning, 28 August, the SADF returned to Ngiva and looted the bank, stores and people's abandoned homes before withdrawing again to Oshakati.

A young Angolan pioneer, Zeca, one of a group in an MPLA camp, was burned to death with one of those petrol bombs; a FAPLA Commander, Comandante Kalulu, was also killed.

The South Africans had excellent intelligence for their Ngiva attack. They were accompanied by half a dozen PIDE officials who took them to the homes of MPLA supporters – FNLA, still present in the town, was untouched.

In the wake of the Ngiva massacre, FNLA and UNITA along with a group of Namibians recruited by UNITA, attacked the wounded FAPLA garrison and drove MPLA out of the Kunene capital.

Meanwhile, the South Africans were also active further east. The People's Movement had begun voluntary military training for supporters south of Lubango in the Jamba area. Political work carried out by workers of the Companhia Mineiro do Lobito (a Krupp subsidiary mining iron ore at Kassinga) had built up a solid MPLA base of support in the area. Heading the political cadres was Faustino Muteka, an Umbundu, whose brother was active in Huambo mobilizing peasants for the '*Frentes de Kimbo*' (Village Fronts) and later murdered by UNITA. Military training started with carved sticks until rifles could be smuggled to them in the back of a Peugeot van. Jamba was a strategic area of criss-crossing tracks linking the border area with the rich farming lands of Huila, and the central highlands further north. Pretoria was particularly interested in gaining permanent road access through Jamba to supply the Huambo area; fighting was thus constant between UNITA and MPLA in this area from August 1975.

Advance reconnaissance was regularly carried out by the Jamba training camp southwards into the Cuvelai area. A FAPLA officer, a former Portuguese commando with considerable military experience, spotted armoured cars one day in September. The South Africans had set up a training base for UNITA between Tchamutete and Cuvelai, which allowed them to keep a closer watch on the movement of SWAPO refugees still streaming out of Namibia. They had also established a regular supply route north from Runtu, a major SADF air and ground forces base in Namibia.

A mixed force of ELP (Portuguese Liberation Army, fascist military under the honorary command of General Spinola) UNITA and FNLA now attacked the MPLA Jamba training camp. Numbering almost 2,000 and well equipped by the SADF, the mixed troops routed the MPLA trainees. Later, from the hills, the survivors watched their fuel supplies being carried off in South African lorries. During September all over central and southern Angola white troops and sophisticated South African weapons began to appear. South African fibreglass bazooka casings were found, armoured cars and South African mortars and light artillery were rushed into Angola, handled mainly by Portuguese ex-army commandos (many from Mozambique), while a small core of South African intelligence and military personnel were in key UNITA towns.

Unchallenged in the majority of provincial capitals from Cabinda in the north to Luena in the east, Lubango in the south and Luanda itself, the MPLA was in a clearly buoyant position; its small, ill-equipped forces had responded courageously to the murderous and massive FNLA influx from Zaire. Previously, the only fighting forces of note in the centre and south were the FNLA-Chipenda squadrons (Chipenda's Eastern Revolt faction had finally left MPLA and joined Holden Roberto). UNITA's 'army' was a rabble of ill-trained youths with no guerrilla experience. The few guerrillas deployed against MPLA on the eastern front during the first war of liberation were too few to make any impact on organization or discipline in the UNITA ranks. Some, like one of Savimbi's former bodyguards, had deserted to MPLA.

Towards the end of September in Cela, near Huambo, a strong and organized fighting force equipped with light artillery attacked FAPLA. 'They had South Africans and Zaireans with them by this time – we knew this from our behind-the-lines intelligence in Huambo. They used field guns and 120mm mortars and sophisticated military strategy.' But in spite of the fresh outside intervention on the southern front and the Zairean battalions deployed in the north, in early October MPLA still ran 11 of the 16 provincial capitals. Huambo, Bié and Menongue were with UNITA, and Sao Salvador and Uije with FNLA.

The FNLA had failed to pierce the MPLA's northern front line running eastwards from Luanda to Malanje. Fighting on the northern front fluctuated up and down the 'coffee road' around Ucua east of Caxito. The Benguela railway was largely in MPLA hands: UNITA controlled sections around the city of Huambo, Bié and the stretch at Cangumbe its main eastern base camp. MPLA units began thrusting towards the heart of the central highlands, anxious to forestall further foreign intervention before Independence Day. Ill-equipped, the FAPLA were optimistic: they had, after all, held their ground against far superior numbers of troops so far. They stood ready, small groups of men led by young Angolan officers with experiences either of the guerrilla war or former military service with the colonial army. Huambo was in UNITA hands and the South African military was already there.

In the last week of September, FAPLA, at Vila Nova do Queve, Monte Belo and Ussoque, Cuma, Catata, Cacunda and Chipindo began to advance. The first target was a South African military and supply base that had begun forming shortly before at Chicomba, just south of Huambo.

On 4 October the inhabitants of Nkurenkuru, a small village in Namibia on the south bank of the Cubango river, found their main street clogged by a South African Defence Force convoy. It rumbled in from the east and ground to a halt. First came camouflaged SADF armoured cars followed by small, armoured assault vehicles.

Then came the South African troop transporters, and behind them, vehicles 'like cold storage vans', and field radio units. To the onlookers' surprise a contingent of uniformed Portuguese came next, following a truck flying the Portuguese flag; behind them were transporters full of French soldiers whose uniforms were of the same design as the South Africans, but green instead of brown. Many of the soldiers of the strange column wore MPLA badges.

During the halt, a young South African soldier asked at a house for water. While he was drinking he asked how far it was to the Angolan capital; 2,000 kilometres they replied. They were Angolans and the soldier broke into fluent Portuguese. His parents, the Matosos, had emigrated years before to South Africa. Among the Angolan family were teenage girls who had fled the UNITA terror in Bié barely a month earlier. One of them, Filomena Bernardo, was a 16 year old trained FAPLA fighter who had escaped a UNITA firing squad, been raped and assaulted and fled south. The column rumbled out of Nkurenkuru west towards Ovamboland and the main border crossing point at Santa Clara. Later that day, the Nkurenkuru South African garrison crossed into the Angolan border town of Cuangar, linked to Namibia by slow moving ferry, and handed out new NATO FN rifles, delivered by the convoy, to FNLA and UNITA troops stationed there.

Before nightfall Filomena and her sister went down to the river. They found Matoso and another white South African soldier, both dead. 'They had killed themselves.' Whether it was suicide or summary execution of men who did not want to fight in Angola, these young South Africans made their stand. They fell before they had touched Angolan soil.

The Battle for Luanda

From early October the UPA-FNLA offensive to take Luanda from the north was on. They drove MPLA out of Caxito, back towards the capital with far superior numbers of men and weapons. MPLA blew the bridge across the Dande river and opened the sluice-gates of a small dam 60 kilometres east at Quimia, to prevent the enemy's armoured cars from fording the river. Reliable information from prisoners spoke of a massive build-up for the Luanda offensive, including crack troops from Zaire's Kamanyola division, mercenaries and even 300 Chinese standing by in western Zaire.

The northern front seemed to hold the key to the fate of Angola. At all costs Luanda had to be defended for the declaration of Independence on 11 November.

On 4 November Armando Sousa, working at the National Bank of Angola received a letter from the transition government Premier, Lopo do Nascimento, ordering him to report to the Northern Front immediately.

Lopo do Nascimento was one of the movement's leading clandestine political workers who had remained in Luanda throughout the anti-colonial struggle, and was now playing a key role in bringing together the guerrillas and external wing of the movement with those who, like himself, had survived in the townships, working for the colonial business community. Armando Sousa, a *mestico* (Angolan of mixed parentage) from the petty bourgeoisie, had been trained as an artillery gunner by the Portuguese while on national service in Guinea Bissau.

> I was at the front the next day, stationed on the low hills above Kifangondo, getting the hang of the equipment. We still only had anti-aircraft guns, and we realized our only hope was to train them straight down the road and beat them back with direct fire . . . . There were one or two Cuban instructors up there, but the main body of Cuban troops had not yet arrived and it was we Angolans who had to make do with the little training we had.

Probably this partly accounted for some of the FNLA-UPA optimistic assumption that despite the unfavourable terrain, they would break through to Luanda.

> Their problem was 11 November [said Commander N'Dalu, a guerrilla veteran on the northern front]. If they tried taking Luanda from the other more easterly road, which would have been viable militarily, it would have taken from two to three months: Kifangondo looked the best way but it meant they had to enter a corridor of 500 metres, where the road forms a straight dyke through the marshes, and where they could not disperse their troops. This was where we had the advantage: we were on the heights. They seemed to have banked on getting through somehow to Kifangondo, and the Luanda water pumping station, cutting off Luanda's water supply and forcing our surrender.

Rumours that Luanda was without water had been circulating for the previous two weeks in Lisbon. 'They said water was getting to Luanda by air from Uíje through the good offices of the FNLA – this helped us understand what the objectives were.'

The main offensive from the north began on 8 November, with artillery fire and exploratory advances by armoured cars. MPLA's infantry, deployed ahead of the escarpment where Sousa and his anti-aircraft guns were positioned, skirmished with the advancing troops whose armoury was beaten back by the artillery. Far from smashing through the MPLA lines and walking into the capital, the FNLA-Zairean columns were becoming bogged down and discouraged. A Portuguese mercenary in FNLA ranks reported:

> From what we could see, it would only be possible to get through with heavy artillery and tanks. The only possible help free from future compromise was the South Africans, since they had, with UNITA, already advanced hundreds of kilometres into Angola. South Africans were contacted and on the night of 8 November, two Hercules C-130 planes of the South African Air Force touched down in Ambriz. From their bellies a group of about 20 soldiers jumped, impeccably uniformed and in a rapid operation, two gigantic weapons and three 140mm Howitzers were rolled down the back ramp trailed by trucks carrying more than 1,000 projectiles! . . . .
>
> According to the South Africans 24 shells would be enough to neutralize the Kifangondo defences. Around 10 o'clock on the 9th we started mounting the South African battery under the shelter of Morro do Cal. At the same time a 130mm Zairean fieldgun was put into position.

There had been heavy fighting all day on the 9th. Now the South African and Zairean batteries were in position for the final onslaught: there was only 24 hours more to go.

Attemps to create panic in the city, behind FAPLA lines, had failed. A light plane had air-dropped leaflets calling on 'Portuguese and Angolan brothers and the people of Luanda' not to be alarmed at the prospect of the imminent arrival of FNLA-UPA, the people 'would not be molested'. The city emptied as people took refuge in the south, the artillery fire could now be heard in the commercial downtown area; but the atmosphere was serene, confident and busy. Western newspaper correspondents were alarmed, some insisted on flying out on the eve of independence. But in the *bairros*, the militias were drilling, the children practising independence songs, and at the Palacio do Povo there were feverish, final preparations for the historic day.

Reports from the front 12 miles away came nightly as weary FAPLA officers returned to the city for a quick meal and a few, snatched moments with their families: their main complaint was of mosquitoes, christened now and for the remainder of the northern front fighting 'the B52s'.

News from the south, of the SADF advance was grim, but on 9 November, a new confidence was in the air. The handful of Cuban correspondents were in an almost jaunty mood reflecting the decision, taken in Havana on 5 November at a Communist Party Central Committee Meeting, to send a volunteer force to defend the Angolan revolution. Heavy weapons were at last coming in from Moscow, and on the night of 9 November the first BM21 40-pod mobile 122mm rocket launcher 'The Stalin Organ' was secretly driven up to Kifangondo and positioned under cover of darkness to target the enemy artillery. 'Our troops didn't even know about it: only General Staff Headquarters.' The BM21s had arrived at dawn that morning – in the nick of time.

At 5 am on 10 November UPA-FNLA launched their final advance on Luanda. Zaire was fielding three infantry battalions, or 3,000 men, on the northern front. About 200 Portuguese mercenaries were deployed in command and spearhead positions. The Zaire army had also contributed at least 12 AML armoured cars with crews totalling around 100 men, a 130mm Howitzer, an M-106,7 battery and a shelling squadron numbering a further 100 or so men and bringing the Zairean contribution up to around 3,500 men. FNLA had four infantry battalions, a company of 160 mercenaries, an AML Squadron, an M-106,7 battery, totalling altogether some 3,300 men on active military duty.

The enemy artillery opened up first. 'There were two kinds of firing – psychological and ballistic. The psychological shots were intended to fall round the city and panic us: people would not realize the guns firing the shots could be 30 kilometres away.' Shells fell near the Petrangol oil refinery, well within the industrial suburbs of the capital, and others at Grafanil, the major suburban military base where a woman was killed.

> The plan was to let them fire. Then we would return simulated fire to trick them – we couldn't pretend not to be there, so we fired pot shots now and again from a small gun, and a few mortars to create an impression of general weakness and disorganization. Santos e Castro, [the Portuguese Colonel who was Commander-in-Chief of the UPA-FNLA and mercenary force] was taken in. Anyhow he'd thought out his plan badly [Commander N'Dalu recalled]. We knew the 500 metre corridor was our trump card: our idea was to let the armoured spearhead through the corridor and fire on the last of the armoured cars to block off the whole column. But when they began to advance, one of their AMLs opened fire and hit the parapet of one of our gun emplacements. The comrade returned fire which messed up the plan and we only destroyed two of their armoured vehicles. Then we opened fire on their artillery positions with the BM21. The first salvo of ten shots silenced everything in one go.

The UPA-FNLA and South African artillery was never fired against Luanda again, and was withdrawn hastily northwards where the South African, Portuguese and Zairean crews were safe. The MPLA used the Stalin Organ only against enemy artillery; so it was hardly fired again on that Northern Front.

The noise of the multipod rocket launcher was fearsome: and the direct fire from the anti-aircraft guns down the road swept the terrified UPA troops into the surrounding Kifangondo marshes. Panicking, jumping from their trucks, they fought and slithered in the deep mud swamps. The mercenaries desperately manoeuvred their vehicles to escape by road but many were forced to flee on foot, making no attempt to regroup their demoralized rank and file. The toll of the 'suicide column' led into death by Colonel Santos e Castro, lay in the Kifangondo marshes. But Luanda was safe: Independence was declared that night and the flag of the People's Republic slowly hoisted to the masthead in May Day Square.

Boer Invasion

In September FAPLA military intelligence had received reports of unmarked helicopters unloading weapons and supplies deep inside Angola at Chicomba, south of Huambo on a small, dirt road. Orders had gone out to advance on the Chicomba area and take Caconda, thus joining up the central and southern front in the shortest time possible. For Agostinho Neto, the Chicomba intelligence confirmed his analysis that South Africa was preparing to further escalate its intervention.

On 18 and 19 October peasants in the border area and Portuguese traders still active in the extreme south, reported that Nord Atlas aircraft had begun unloading troops. Mark II on the Angola-Namibia border was the place where the planes were unloading white and black South Africans. But, the informants said, the blacks had whites' features; they were white painted black. Throughout September scattered but growing reports of movements of white forces in the Moçamedes and Virei areas further west had been coming in. But the whites had been identified as Portuguese: a mixture of well-known settlers and outsiders, former commandos from other African colonies – especially Mozambique – recruited by South Africa as they left the country before its independence in June. This Mark II business was different.

On the night of 19 October, the FAPLA Ngiva Commanding Officer, Comandante Franca, left the town with his troops on eastwards patrol; it was occupied from the west by white troops. The white column was accompanied by UNITA which stayed in Ngiva while the white force pushed north. Suddenly the southern command in Lubango was flooded with reports of white troop movements. In western Kunene, a white force, predominantly settlers, reinforced by mercenaries and South African weapons began moving towards Moçamedes. On the 20th, two columns of the South African Defence Force crossed into Angola. One entered Angola west of Namacunde, branched east to Chiede and went on to take Xangongo (ex-Roçadas). The second column, spearheaded by AFVs, moved rapidly out from Ruacana in a two-pronged attack north.

Part of the column moved in on Xangongo to join up with the Namacunde division. The rest pushed straight on north, to take Cahama, a strategic cross-roads town and the gateway to Huila province along the only tarmac highway from the border. From there they thrust a further 9 kms to Humbe and paused. It was 9 pm on 21 October when the news reached FAPLA General Staff in Lubango.

The FAPLA Southern Front command was in disarray. No heavy weapons were available, (and nobody trained to use them if there had been), capable of withstanding attack by the regular forces of the best-armed military on the African continent. MPLA had not a single armoured car on the Southern Front to stand up to the dozens now rolling through Kunene and Huila under South African command. Artillery was almost non-existent in the FAPLA lines, until a matter of days before the invasion. Unfortunately, the limited number of pieces that had arrived from Moçamedes that week were non-operational: there were no gunners for the 122mm Grad P. The FAPLA infantry in Kunene had taken to the bush realizing the uselessness of firing rifle shots at this massive, motorized, armoured advance. No major road-block was organized between Humbe, where the SADF was ensconced, and Lubango, FAPLA Southern Front General Staff Headquarters.

The South African Defence Force cut through FAPLA's southern front-line with almost no fighting. Leading FAPLA commanders, such as Kalulu and Cowboy, had been killed in the murdering forays by the South African forces during August and September, and in early October as they tested the strength of the MPLA in Kunene, the gateway of the north.

Clearly FAPLA were not operating any heavy weapons and had little ammunition for their small arms. During the constant fighting around Jamba and Matala, FAPLA had been forced to retreat several times owing to lack of ammunition. FAPLA was not a regular army, but a makeshift affair centred on the First War of Liberation guerrilla cadres and the MPLA supporters from the cities who had done service in the Portuguese colonial army. Volunteers with little or no military experience swelled the ranks. General resistance and military service was declared only on 23 October 1975, as the extent of South African aggression became clear. There was a void between the senior officers and the rank and file, there were no middle ranking officers and cadres, so vital to the efficient conduct of military operations.

Reinforcements were immediately despatched to the dam at Matala (that supplied Lubango's electricity and water). All commanding officers for the Southern Front were assembled, and there was a glimmer of hope that reinforcements might come from Benguela and the Central Front Command. The arrival from Moçamedes of the Grad P without gunners had been a terrible moment. On 22 October, around 11 am, reports began coming in of an enemy group of 13 AFVs and troop transporters pushing north from Humbe. They met brief resistance from a FAPLA roadblock at Chibia (ex João de Almeida). Hopelessly outgunned and outnumbered, FAPLA withdrew

Meanwhile, through the beautiful rolling farmlands high on the Lubango plateau near Humpata, other South African AFVs were closing in around Lubango.

At 9 am on the 23rd the firing began. FAPLA managed, briefly, to gain nominal control of Humpata heights, and spirits rose slightly, encouraged by messages from Benguela that a relief convoy had started out, including a few artillery gunners, some of whom were Cubans from the Benguela training camp. Orders were to hold Lubango as a defensive line at all costs; reinforcements were due in mid-afternoon and a plane had been despatched with weapons.

The local radio station began broadcasting appeals to those with cars and buses to drive out and meet the convoy, bringing them to the beleaguered city as quickly as possible. The Radio Clube de Lubango, a local settler commercial radio station, had been taken over by MPLA supporters who had formed a citizens radio service under a young Angolan, Nelson Bandeira: he was to stay on the air till the South Africans entered the city. The relief column never reached Lubango. At mid-morning the South Africans broke the FAPLA roadblock 11 kilometres south of the city and the soldiers fell back to a second defence line two kilometres further in. There were many dead. In the city limits, especially in the working-class suburbs of Mitcha and Santo Antonio, the military were distributing weapons for a last ditch stand by militias and civilians. Meanwhile, radio-telephone conversation intercepts of pilots speaking English were reported from the airport.

The firing grew heavier as the city went to the barricades. Around 1.30 pm the second defence line ceded. Covering his troops' retreat with a mortar, Commander Dack Doy died firing at the enemy AFVs; he was the only man at the frontline experienced in handling the mortar.

Shortly afterwards, the Benguela relief plane contacted air traffic control: it was instructed to land as fast as possible; the airport was still safe. Hardly had it touched down, at 2 pm, than South African AFVs, moving in from the north, began to shell the airport. A small group of Angolan gunners had disembarked, and a few weapons had been unloaded. To save the arms, the plane hurriedly took-off back north, with the news that the airport was now under South African control. An MPLA pilot, Azevedo, and Carlos Mangas a militant, had come to Lubango to collect information for the central front HQ in Benguela. The Lubango FAPLA command urged them to make a dash for the Lubango airport and try to take off in their small plane before the South Africans had completed encirclement of the airfield and Lubango.

As Mangas, Azevedo, and his Swiss wife, drove up the last hill before the airport, a group of South African AFVs suddenly appeared in the road ahead, cutting them off. Hit by machine gun fire, the car swerved and halted directly in front of the advancing column. For the next two hours, Azevedo and his wife – who died within an hour of each other – lay in the wreckage as the South Africans deployed themselves around them. Trapped and bleeding but not badly hurt, Mangas feigned death and observed the invading force.

He counted 42 AFVs, some cream and brown for desert war, others camouflaged green and daubed 'FNLA' in white, followed by camouflage-decked Bedford military transporters carrying Portuguese ELP and Bushmen contingents wearing FNLA Chipenda insignia. (The Bushmen had been deployed as reconnaissance and infantry by the Portuguese in the first war of liberation.)

By mid-afternoon all hope had gone. The Benguela relief column had not got through in time. The airport was in South African control and the hoped-for plane had not unloaded its cargo. The city people threw up a desperate and last minute defence, manned by militias, civilians and children – the MPLA pioneers, armed with their fantastic little guns, home-made from chickenwire, rubber bands and sticks and able to fire live bullets. FAPLA was in complete disarray, its operational commander dead. All efforts now were directed at an orderly military evacuation of the city.

FAPLA now had orders to set up a defence line as close to Lubango as possible. The choice was Cacula, 70 kilometres north on the main highway to Benguela. That night FAPLA bivouacked 36 kilometres out of Lubango. Matala, Quipungo and Vila Branca were still free; further north at Caporolo, a force of 200 men, with a handful of Cuban instructors from the CIR guarded the Benguela heights. Aside from Caporolo, there was nothing but the Catengue CIR, with its fresh trainees and Cuban instructors.

Confusion about the strength and nature of the South African advancing force persisted in Benguela, where Jorge de Morais 'Monty', a guerrilla veteran, was in command of the Central Front. Monty moved south to see the situation for himself, exasperated at the contradictory reports from refugees and seriously concerned by news from military intelligence. Even now, 25 October, barely two weeks before Independence Day, there was no effective barrier to halt the invasion. Some even doubted that a full scale South African invasion was underway, dismissing the facts as 'exaggerations'. If the South Africans had pushed ahead, Angola might have been theirs. But the West's plan was for taking Luanda by the northern black force.

The armoured columns forced the FAPLA at Cacula to retreat. A general retreat north began, abandoning Matala, Quipungo and Vila Branca and thus opening up the road between the Namibia border and Savimbi's headquarters in the central Highlands.

On 28 October Neto was fully briefed on the disastrous situation. There was no time to be lost; help was needed quickly. On the 29th, FAPLA's Dora Squadron moved south from Quilengues and reoccupied Cacula. The SADF again clashed with them, but this time they lost two AFVs to FAPLA fire. These were probably the first SADF losses in the invasion.

Back in Benguela, ammunition had been running low for some weeks, as the Benguela command was supplying FAPLA lines trying to push through to Huambo. Fighting had been sustained and available infantry was now limited. Many FAPLA soldiers were fresh from the CIR, set up in October with Cuban instructors, and had only a few weeks training behind them, mostly political groundwork and no combat experience. There were B-10 guns with a small supply of shells, 60mm and 82mm mortars and the 122m Grad Ps, also with shells: but no trained gunners. The Cuban instructors could operate them, but the only Angolan Monacaxito gunner, *Comandante* Graça, had been killed at Cacula.

With the second fall of Cacula, the advancing columns could now fork right to Huambo or left to attack Benguela. There was an attempt by MPLA to defend Quilengues, but the South Africans' AFVs came up east of the town in a flanking movement that indicated their accurate knowledge of the terrain. This was not surprising since several, leading local settlers had been recognized in the Lubango force.

Chongoroi, next stop on the road, was indefensible. Presumably the South African columns had received intelligence that the Caporolo force had set an ambush above the town and that the bridge was mined, because they swerved west on to track roads dodged Caporolo and headed for Catengue. Their plan was to join up with the second South African column that had been landed by air in Huambo and was now moving westwards on the main Huambo-Benguela road. Once they had moved jointly on Benguela, they would set their sights on the capital.

On 28 October the Huambo column started out for Benguela. On the 30th it defeated a small FAPLA force at Luimbale. And they moved slowly forwards towards Caluita where FAPLA were again digging in.

November 3rd dawned hot and airless. In the Catengue hills, the young, raw recruits from the CIR gathered to defend Benguela, the 'red city', MPLA's city. They came from all over the country: from Cabinda, from north and south Cuanza, western Huambo and even from Kunene and Moçamedes. A group of Mocubals from the Moçamedes desert planned to move south, and set up a CIR near Kaito when they had completed their training.

Armed only with rifles and led by their Cuban instructors, the men strung out across the dry hills facing the advancing 140mm field guns of the South African artillery deployed for the first time on the south front in the attack on Benguela, to cover their AFVs moving forward in the dust. As the Catengue trainees fell, in more than two and a half hours of blanket bombardment, other FAPLA were dying in Caluita: the two-pronged attack on Benguela had begun.

That day, Commander Sapu lost 723 men in two hours – seven companies fighting against impossible odds: the heroes of Caluita and Catengue. Cuban instructors, the first to die in Angola, fought side by side with their trainees till they fell.

Not even a 75mm mortar had been fired to defend Benguela: there were none. In sharp contrast, the South Africans had dispensed with infantry and were by now moving forward with armoured vehicles and artillery. Air reconnaissance had spotted a force of AFVs in the Pundo mountains above Lobito. There was a strong likelihood that Benguela would be cut off. The evacuation of the city began: it was disorderly and bitter. Angry soldiers kept limping in from the front calling for reinforcements to help their comrades still holding out in the hills to the east, falling back as the South Africans advanced. There was no transport to bring back the wounded; troops were running out of ammunition; the Benguela command was a shambles. There was not enough transport to evacuate the troops and the civilian population was in full flight, MPLA supporters were running for their lives fearing more of the savage reprisals they had suffered for their convictions earlier in the year, when FNLA and UNITA had briefly lodged in the town. Women with bundles on their heads, children on their backs, trudged along the road north, accompanied by weary soldiers. Their aim was to stop at Ngunza, but no one knew how far or how fast the South Africans' armoured cars would travel that night. Shortly after midnight, Benguela was deserted.

Again the SADF hesitated. On the morning of 4 November, a FAPLA jeep screeched into Ngunza and angry soldiers jumped out, shouting for help. Benguela was still unoccupied. A force of volunteers was assembled and moved back south towards Benguela, but when they reached the outskirts of the city in late afternoon, shots greeted them. A small force of South African armoured cars had occupied Benguela airport, on the south side. 120mm Monacaxitos were set up and a dawn attack planned by FAPLA. A small force of soldiers under the command of Mundo Real, a veteran and former Chipenda supporter who had rejoined MPLA, waited on the beach. A second infantry group hid in the Benfica area and Monty and a third group was to engage the enemy in a frontal attack. Under the Angolans' fire the South Africans fled from their exposed position on the airport apron. Four AFVs and some 140mm guns were left behind; but covering fire prevented FAPLA from capturing the abandoned weapons. Shells were falling in the city limits and the armoured column was again moving towards Pundo cutting off FAPLA's retreat: a second evacuation was ordered. Civilians who had rushed back to defend their city had now to be told that they must again head for Ngunza. A retreat made the move bitter as news had come that day from Porto Amboim, north of Ngunza, of the arrival of the first Katiushas, the 40-pod mobile 122mm rockets that were to provide FAPLA with a response to the South Africans' 140mm Howitzers.

Cheered by their temporary success the rank and file were reluctant to retreat. But Lobito reported South African controls at the city edges. FAPLA and the people of Benguela had to slip through the enemy lines in the dusk. A Greek ship in Lobito port had taken on FAPLA and MPLA supporters earlier in the day in response to an appeal by the Greek-born Angolan Governor of Benguela. Others fled on foot or by whatever vehicle was available on the tracks skirting Lobito; some went into hiding in the fisheries. Several Cuban instructors who had managed to escape, were taken in by peasants and fishermen and hidden from the enemy until they were able to rejoin MPLA north of the Queve river. The first arrivals in Ngunza, around 11 pm on 4 November, met other frustrations. The Katiushas had arrived safely in Porto Amboim – but without ammunition! Once again the defence of free Angola was to be undertaken by infantry.

3. War on Two Fronts

Ambushes were deployed along the road to Ngunza as the Southern Front commanders prepared for a last ditch stand to save the capital, Luanda. No one now doubted that the South African columns were spearheading a concerted western attack against MPLA and People's Angola. It was 7 November. The only weapons available to defend Ngunza were those salvaged from the Benguela retreat. The soldiers were demoralized and afraid, with Caluita and Catengue fresh in their minds. Amongst the troops moved the Political Commissars, outstanding among them Kassanje, Chief Commissar for the Front. Meanwhile civilian refugees were pushing ahead, struggling to cross the Queve river, and finding shelter in the villages along its northern bank. North of the river too, FAPLA was regrouping at Porto Amboim, a small coffee seaport with an airstrip. Weapons were at last being unloaded there on the shore. There was daily air traffic to the capital, and road communication with Luanda was a three hour drive on a rough but fast dirt road.

On 10 November, Monstro Imortal was sent from the Luanda High Command to Porto Amboim to take charge. He at once sent back a despatch which reached Luanda shortly before midnight, in the hands of a young FAPLA Officer. He rushed to May Day Square and as Agostinho Neto stepped from his limousine and moved towards the platform, handed him Monstro's message: the Southern and Central Fronts had fallen. Aviation was the only way to halt the South African advance. Ngunza was under South African artillery fire.

On 8 November, the day after FAPLA reached Ngunza, Pretoria began to direct heavy artillery fire over the whole Ngunza area. With its back to the sea and riddled with access roads the town was impossible to defend. But FAPLA, aided by a handful of Cubans from the Benguela retreat, set up B-10s and mortars, and some ammunition was now coming through from Porto Amboim. The South Africans shelled from dawn to dusk, civilians fled north and finally, FAPLA was forced to pull out to the surrounding hills. On 13 November, the commanders watched the South Africans occupy the town.

> We were up on the hill where we had a general view of Ngunza. Our retreat had begun after lunch. They entered around 7.30 pm. They came only in AFVs. We counted 58. We counted the little campaign

lights on them. They came so quietly, and behind the trucks with the 140mm guns. Then we left the hills and went down to Porto Amboim.

Morale was shattered. Hundreds of soldiers had died and it all seemed useless. The South Africans were pushing ahead as fast as ever. Luanda had only narrowly escaped the FNLA, and the officers were down here in the south losing. Luanda was now threatened again, this time from the south. Although some Katiushas had arrived there was still no ammunition. On 14 November in a mood of complete despair, Commissar Kassanje called for volunteers. Against all his comrades' earnest pleading the Commissar headed back south across the Queve with his men, towards Ngunza. They had gone barely four kilometres when they were mown down by South African artillery. It was suicide – they were armed only with AKs, against the Howitzers.

At this critical moment the first groups of special Cuban combat troops disembarked at Porto Amboim.

Cuban Commander Captain Esteban Manuel stepped out of an old Dakota at about 4 pm on 14 November in drenching rain. There to meet him was Commander Rosas, a white Angolan FAPLA in his 50s, a trained engineer and a man who had spent his life avoiding PIDE, as a progressive member of the white community in Benguela.

After a briefing with Commander Arguelles, head of the Cuban military, and other FAPLA officers, it was decided to proceed immediately to blow the Queve bridges. Rosas and Manuel started out with their men and explosives in the darkness and rain towards Gabela, where the main bridge lay at Sete Pontos. They reached Gabela around 10 pm and pressed straight through the sleepy coffee town to Sete Pontos. The bridge was blown that same night and a Cuban company deployed there. The first special Cuban forces had gone into action on the Gabela-Porto Amboim front.

Two other bridges were then destroyed: at Caxoeiras, closer to Porto Amboim, and at Porto Amboim itself. An ancient ferry at Kambalu had been inoperative for years. The river Queve halted the South African advance.

As for the vast quantities of Soviet weapons and thousands of Cuban troops that Western intelligence was meticulously reporting to the press – they simply did not exist at this stage.

Cuba's Contribution to the Victory

Angola was not the first African country where Cuban combatants committed themselves to fight in defence of revolution. Cuba fought alongside the FLN in Algeria in 1963. But it was the US intervention in the Congo that marked the decisive Cuban commitment to active solidarity in Africa. In December 1964, Ché Guevara told the UN General Assembly 'We, the free men of the world, must be prepared to avenge the crimes committed in the Congo'. And at the ensuing Afro-Asian Solidarity Conference in Algiers he called for African unity and solidarity against imperialist strategy in the Congo. He criticized peaceful coexistence and declared 'the Socialist countries have a moral duty to liquidate their tacit complicity with the exploiting nations of the West'.

The Colombian writer, Gabriel Garcia Marquez traces Ché's steps to Africa:

> On 25 April 1965, he gave Fidel Castro a farewell letter resigning his rank as Commandant and everything else that tied him to the government of Cuba. On the same day, travelling alone, he took a commercial flight using a false passport and name but not altering his appearance . . . three months later in the Congo, he joined 200 Cuban troops who had travelled from Havana in an arms ship. Ché's mission was to train guerrillas for the National Revolutionary Council of the Congo, then battling with Moise Tshombe, the puppet of the Belgian colonialists and international mining companies.

From April to December 1965 Ché stayed in the Congo.

> Not only training guerrillas but also directing them in battle and fighting alongside. His personal ties with Fidel, about which there has been so much speculation, did not deteriorate at any time.
>
> The two kept up regular and cordial contacts through very efficient systems of communication. When Moise Tshombe was defeated, the Congolese asked the Cubans to withdraw, to make the armistice easier.*

In 1966, shortly after the Congolese struggle, Agostinho Neto left for Havana, accompanied by Hoji Ya Henda and other young military cadres of MPLA.

Cuba offered Neto substantial aid for Angola's first war of liberation. But he declined, believing it important that his guerrillas' instructors be fellow Angolans. A growing number of civilian cadres went to Havana for education. Cuban doctors and instructors were playing an important internationalist role with the PAIGC in Guinea Bissau against Portugal's fascist colonial army. By the time of the Alvor Independence Agreement in January 1975, the Angolan revolutionaries had a decade of observation and experience of Cuba's revolution and its internationalism. There was a deep understanding on both sides of the crippling nature of illiteracy and exploitation. Angolans in Cuba, like their fellow Mozambican, Zimbabwean and South African exiles studying there, were inspired by the dramatic changes wrought in the fabric of Cuban society. These experiences renewed the determination to fight for what is right – for dignity and freedom, health and employment.

In May 1975, seven months after the beginning of the slow invasion of Angola by Zairean and Portuguese mercenaries, two months after the FNLA launched its terror campaign in Luanda, Agostinho Neto met Cuban

*Quoted passages here are the author's own translations.

Commander Flavio Bravo in Brazzaville. The Angolan leader clearly understood that whatever efforts the MPLA might make to bring Angola to Independence with a united government as envisaged under the Alvor agreement, this would not be permitted by the Western powers, whose objective was the complete elimination of MPLA. So Angola's revolution would have to be defended. Neto's priority for his country, then, as always, was full independence from all forms of foreign dependence. He wanted help to train Angolans to defend themselves. His first request was for shipments of light arms, and more talks.

In August, a year after proclamation of FAPLA, the People's Armed Forces for the Liberation of Angola, a Cuban delegation led by Comandante Raul Diaz Arguelles arrived in Luanda. Neto requested practical help in military instruction at four new Centres for Revolutionary Instruction (CIR) FAPLA was setting up. The Cuban troopship *El Vietnam Heroico* docked in Porto Amboim on 4 October, and instructors went to the four CIRs, at Dalatando, east of Luanda, Benguela Saurimo in the north-east, and Cabinda. Weapons arrived aboard *El Coral Island*, docking in Porto Amboim on 4 November.

By the time the Cuban instructors landed in Porto Amboim, South Africa's Defence Force and helicopter-borne commando units had been in action inside the country for over two months, since their July attacks in Kunene. Throughout September, movements of white troops, signs of South African logistic military and intelligence aid to FNLA and UNITA in Huambo and Bié, had been multiplying.

Why did MPLA not request aid on a far larger scale at this stage, as eventually it did in November? Agostinho Neto had been convinced ever since the Sal conference in September the previous year that the aim of the Western powers was to eliminate his movement. Sal, where Zaire's President Mobutu, Portugal's then President Spinola, Jonas Savimbi and Holden Roberto, and MPLA renegade Daniel Chipenda, met in secret to plan Angola's future, was now culminating in a clear military alliance, armed by the NATO countries and backed by the world's three foremost imperialist powers, the US, Britain and France, to crush MPLA.

Neto was well aware of the underlying long term subversion of the liberation struggle that had precipitated Angola's independent neighbours, Zaire and Zambia, into supporting FNLA and UNITA – the forces of oppression and neo-colonial subjection – instead of MPLA, who represented the forces of freedom; he had surmounted the MPLA leadership conflict provoked by Daniel Chipenda and the ambitious, anti-communist intellectuals of Andrade's Active Revolt faction. And having suffered the ensuing loss of confidence from MPLA's traditional supporters, had fought back to create fresh unity and strength, centring on the cadres of the ideologically clear and militarily active Eastern Front. But they alone could not defeat a massive South African invasion.

Yet many MPLA cadres doubted that such a massive attack by Pretoria would take place. The Southern African detente exercise was in process. In

1974 the South African Premier John Vorster went, in secret, to West Africa, and met the Presidents of Ivory Coast, Senegal and Gabon; later, he made his famous 'Give me six months' speech, promising to change South Africa. In Zambia, talks on Zimbabwe's Independence took place, involving President Kaunda and South African leaders, after Kaunda's 'Voice of reason' appeal to Pretoria in October 1976.

In the midst of the detente exercise in Southern Africa, Botha made the astonishing statement at the United Nations that South Africa was opposed to racial discrimination, and mounted a major publicity stunt in Smith's Rhodesia around a fictitious 'withdrawal' of the South African 'police' units operating there. Mozambique's Independence in June 1975 went by without South African intervention; travellers from Rhodesia even reached Maputo for the celebrations via Jan Smuts airport, Johannesburg.

In August 1975, came the momentous Victoria Falls conference between Vorster and Kaunda. For over a year – since the Portuguese Armed Forces coup – Zambia's President had been under increasingly intense pressure to co-operate with Pretoria. Zambia's economy, as usual, was in a critical state – dependent on injections of Western credit. Since the Benguela railway, its lifeline, was obviously threatened by war in Angola, Zambia had, therefore, to envisage using the southern route to the coast through Rhodesia and South Africa.

The diplomatic front seemed to be Vorster's chosen – and potentially successful – mode of operations. On 16 October 1975, President Felix Houphouet-Boigny, addressing the 6th Congress of his PDCI Party in Abidjan, Ivory Coast, having previously called for dialogue with Pretoria, made an outright plea for diplomatic relations between Black African states and South Africa, along the Malawi model. On the eve of their Angolan invasion, the racists in Pretoria had won a major diplomatic victory, which, had it gone through, would have had serious consequences for Africa. Accordingly, it seemed to many unlikely that the Generals in Pretoria would sweep such achievements aside and march their men into Angola.

The strength and size of the South African armoured columns operating in Angola in October came as a shock: within ten days it was clear that urgent outside help was needed to defend free Angola.

The MPLA Political Bureau met in emergency session, and following a full briefing on the collapse of the Southern Front and the South African advance upon Benguela, heard Agostinho Neto's suggested strategy. There was unanimous agreement with the Neto plan. Henrique Santos 'Onambwe' was entrusted with the task of bearing a request for help to Cuba. On 5 November, the Cuban Communist Party Central Committee met to discuss the Angolan request. Benguela and Lobito had fallen to South African columns the previous day. The Cuban Communists were informed of the deaths of some of their people on the hills of Catengue, while fighting alongside their Angolan trainees from the Benguela CIR, and given all the available information on the strength and nature of the South African military invasion, and asked to make a decision within 24 hours. But there was no hesitation: the first volunteers left Havana at 4 pm on 7 November, all chosen personally by Fidel Castro from amongst his most trusted comrades.

Castro said later:

> We simply could not sit back when the MPLA asked us for help. We gave MPLA the necessary assistance to prevent a people fighting for their Independence for almost 14 years from being crushed. It was our elementary duty, our revolutionary duty, our internationalist duty to give that assistance to MPLA regardless of the price.

The Soviet Union was involved neither in the Angolans' decision to turn to Cuba for help, nor in Cuba's decision to send their combatants. The Soviet Communist Party was informed of the Cuban Central Committee decision, after the 5 November emergency meeting. The Red Army role, decided by the MPLA, was to supply the weapons that Cuba's regular army FAR, *Fuerzas Armadas Revolucionarias*, knew how to use, and which would equal the South Africans' fire power. According to one Western source, the Red Army offered to send 400 military technicians to Angola, but this was declined in the belief it might provoke further escalation in US involvement in the war.

As the first 82 volunteers boarded a Bristol Britannia for Luanda, MPLA's Commander Onambwe embarked on a Caribbean diplomatic mission to organize fuelling posts for the ancient aircraft. Predictably, he encountered the full force of US opposition: Georgetown, Guyana, was a route soon closed by Washington's threats, as was Jamaica. Eventually Cape Verde was the only possible stopover and, in response to US orders, the oil companies began limiting air fuel supplies.

Three boatloads of volunteers were at the Havana docks. Early Cuban volunteer units were recruited by means of cables requesting men on the First Reserve lists (former FAR members) to report to local military committees; they were told a volunteer force was being formed, and given some days to make their decision. Thousands also turned up unasked.

The first two plane loads of Cuban combat troops arrived in Luanda on 10 November, as South African 140mm Howitzers stationed 20 kilometres north of the capital were lobbing shells at the FAPLA base at Grafanil, on the capital's outskirts, while bitter fighting raged at Kifangondo. The Cubans went straight to the front. The first Soviet BM21 multipod rocket launchers had gone to the Kifangondo escarpment, and the Cubans had brought light artillery, three 75mm field guns and three 82mm mortars. Their mission was to defend Luanda at all costs until further reinforcements arrived by sea. On the night of Independence, the Cuban journalists predicted a 'qualitative and quantitative change' in the war.

After the routing of the FNLA at Kifangondo, it was clear that part of the small Cuban combat force had to be rushed south to meet the SADF. The decision was forced by the fall of Ngunza on 13 November. On 14 November at Porto Amboim, the first Cuban combat forces joined the Southern Front. The first three Cuban troop ships, carrying an artillery regiment, a mechanized battalion and recoilless guns, docked in Angola on 27 November.

The East Holds Fast

In the east, the river Cassai formed a natural barrier to the South African advance. North of the river lay Angola's diamonds, mined by a consortium of Portuguese, US and South African interests. This had been a no-go area for MPLA's guerrillas, but south of the diamond area in southern Lunda province and Moxico, the same Lunda-Chokwe peoples had provided the backbone of the MPLA guerrilla force and their peasant supporters from 1966 onwards. Veteran commanders like Dangeureux, Tchizainga and Liberdade all came from the area. Recruiting was easy.

The first shots had been fired by MPLA at Kakwezi against a Portuguese military patrol in 1966. At that time Luso was a small village, known as Luena,* on the Benguela railway linking Zambia and Zaire to the Atlantic. The area became MPLA's target as Luso was built up into a garrison town against them. Iko Carreira and his group blew bridges, attacked military convoys but not the railway line: this would have harmed Zambia which was the MPLA rear base. Peasants were walking 400 kilometres there and back for weapons.

In 1970 the guerrillas penetrated north into Lunda. Liberated areas were now being organized with peasant militias to defend them. Defoliation by Portugal followed. PIDE swept through the villages looking for underground MPLA workers. Older men were mobilizing the youth to join the guerrillas, and acting as go-betweens ferrying information and food. Pedro Kalundungo was arrested in Buçaco in August 1970, charged with passing information to MPLA guerrillas, and beaten until he was blinded in one eye. He was then taken to the political prison at Sao Nicolau where he stayed until 25 April 1974. He was imprisoned yet again in Luena, by UNITA, after it fell to the South Africans.

Now, in 1975, the counter-revolutionaries needed the railway line. It would have solved their supply problems and allowed fuel, food, weapons and ammunition to flow in from Zaire and Zambia to the central highlands. FNLA had brought Zairean units into Moxico and tried to dislodge MPLA from Luena, Cavungo and Cazombo. They failed and were withdrawn in August 1975.

That month marked a key change in the centre-east situation. The Portuguese army had watched Portuguese mercenaries, PIDE agents and fascist military and civilians help UNITA throw MPLA cadres out of Huambo and Bié. When UNITA gunmen hauled local MPLA leaders off a plane organized to evacuate the Movement to Luanda, army officers and the International

*The original African name – Luena – was restored after Angola's Independence.

Red Cross stood by. Those men were later murdered. After the MPLA evacuation, the Portuguese army withdrew, leaving their entire arsenal to UNITA. Mercenaries were flown in from Johannesburg, together with SADF officers, intelligence and logistics experts.

The Portuguese Panhard armoured unit from Bié, operated by the mercenaries, then spearheaded an offensive against MPLA further east in Luena. The revolutionaries had rifles, but little ammunition. They also had 82mm recoilless guns and 122mm rockets; but no armoured vehicles. Luena command went into action. Two Land Rovers were found and driven to the railway workshops where metal plates were soldered on. Morale rose. Then the guerrillas remembered the diamond mining company's armoured cars; they went north and found three. Only one was roadworthy and reached Luena after overturning on the way. Eastern Front Armoured Corps was formed: two Land Rovers, a captured UNITA armour plated Willys jeep with UNITA gun tripod, the Diamond Mine contraption, and a Caterpillar bulldozer, its shovel raised and soldered into a fixed position with a gun mounted upon it. The Corps drove round Luena as the people cheered wildly.

Commander Dibala was desperate for ammunition. 'As soon as we cleared the enemy out of the area, we ran out of ammunition and were forced to fall back into Luena again. We could not hold our forward positions.'

The easterners held out as best they could and not until December did the South African Defence Force advance against them. Now, in mid-November the southern front was where the Boers were. This was the main theatre of operations, and where Cuba's contribution was most effective.

FNLA Falls Apart

After the Kifangondo disaster, there had been fierce recriminations in the UPA-FNLA military camp. The Portuguese mercenary high command, led by Santos e Castro, was in disgrace and Holden announced that he would take personal command of his troops. Fresh mercenaries – from Britain and the US – were rushed in to support the northern team. Mobutu's crack Kamanyola Division had been thoroughly discredited and there were reports of pro-MPLA demonstrations in the Kinshasa townships.

Wilfred Burchett and Derek Roebuck in *The Whores of War* told the full story of the British and American mercenary venture. South Africa openly put its army into the field against the People's Angola; Britain, the United States and France resorted to mercenaries – 'a faceless and bottomless reserve of cannon fodder, not identifiable with governments and their policies, immune to public criticism and debate. The perfect substitute for the expeditionary forces.' The British and American mercenaries' command was equally as disastrous as the Portuguese had been; their disregard for morality and human life probably exceeded that of the Portuguese.

'Special Commandos', as the Portuguese mercenary contingent preferred to call themselves, were contemptuous of their Anglo-Saxon colleagues. One

Portuguese mercenary wrote:

> One English mercenary wanted information on Tomboco so they could go and occupy it showing he understood nothing about war – just because the Cubans weren't there yet. It was like they were playing parts in a film with an all-star cast. In their self-appointed role as gallant heroes the English advanced on Tomboco and were mown down like chickens.
>
> A truck on arrival went smack into an enemy tank and around 40 men in it died instantly: many of whom had only arrived in Angola from England three days before. The majority of these mercenaries hardly knew where they were or whether the war was being won or lost. They hadn't even had time to find out that the Angolan war wasn't a London bar room brawl. (Author's translation.)

The north of Angola was proving difficult to colonize from Zaire. Weapons were plentiful, but personnel with a will to fight for Holden were not. The invading army was met with caution and cunning, as thousands of peasants sought to safeguard their tiny assets. Decades of colonial exploitation had seen all fertile land expropriated for coffee, and the labour force made dependent on the plantation store for food supplies. These supplies had long since stopped coming in, and the peasants were near starvation. The western coastal belt was scantily populated and barren, and the occupying troops were forced to scrounge and pillage. This not only increasingly diverted them from military duties but hardened Angolans' resolve against them. Rations flown in by Hercules C-130 transport planes to the big Portuguese-built air bases at Negage and Toto had to be transhipped hundreds of kilometres along a route made more precarious by dependence upon numerous bridges over the small rivers that criss-crossed the region east-west to the coast.

The rank and file were left to fend for themselves and logistics concentrated on weapons supplies – huge arms dumps were captured at Caxito, Nambuangongo, Negage, Ambriz and Toto – and perks for the white officers. MPLA troops were able to enjoy ther mercenaries Christmas rations flown in from South Africa as they moved north, liberating Uíje and Zaire provinces. (Rations for 75 British mercenaries fed a FAPLA company and the local town for more than a month in one UPA base.)

The Zairean troops began to stage mock enemy attacks in order to flee an imaginary FAPLA advance still faster. This had begun in Porto Quipiri, after the Kifangondo battle, with discreet 'avoiding action'. Holden Roberto, visiting the front, was handed a written report on the 'cowardice of the Zairean battalions', which he disbelieved. Admonishing the Portuguese mercenaries for their lax command he called on the Zaireans to fill the breach.

> Brave and fearless, the Zairois jumped into their armoured cars and crossed the Porto Quipiri bridge towards the enemy lines under Holden's gaze. A few commandos (Portuguese mercenaries) followed . . . . When

> they came out of the bend beyond the bridge, they found the brave Zairois and their armoured cars in hiding behind the Church, some already on their way back towards the rear,

the bitter Portuguese reported.

At Asfalto Hill further north, where Santos e Castro made a final attempt to marshall his forces, the Zaireans fired off a mortar, feigning an enemy attack. They succeeded in forcing a retreat the following day and, the Portuguese mercenaries reported

> their subsequent action was to take the shortest possible road to the Zaire frontier, looting whatever they could lay their hands on. Their armoured cars were unable to open fire because of the bicycles, radios and furniture festooning the gun turrets. They were involved in armed robbery and rape.

The Portuguese mercenaries were making their own plans, and Santos e Castro shortly made off with the $350,000 CIA payroll, that according to John Stockwell, the CIA taskforce chief, was intended for the full Portuguese contingent.

By mid December Zairean and FNLA forces had begun sabotaging their own guns. The Portuguese mercenaries complained that

> the barrel of our AA guns were repeatedly stuffed with charcoal and wood, weapons were left lying around and there were suspect footprints near the river Onzo leading towards the enemy lines. There were traitors infiltrated into our forces.

The FNLA-UNITA Government

In an effort to divert attention from the military situation at the end of November, FNLA's press officers took correspondents on a guided tour of the FNLA-UNITA zone, which was supposed to end in a triumphal ceremony announcing the formation of the FNLA-UNITA allied government. In contrast to the post-independence appointments and orderly administration in MPLA's Angola, almost nothing had filtered through on how the Western-backed alliance was functioning.

The party left Kinshasa in a Fokker Friendship hijacked from the Angolan airlines. The first stop was Ambriz, at that time military headquarters for Holden's forces; many black troops and some Belgian and French journalists were hanging about. 'They had been there for some time as they had expected to accompany the victorious UPA entry into Luanda' an African journalist member of the press party recalls. 'There were Portuguese mercenaries and I met an American colonel, about 60 and balding. Holden was in Ambriz but we didn't see him.' A few days earlier, on 24 November, a first announcement of a joint government was made. AZAP, the Zaire News Agency reported from Carmona that 'the government of FNLA and UNITA formed on 11 November was announced last night, 23 November. It comprises two nominated Prime Ministers who will be holding office successively at one month intervals.'

Predictably, the two Premiers were Johnny Eduardo and José Ndele. The press party from Kinshasa, anxious to find out more about the government, proceeded to Carmona, took Daniel Chipenda on board and headed south.

> Chipenda's mission was to explain to the masses in the south why he had allied himself with FNLA. In Kinshasa, earlier, it was known that Chipenda wanted to join FNLA as the head of an 'MPLA-Chipenda Faction' but he had been forced to abandon the idea in exchange for nomination as FNLA's 'deputy secretary-general'.

Landing in Serpa Pinto, the party hung around while the pilots flew off to South Africa to refuel. 'We saw South African troops there but when we spoke to them in English they wouldn't reply.' After two or three days, during which Chipenda held public rallies and spoke against MPLA, the party left for Mocamedes, Angola's major southern Atlantic port and a key supply depot. They made a brief stop in Porto Alexandre, to boost local morale: 'there were a lot of whites in uniform complaining of fuel shortages'.

They proceeded to Lubango where the airport had been cleared of all South African troops, and Portuguese guarded the area. The Grand Hotel was swarming with Boers. After a big Chipenda rally the party moved on to Lobito and Benguela. There was no rally in Lobito – only a good deal of drinking and festivities. Finally they left for Huambo.

> As we got off the plane in Huambo the FNLA soldiers came and spoke to us in Lingala – they said this place is no good, there is a lot of tension, we are constantly being provoked by UNITA and at this very moment several of our brothers are in the morgue. You must tell our leaders about this problem we may have to open fire.

Holden arrived the following day but Savimbi did not go to meet him at the airport. The tone of Holden's speech to the crowds was conciliatory, he said '*Viva Kwacha*', the UNITA slogan, but the talks between the two leaderships dragged on. 'There was no agreement and we [correspondents] had been waiting for days. Everyone was fed up. They had taken us all round the country because they couldn't agree.' Finally something was cobbled together and Chipenda and Nzau Puna addressed a large crowd from the Huambo Governor's palace. Neither Savimbi nor Holden appeared, and the two deputies jostled and interrupted each other.

On the way back, some of the press party lunched with Holden in Carmona.

> He was very talkative. He told us the Zaire Embassy in Paris knew of

documents saying if MPLA came to power in Angola, Mobutu would be on his knees. A soldier came in and handed a document to Holden. He read it and then told us Ambriz was threatened or perhaps already occupied by FAPLA. Earlier the ORTF (French radio) correspondent had called me into his room and said he'd heard the news on his radio. We flew straight out to Kinshasa with Holden. He never entered Angola again.

The Queve Front

The South Africans had desperately needed to cross the Queve river and take Porto Amboim on its northern bank. From there, they could have reached Luanda in a couple of hours, with only one more obstacle, the Cuanza river.

Several times they claimed to have taken it. But this small, coastal fishing port nestled in sandy hills just out of bombing range of the 140mm Howitzers, thanks to a high hill between the town and the river mouth. FAPLA were dug in along the beaches against possible sea attack. Shells fell within a mile of the town centre where thousands of refugees from south of the river were squatting in back yards or camping in warehouses. The Cotton Company building had been offered to the Cuban arrivals and FAPLA officers were billeted in the former Portuguese District Officer's residence, when the old cook had taken a new lease on life and served up army rations with encouraging talk far into the night. The small airport hummed with activity.

As November wore on into December, heavy weapons were camouflaged on the hill behind the town in the open cotton store behind bales of raw cotton which caught fire at one time and burned for several days. Nobody cared, except the MPLA official – who knew its value – and the firemen fighting the blaze. Cotton was hated in Porto Amboim, Ebo, Nhia, Kariango down through to Cela. Cotton was cultivated by force, each peasant had to deliver cotton every year, and was paid nothing. In the stifling dusty valleys of Ebo and Porto Amboim, were the tinroofed cotton stores, and the miserable, abandoned hovels, where a man could not stand upright and there was barely room to lie down. By the end of November that year King Cotton was dying.

The Queve valley was to produce the most organized mass resistance to the enemy seen in the war. The people had turned to the MPLA, realizing its opposition to their exploitation. As the peasants and agricultural wage labourers of the Central Highlands who came to know the MPLA responded enthusiastically, organizing themselves into Village Fronts and self-help communities and ignoring the tribalism of the UNITA activists, so in the Gabela area, an ethnic transition area between Kimbundu and Umbundu, tribal identity was irrelevant, only an individual's history as oppressed or oppressor was of importance.

UNITA and FNLA both tried and failed to gain support in this rich farming belt. A local man said:

> Why are these people so militant? In Cuanza Sul province the settlers and traders were exploiting us stupidly. The District Officers, Chefes de Posto, were making slaves of the peasants through contract and forced labour in the cotton fields. Pregnant women were put to clearing the roadside bush and working in the *Granjas*, which were farms producing cotton and run for the benefit of the local administrator to supplement his income. They killed men, women and children here in the 1961 massacres. In the people's minds, all this is burning. When MPLA called for independence, the people jumped at it. They saw the Portuguese trader solely as an enemy. We couldn't stand these men. We remembered the massacres, the suffering, the exploitation. Later, when the three organizations came to the area, the others brought military contingents but we didn't. We were political organizers moving amongst the people, showing them the line. Then the Portuguese traders contacted FNLA and UNITA and asked for protection. We had the full support of the people, we had nothing to be afraid of. But the traders with their FNLA and UNITA bodyguards were constantly threatening the people.

Throughout 1975 until September, the reactionary settlers and traders and their FNLA and UNITA backers and bodyguards waged a resistance campaign against the revolutionary changes being wrought by the people. Many settlers retreated from the immediate Gabela area to the nearby *colonato* (settlement) at Cela. Symbol of colonial exploitation, Cela had been set up in the late 1950s, as a white small-holding community. With its enormous church, complete with stained glass windows, and commemorative plaques marking the ceremonial visit of President Salazar, it became a centre for settler military activities. Later it was occupied by the SADF who used it as a logistics base and landed their C-130s at its airport.

As the year wore on, most settlers left for Portugal on the government-financed air lift. In the Gabela-Cela area, Portuguese troops spread the alarming news that any whites who remained did so 'at their own risk'. A panicky convoy left for Luanda. Months later, in one house in Gabela, there were still false teeth in a mug on the bathroom shelf.

In September, the emergence of settler and commando-led mixed forces armed with South African weapons, signalled a counter-revolutionary offensive in Cela. MPLA was forced back to a line running south of Kibala on the main highway, eastwards through Kariango and Mussende, westwards through Ebo to Porto Amboim.

This was the front that defeated the South African army. The Queve river saved Luanda from the original attack by the Zulu column. But fierce and bitter fighting for more than two months stopped Pretoria from winning ground.

South Africa Defeated

On 14 November, the day after the fall of Ngunza, the situation seemed hopeless. That morning, Kassanje's suicide column, which he had led back south, had been wiped out by the South African artillery. In the dismal rain, even the new arrivals from Cuba seemed inadequate to stop the South African war machine. But on the 15th, after the bridges across the river had been blown spirits lifted.

A Volkswagen appeared on the south bank at the Porto Amboim bridge – already blown that night. Two men dressed as priests got out to inspect the damage; FAPLA opened fire and the 'priests' withdrew. Shortly afterwards five armoured cars nosed into view: the Zulu column of the South African Defence Force. Porto Amboim's first BM 21 was ready for them: all five were destroyed. The Zulu column then skirted round eastwards. Later that day it attacked Caxoeiras bridge – a 55 kilometre detour on track roads – but that also had been blown by FAPLA-FAR at 3 am that morning. The Zulu column then dodged 36 kilometres east to Sete Pontos, but Commander Rosas and his Cuban allies had blown the bridge shortly before dawn.

The invaders took the one route open to them: to return south to Santa Comba, cross the Queve there and move back up its north bank to Ebo, midway between Gabela and Kibala and about 20 kilometres south of the tarmac road. The Zulu column got to Ebo on 18 November; having left its infantry behind it now comprised a spearhead of artillery and armoured cars only.

Unaware of the Zulu column penetration behind their lines a small FAPLA force under command of a local man was still holding out to the south in Cela and Alto Hama. A heroic offensive by these Angolans was underway on their own initiative, since all contact with the Central Front command had been lost. Their aim was to push through to relieve Benguela and Lobito. On 8 November their advance scouting parties contacted the South African columns south of Cela. FAPLA decided to hole up on Tongo mountain, where the main road runs through a narrow cleft. On 16 November the South Africans occupied Cela and began firing on FAPLA on Tongo. After ten hours of shelling, the Angolans fell back on foot through the bush. They had no heavy weapons, and survivors rejoined the front at Ebo or Kibala.

After the fiasco of 15 November, the Zulu command was now receiving impatient signals from Pretoria. South African and Western press reports were informing the world that the Cambambe dam at Dondo was occupied by 'UNITA and FNLA' and that Luanda's water and electricity supplies were consequently cut off. But on the ground, the Zulu column was still more than 100 kilometres south of the strategic dam, and making little headway.

Moving further and further east, in an attempt to outflank the Gabela-Porto Amboim resistance and avoid the Queve barrier, the Zulu column now opened up a new direction towards Kalulo, north of Mussende. This seemed a possible way to reach Cambambe since there were numerous, reasonably good track roads leading north and no major rivers. FAPLA's small infantry squadron at Mussende put up a gallant but impossible defence; there were very heavy casualties. The MPLA command decided to throw up a strong defence line on the Mussende-Kariango front, and reinforce the Dondo defences, where a Cuban logistics headquarters was beginning to operate. It was essential to safeguard the dam.

In Huambo, Western correspondents were waiting for the UNITA victory. *Newsweek* reported the 'pro-Western forces' had a 'substantial military edge'. There was still no coverage of South Africa's intervention. Correspondent, Andrew Jaffe, whisked from Lusaka by Hawker Siddeley Lear Jet, piloted by Britons who told him 'you can say we work for MI 6 1/2', quoted Savimbi: 'Today I have armoured cars with no drivers. If MPLA has ten bazookas, I have 20.' Queried about South Africa's 'support', Savimbi retorted, 'Here I am fighting Communism, trying to stop the Russians from taking over Angola, and you hold me up to ridicule. What's the matter, don't you want to live in a democracy?' Jaffe wrote:

> Savimbi met us, ordered passion fruit cocktails and introduced us to Major-General Samuel Chiwale, his Chief of Staff. The two men claimed that the war is nearly over. Savimbi's troops, supported by a white-led armoured brigade from Holden Roberto's National Front for the Liberation of Angola (FNLA) have rolled up their enemy's entire southern flank. Chiwale, a tall slender man with a Clint Eastwood squint, nonchalantly ticked off the gains. 'Yesterday we were in Novo Redondo; today we are in Port Amboim' he said. 'We are already on the outskirts of Dondo (where Luanda's power is generated) but we don't turn off the lights. Not yet'.

South African artillery was pounding the north bank of the Queve. West of the Kibala road, the Zulu column had little infantry, but heavy concentrations of field guns and armoured cars. FAPLA's response was geared to its fighting strength: still weak both in weapons and skilled troops to operate them. The people of Ebo, Kambalu, and Porto Amboim began daily intelligence gathering. Crossing the river in their small boats, they worked their fields of beans and maize on the south bank, lulling the South Africans into complacency. Willem Steenkamp of the *Cape Town Highlander* wrote of

> black peasants who still tilled the land. Rooted so deep in the fertile red soil that they were virtually a part of it, they could not conceive of doing anything else but follow the slow relentless cycle of the seasons. They sowed, they reaped, they bore their babies and buried their dead . . . .

They informed on South African troop movements and led sniping parties but Steenkamp in his book *Adeus Angola* was ill-informed on this aspect of the Angolan peasants' daily activities: 'they turned their backs on the intruders and pretended . . . that no strangers walked their land . . . bending dreamily to their ancient tasks.'

All along the front as far as Huambo, MPLA's peasant supporters, Kimbundus and Umbundus regardless of tribal origin, infiltrated enemy-held villages and FNLA and UNITA barracks. Caught up in the web of tribalism it had itself woven, UNITA rarely suspected Umbundus, and even Umbundu speakers were regarded as at least 'Umbundu-ish' and unlikely to be MPLA activists.

FAPLA Commander Sapu, now involved in reorganizing this central front after the disasters of Caluita and Catengue, came to know the people well.

> In all these villages along the Queve, our frontier, the villagers were organized. We found them already organized and they demanded weapons from us. We had to provide guns, ammunition and training because they had already formed up volunteers for militia duty. They stayed there with us, under the shells. The daily bombing was against them, as well as against us soldiers. They resisted, and they controlled the area. When people crossed the river, fleeing north from the South Africans, they helped them, found out who they were, and if they were infiltrated from the enemy. They organized themselves into action committees and later they received some support from the MPLA Refugees Commission based in Porto Amboim.

In FAPLA, local men volunteered to train as deep reconnaissance scouts. One, Manuel José Horacio from Ebo, a former worker in the Cela milk factory, who had gone to Luanda and become caught up in the war, joined FAPLA and fought at Kifangondo. FNLA and UNITA retaliated by murdering his parents. Now back in his home area, he led a seven-man, deep reconnaissance unit foraging behind enemy lines and fraternizing with UNITA and FNLA to gain knowledge of troop movements. From December, his unit was supported by two Cuban radio operators who maintained contact between Manuel and his colleagues in the villages, and the Front Command.

There was encouraging news; FNLA and UNITA were squabbling amongst themselves. Towns and villages in occupied territory were in miserable condition, there was neither food nor fuel, and UNITA had raided the Lobito bank vaults and recirculated old, cancelled bank notes. Vehicles were running on paint-stripper, and soon ground to a halt. Apparently no attempt was made to organize local government. Top cadres like Jorge Valentim, governor of Lobito, engaged in gestapo activities and neglected administration. The 'troops' fought each other. In Ngunza, UNITA was evacuated in order to end the strife, but the FNLA left behind with the South Africans refused to go to the front to fight.

Clearly, the South African offensive was becoming bogged down. Three weeks had gone by, and although most Western news media were dutifully sceptical that Pretoria's troops were inside Angola, and were relaying Savimbi's claims that this had nothing to do with him, a steady trickle of reports on the South African invasion began to have an effect on world public opinion.

On 9 December, a South African air reconnaissance plane was shot down over Caxoeiras bridge. The only survivors in the burnt out wreck were a Luger and two Browning pistols. A few days later, Pretoria announced the death of some officers in the Namibia operational area.

The third week in November marked a fresh offensive by the South Africans against Ebo, and heavy fighting north of Mussende. Ebo was a no-mans-land between the two lines. FAPLA-FAR prepared the strongest defence line they could muster, aware that Ebo was their weak spot, where the Zulu column armour could pierce north of the river, on the shortest and fastest route to Cambambe dam. On 23 November the South Africans attacked in strength. First they made contact with artillery fire, then moved up the armoured cars; bombing began promptly at 8 am. South Africa conducted its war in 'normal working hours'. As usual, bombing continued until midday; normally it would have been resumed at 2 pm until around 6 pm. But for the South Africans the 23rd proved to be an exception. They had 75 AFVs, their artillery and other vehicles, all caught up in the fluctuating advance and shelling. The Angolans had one BM 21 Stalin Organ, a 76mm fieldgun and two armoured cars, two companies of FAPLA infantry and 60 Cuban combatants. The Angolans and Cubans were deployed in alternate groups along the hillside, dug in, in ambush.

South African and FAPLA-FAR infantry clashed in the early afternoon. The South Africans lost about 30 men and eight armoured cars before they began a disorderly retreat; trucks with ammunition, food and uniforms were abandoned. Their aim had been to advance as a single column and capture Gabela or Kibala; instead, they remained spreadeagled across a dozen track roads.

The invading column now turned its attention to Nhia, while FAPLA-FAR followed up the retreat by occupying Ebo. On 11 December FAPLA-FAR had to withdraw from the Nhia line. Cuba's Comandante Raul Diaz Arguelles, Commander of Internationalist Operations in Angola, was killed during the fighting. To save time, he disregarded advice from scouts to avoid the Hengo track road, which had been mined by the enemy; his jeep hit a mine, and he died instantly.

Retreating from Nhia, FAPLA-FAR blew the Catofe bridge and resolved to make Catofe town their defence line. But early on the morning of the 12th, while they were still regrouping, the South Africans, having patched up the bridge under cover of darkness, launched a surprise attack. Angolans and Cubans, caught off their guard, suffered the heaviest casualties in a single battle in this second phase of the war. But Catofe was held. Once more, the Zulu column had failed to dislodge the revolutionaries.

The South Africans moved their main thrust back east to Mussende. However, the Central Front command's orders to strengthen the line from Mussende to Kariango had now been carried out and this fresh South African offensive was too late. Between 15 and 22 December the front stabilized, with little advance either way.

MPLA guerrilla groups were now active behind the South African lines.

Led by the 'dreamy' peasants, they laid mines and ambushed traffic moving up from the south. Small guerrilla bases were scattered through the Fazendas up the road east of Kibala and south towards Cela. Parties of South African troops moving out from Ngunza fell into ambushes in the low-lying farmland, the guerrillas hidden in banana plantations.

On 23 December FAPLA scouts reported that a major new South African offensive was underway. A 12 kilometre column was once again heading for Ebo from Kissobe to the south. From a neighbouring hill FAPLA watched the column and estimated 130 vehicles, of which probably a third were armoured cars. The trucks contained South African, Portuguese mercenary and UNITA infantry and, as FAPLA discovered in Bimbe, after the battle, washing machines, stoves, boots and uniforms: it was an occupying column. Women were also brought along. The column reached Bimbe shortly before dawn. At 5 am it set out for Ebo. FAPLA was dug in on the northside of Ebo in a carefully planned ambush. The road leaves the village, dips down to a bridge over the river and then rises again. FAPLA and Cuban combatants were waiting, hidden, at the top of the rise.

The South African column lumbered forward from Bimbe and opened up with everything it had. Artillery reconnaissance fire, mortars, making as much noise as possible. FAPLA stayed silent. The firing continued until the column entered Ebo village and then stopped. Field guns were mounted at the Ebo village outskirts, logistics began pottering about and women accompanying the column set to work. FAPLA were incredulous.

> They had brought their women and everything. We were saying the only thing missing was the TV set. There they were unloading their junk, and mounting their field guns happily. They didn't seem to know we were only a couple of kilometres away and they began firing wild blanket shots. Next thing they decided we were in Alambiri, five kilometres further off, and began firing on the mountain there, where we had an artillery position and reconnaissance and communications equipment. They shelled and shelled away but we didn't fire a single shot. They thought nobody was around and began moving into our ambush.

An RPG7 anti-tank shell hit the first South African armoured car, piercing the radiator, the driver's chest, set fire to the petrol tank and hit the armoured car behind. The revolutionaries had all seven leading armoured vehicles under fire from their 76mm guns while their BM 21, stationed 18 kilometres back, opened fire all down the column. Fourteen South African armoured vehicles were put out of action and abandoned, along with troop transports and officers' cars. FAPLA remained in ambush until the following day. The number of enemy dead could not be confirmed because the South Africans went back for the bodies. Two white South African bodies were recovered from armoured vehicles; over 200 black, Angolan soldiers – Boer cannon fodder – were killed in the infantry transports. The quantities of uniforms and weapons recovered in the bush suggest this number was an underestimate.

In the second battle of Ebo the South African army were losing too many men and not gaining any ground. Their Angolan allies were not only militarily ineffective but fought amongst themselves, turned on white civilians, wrecked property, looted settler homes and farms and rampaged through the countryside. While Savimbi and Chiwale sipped cocktails in Huambo and Bié and posed for Western journalists, their People's Democratic Republic of Angola was disintegrating. Pretoria's invasion was no longer a secret: MPLA had presented a group of South African PoWs in Luanda on 16 December. Young national servicemen, they described their capture near Cela, 1,000 miles north of the Namibia border. Other pressmen with UNITA had filed reports of the South African military presence in Lobito and Benguela, Huambo and Bié. International outrage provoked a nervous reaction from the imperialist powers a tendency to renege on all but clandestine support for Pretoria and its Angolan friends.

At the frontline, South African troops experienced increasingly daring forays by FAPLA. Scouting parties, with silencers on their guns, picked off the young South African troops. Air reconnaissance was becoming hazardous: two helicopters and a couple of light planes had been shot down on the Ebo front. A local militiaman, who shot a helicopter gunner, was knocked to the ground as gunner, machine gun and magazines fell out of the sky on top of him!

From 5 January, the South African army began a slow reatreat back towards Huambo, leaving only artillery and armoured vehicles to cover their forces withdrawal. As FAPLA-FAR consolidated their positions from Balaia through Ebo and Kibala, South Africans remained guarding the Tongo mountain pass that dominated the highway south to the central highlands, from Catofe.

FAPLA dislodged them from Tongo on 18 January. Firing on the South Africans' position began at dawn, then infantry moved up the north side of the mountain and the assault began. The South Africans abandoned the position that afternoon and never seriously attacked again along the entire front.

Three days later, on 21 January 1976, Pretoria ordered its defeated army to retreat towards the border, 1,000 miles away.

4. Victory to the People

FAPLA's Counter Offensive North

The MPLA counter offensive on the Northern Front did not get underway until almost a month after the decisive Kifangondo battle, but it met little organized resistance from UPA-FNLA. Such resistance as there was, MPLA discovered, centred on pockets of mercenaries with 105mm and 106mm recoilless guns mounted on jeeps, armoured cars and some heavier artillery still in action, but they were mainly employed in defensive mine-laying to hinder the FAPLA's advance.

On 6 December, FAPLA returned to Caxito, the crossroads town north of the capital that had changed hands so often that year; it would not fall into UPA hands again. Fourteen tons of weapons were taken, and the First and Second Infantry Squadrons moved on, accompanied now by tanks, and the Stalin Organs with Cuban crews. The heavy weapons proved to be unnecessary, however, and it was the young army's infantry, spearheaded by shock troops of veteran guerrillas and young recruits armed with AK47s and G-3s, rolling down the roads in ordinary trucks that kept the UPA force on the move.

'This was a war for bridges' recalls Commander Ndozi who led his column from Kifangondo to Soyo on the Zaire estuary with the loss of only one man. 'Our shock unit was a mixture of veteran guerrillas and young recruits – they didn't even move in armoured cars.'

There were two hours of real fighting at the Onzo river, below Nambuangongo, which turned out to be a major supply base. After Nambuangongo the columns split, with Commander Ndozi heading north-west to Ambriz, UPA-FNLA military General Headquarters, and the second column going on to take Uíje provincial capital of Carmona (now Uíje). There was further resistance at the Negage airbase a few miles from Uíje, but by 3 January it was all over. On the 4th, FAPLA walked into Uíje – the proposed capital of Holden's Angola, whose fall to the MPLA was the final blow to the morale of the UPA-FNLA forces.

Meanwhile, Commander Ndozi's column using amphibious landing craft forded the Loge river to Ambrizete, which had been occupied along with Ambriz on 13 January. In a film shot of the advance, supply boats landing on the beach at the seaside town the following day were welcomed by the townspeople who waded out waving and giving MPLA's victory sign. 'Why is the baby crying?' a FAPLA asks a thin young mother '*É fome, Camarada*' (It is hunger comrade). The children are hungry and sick, she complained, they have been without food or medical care.

From Ambriz and Ambrizete, the Ndozi column was catching up with the enemy forces who were being pushed inexorably into a corner: Soyo on the Zaire river estuary. Their only way out would be by air or sea. But FAPLA had to deal with mines, laid down by the mercenaries, and there were frequent halts for the engineering units to throw up bridges: 'What we usually did was throw up earthworks with culverts for the river to pass through. Of course this only worked with small rivers'. One Bailey bridge was constructed in the Soyo advance, and this had to be reinforced for the tanks to pass.

Ndozi's column had a tank force attached, manned by Cuban volunteers.

> In my column the majority of the Cubans were tank crews though we had some logistics experts and some artillery gunners and seamen for the boats. From January onwards we started training Angolans in the tanks so that for every tank crew of five there were three Cubans and two Angolans learning. By the time we reached the frontier the Angolans were driving!

The front was a training ground in other ways too, whenever there was a halt, captured weapons would be examined and tested; US anti-tank weapons were especially appreciated.

The final assault on Soyo took the town completely by surprise.

> They were expecting reinforcements and when we came in some chaps from the UPA positions ran out to meet us: they had lost contact with the General Staff Headquarters which was in Mbanza Kongo. The British mercenaries were still there: one was killed, we captured Barker and the rest got away by boat.

It was all over. Mopping up operations continued through to mid-February and on 6 March the Noqui border post with Zaire was the last point to be formally occupied.

Luso Column attacks MPLA

Forced to defend their positions actively on the central front, the South Africans resolved to push on and gain control of the entire Benguela railway; giving them the option of dividing the country in two and leaving MPLA temporarily in control of Luanda and the north.

MPLA was still holding the easternmost section of the international railway line, from positions west of Luena to the Zaire border. The makeshift Armoured Corps was, however, no match for a concerted attack by 'Luso column' of the SADF, which began heavy shelling of the town at 4.30 am on 8 December. FAPLA held its fire and waited. The Boers sent in a first wave of UNITA infantry which met heavy FAPLA fire and fled. The significance of the dead left behind was not lost on the South Africans whose artillery was hardly out of action for the next four days. The plan, according to a UNITA prisoner, was to capture Luena that same day but if resistance was met, the artillery was to flatten the town.

Radio contact with MPLA Eastern front headquarters at Saurimo to the north was lost. Messages were ferried by battered, private cars. Codes had not been properly organized. Waves of UNITA infantry were again sent in the following day and again beaten back. The shelling continued. That afternoon the South African armoured column came into sight.

Baltasar Missoji heard the HQ radio bleeping and ran in. The radio operator was lying dead over his machine. Pushing the body aside he heard: 'Hello, hello post number one here.' 'HQ here, where is post number one?' He did not know the code numbers. 'Post number one – Luena airport. The South African armoured cars – we can see them!' 'How many?' 'Eight.' 'Hold on. We're coming.' Comandante Dangeureux was listening in by now. They went down to observe the road running along the railway line, beyond the airport.

They were on their only FAPLA troop transporter: a tractor, armour plated at the railway workshops. Spotting the armoured column, Dangeureux ordered the tractor to the airport to transmit the command to evacuate. On the way, the enemy artillery scored a hit; the tractor engine went up in flames.

Heavy weapons were now beginning to reach Angola, but few reached the Eastern Front, because of the emergency south of Luanda. What had been airlifted to Saurimo, had not yet been transhipped to Luena. The FAPLA, aided only by a small group of Cuban instructors from the Saurimo CIR who had arrived that October in Porto Amboim, were again hopelessly outgunned and outnumbered.

The evacuation of Luena began on 10 December, shortly after midnight. Shells were falling everywhere. The civilians had fled at the start of the artillery fire on the 8th. Now FAPLA had to withdraw. But where to? Some suggested staying on and starting urban guerrilla warfare, but the town is small. It was more important that the South African advance north to Saurimo and east to the border, which would have given them control of the entire railway, was prevented.

So FAPLA went north to Buçaco. By blowing the bridge, a defensive position was established to the north on the Biula flank. The South African column occupied Luena but halted, which gave FAPLA time to regroup and organize its Biula position: for the next two months the revolutionaries resisted persistent attempts to cut them out from the east. Teixeira de Sousa, right on the Zaire border, also remained in FAPLA control. Blowing the bridge into Zaire to prevent Mobutu's army attacking, the MPLA forces held on. Meanwhile tanks were arriving from Saurimo with reinforcements of weapons and Cuban combatants. Luena was finally liberated on 14 February.

Fighting in the east had cost many lives. As in the first three weeks on the

Southern and Central front, Angolans alone were involved against the South Africans, with only a handful of Cuban instructors from the local CIR. By the time the Soviet-made tanks arrived, the war had already been won; the counter-offensive was being prepared.

FNLA and UNITA's 'Democratic Republic'

Theoretically, two governments ruled Angola during the war. MPLA's People's Republic was governed from Luanda, FNLA and UNITA were supposed to have ruled jointly as the Democratic Republic of Angola. It was never made clear whether Uije, in FNLA territory or Huambo, in UNITA territory was the capital. As the Zaire news agency reported, a government was not even formally announced until 23 November, two weeks after Independence, and even then there had to be two Premiers who were supposed to hold office on alternate months.

Conflict between the two allies arose almost at once. In Benguela, FNLA and UNITA entered the city on 7 November, after the South Africans. Each hoisted its own flag: UNITA on the railway building and the bank, FNLA on the Town Hall. The assistant to the Provincial Governor, who stayed on, reports:

> They didn't even know who was working here. Most people had left for Luanda with the MPLA. A few of us stayed on. They didn't threaten us in the office but life went on without government or anything. Any problems were forwarded to Huambo. Nobody worked, as we felt unsafe and stayed at home. Private firms didn't want to pay their workers because the UNITA trades union, SINDACO had told casual workers to get taken on as full-time and get full-time pay. On 24 December fighting broke out between FNLA and UNITA with automatic weapons and some mortars. UNITA did have support in the south but they lost it because of their 90 days misrule. Benguela always had food and water and electricity, also petrol. But prices went up. Of the foreigners, the Italian and German consuls never left.

In Lobito, a survivor of the UNITA firing squads testified 'I don't think there is enough ink to record the blood that flowed under their rule'. UNITA carried out organized looting and killing of whites, coloureds and educated blacks.

Problems began when Chipenda arrived in town. There was rivalry between him and Valentim, Savimbi's top man. Fighting between Chipenda's FNLA and Valentim's UNITA also started on 24 December.

> The South Africans helped the whites and the FNLA helped everyone else escape from UNITA. FNLA were encamped with the South Africans up on the hill. On the 26th the FNLA evacuated to Lubango.

> We went into hiding until FAPLA liberated the city on 10 February. UNITA was very racist. Even coloured people with UNITA cards they killed. A mass meeting at the High School called by UNITA was told everyone must carry a UNITA membership card. This is a military dictatorship. UNITA soldiers looted city houses and called on the poorest people in the townships to follow on behind and take the rest.

UNITA soldiers were given no pay, and often had no food. 'UNITA wasn't a liberation movement, it was a movement of killing. They didn't beat up whites they shot us. But they beat up blacks. It was horrible, I don't know how they survived.' Francisco José dos Santos was shot through the lip on Lobito's Death Hill, and left for dead. The firing squad stole his watch and he crawled to safety during the night.

In both Benguela and Lobito, the working people said they had been forced to attend UNITA mass meetings. 'People who went to MPLA meetings went of their own free will. UNITA soldiers forced us to go to theirs. The white business people here were all for UNITA but when the MPLA had left, the whites started crying for the MPLA to come back.'

UNITA organized mass killings at the Bié prison. 'The back wall was covered in blood. The prisoners were taken out and lined up there, beaten up and shot.' The last batch of murders were carried out on 9 and 10 February 1976, as FAPLA approached. When they reached the prison on the 11th they found hundreds of bodies and two mass graves.

Fighting between FNLA and UNITA had begun in Huambo on 22 December and spread to Benguela and Lobito on the 24th. On 22 December Huambo radio broadcast a call from the 'Council of Ministers' under FNLA Premier Johnny Pinnock Eduardo (a cousin of Holden) for all troops to return to barracks and an end to fighting between FNLA and UNITA; subsequent broadcasts from Lobito radio confirmed the fighting had spread there over Christmas. On 28 December UNITA's Radio Clube de Lobito condemned FNLA 'fraud and opportunism' that had led UNITA 'to expel FNLA from the centre and south of Angola'. FNLA was accused of robbery, murder and corruption, of propagating racism and robbing banks. The broadcast said FNLA were left only in Lubango, Moçamedes, Porto Alexandre and Menongue (Serpa Pinto). The provinces of Bié, Huambo and Moxico were described as 'already free of its reactionary presence'. UNITA, it said, no longer accepted military coexistence with FNLA and would permit only 100 FNLA soldiers to remain in Huambo to protect FNLA government staff.

Subsequently, Savimbi followed this up by telling Western correspondents that FNLA and principally Chipenda's faction, were responsible for the armed robberies, assaults, rapes and killings in the Democratic Republic. Hundreds of victims and eye witnesses have disproved this.

At the end of December in Moçamedes, road maintenance workers collected 84 bodies from the streets for a mass burial. Townspeople estimated that 700 civilians were killed in the FNLA-UNITA occupation. At nearby Porto Alexandre, a 32 year old tailor, gave the names of 38 people known to him personally who had been murdered. The MPLA steering committee in Porto Alexandre, formed from local members, thought about 150 MPLA sympathizers had been murdered there in the three month occupation.

When UNITA took control of downtown Lubango, the people fled to the airport for protection by the South African army.

On 11 January hundreds of Moçamedes civilians fled the terror in fishing boats. Two reached Luanda on the 13th with 74 and 71 passengers. A third, the Silver Sky, turned south and docked in Walvis Bay, Namibia.

UNITA's reign of terror continued after FAPLA had liberated the country, and today is the main feature of UNITA 'control' of civilians in the bush.

In Moxico, bands of armed UNITA rampaged through villages on their way to Zambia. On 24 May 1976 UNITA, in a BBC broadcast, claimed that it was attacking Cuban troops and that Savimbi was at the head of an organized guerrilla force. Actually an anti-civilian terror campaign was in progress. Mupita Kussupika, of Cameia on the Lumege river in Moxico, an elder and member of the MPLA action committee said:

> Savimbi was defeated and had to take to the bush. He started fighting against us, the Angolan people.
>
> UNITA fired on our village with heavy weapons, we had to cross the river and flee. Nobody stayed in our village and they occupied it. Everything we had . . . was taken by them . . . . Many people were murdered between March and August 1976 by UNITA. Captain Mandevo was here and in Liangongo during their retreat. He rounded up our women, youth organization, and the action committee. Then he went on to Tchiesso and began killing there. FAPLA was nearby but even so a lot of people were killed by UNITA. Everyone who could ran away, but they were behind us, killing us as they went. They destroyed everything.

Many, different eye witnesses told seemingly incredible stories: a Bié nurse buried alive by UNITA; men and women hauled up before mass UNITA rallies, accused of being MPLA supporters and knifed to death on the spot. This happened not once but many times, and continued in the UNITA campaign of terror against civilians of the People's Republic.

The Western press's lavish coverage of Savimbi and his UNITA reported neither the terror nor administrative, governmental, health, welfare or organizational innovations. Both the last US Consul General and the Portuguese High Commissioner had warned Western governments that MPLA alone had the support of the civil service cadres and that government without MPLA would be impossible. The counter-revolutionary war waged against MPLA since 1975 has fruitlessly sought to prove the opposite. But Washington, London, Paris and Pretoria cannot point to a single, successful civilian government action by their 'Democratic Republic', in its 100 days of rule.

UNITA had its mass organizations, LIMA for the women, the Youth, and SINDACO, the trades union front. LIMA's main task was to ensure women abandoned Western dress and lead swaying, chanting lines of supporters whenever a male leader appeared. The MPLA women's movement co-ordinator in Bié, Elena, was arrested with Gertrude, another member of the women's committee, and other MPLA women activists on 16 August 1975. Gertrude tells how:

> They took us to a mass rally at the Bié Sports Stadium. They presented us to the people. It was done by Alisira of LIMA . . . first she insulted our President. She said we had been tricked into joining MPLA which was the movement of the rich . . . we must wear African clothes and eat African food. Down with the civilized, down with women who wear trousers they shouted. Down with the Portuguese language. Down with pencils.

Gertrude was kept under house arrest but constantly visited the Bié prison where her uncle and brother were.

> I saw a lot of torture. When prisoners were brought there; first they ripped off all their clothes and beat them with whips made of rubber tyres till they screamed. One day I saw Bandeira with a gash on his head and a dirty bandage. He was with Assis and Agnello, an Indian medical student and MPLA supporter. Kapango and Machado called to me from a window. Women prisoners requested sanitary towels. UNITA didn't allow me to hand them over.

Elena, was knifed to death; Gertrude survived by going underground with around 300 other MPLA supporters.

SINDACO involved itself in anything except organizing the work force. It undertook armed robbery of the docks, warehouses and any functioning shops whose owners were suspected of MPLA sympathies. It fixed prices in UNITA stores: one price to its members and another to the people. Under the overall command of Jorge Valentim, SINDACO chief in Lobito, it sought out and eliminated workers suspected of MPLA sympathies. After liberation, when MPLA activists addressed dock workers and began union work there, dockers could not recall SINDACO having undertaken any concrete action on their behalf or asking for their views, or about their problems and what action the union should take.

People's Angola

In the People's Angola during the war and early days of liberation, corresponding to those 100 days of FNLA/UNITA terror, there was no racism, no fear, no arrests, and no beatings and executions. Travellers could drive alone, unarmed and unescorted. People's Neighbourhood Committees in the towns and Action Groups in the villages functioned as local authorities until the government appointed district officials. Peasants sold fresh fruit, eggs and vegetables at the roadside; roadblocks, manned, 24 hours a day, by citizens' committees from the local village, guarded their area from enemy infiltration. Travellers' documents were checked, news – and sometimes cigarettes – exchanged. Villages near the frontline from which FAPLA soldiers had been killed at the front flew the MPLA flag at half mast; occasionally a burial party could be seen. At dawn, all over People's Angola, the new People's flag was run up, traffic halted and everyone saluted it: black for the people, red for the blood sacrificed in the liberation struggle, gold for the country's wealth.

Then everyone went to work. The administration offices were never closed. Post office, government departments in the provincial capitals, schools, hospitals, mother and child care clinics were kept going as best they could while new staff was recruited. In the countryside, Ministry of Agriculture officials plied to and fro assessing crops and organizing marketing. Even three miles from the South African artillery, in the Queve valley cotton-fields, the National Cotton Board van could be seen – once travelling in reverse, to escape from a stray South African shell.

The MPLA's Department of Organization of the Masses (DOM) led civilian organization. It was in charge of refugee support work – distributing food and clothing, housing and jobs – mass campaigns to help schools and literacy work, and organization of the workforce on collective or state owned property. DOM offices in the towns overflowed with volunteer workers and visitors, refugees and peasants seeking advice or help. DOM workers took homeless visitors to their houses, and sometimes the DOM offices themselves were turned into an improvised doss house.

There was always news at the DOM, as travellers came through the enemy lines or returned from the front. By 8 am, seven days a week, the doors were open and the day's work begun. At all hours of the day and night, convoys left to fetch supplies, and to carry news to government and military headquarters. DOM workers contacted outlying villages, hamlets, and local citizens' action groups. They held political meetings to explain MPLA's ideas and the need for hard work to increase production and support national resistance. Long before November 1976, when the official literacy campaign was launched, literacy classes were going strong in the towns and countryside, stimulated by DOM. Militias and underground resistance groups in the occupied zones had organized themselves around the DOM. When the enemy advanced, MPLA flags, books, guns and ammunition were buried, but the DOM's work went on. Action groups met secretly, listened to the radio broadcasts and passed on the real news, of the FAPLA victories. When the victorious liberating army was on its way, secret messages went out on National Radio to the DOM groups who prepared for the troops' re-entry.

While the UNITA army spent most of its time pillaging in the rearguard, FAPLA were at the front. After January 1976 FAPLA jeeps and military trucks and equipment plied the main roads towards the front; soldiers were in the trenches, or in garrison towns: Saurimo in the east, Malanje, Dalatando, Luanda.

The Cubans were dug in with FAPLA, or manning logistics bases in the rearguard, and staking out strategic points in Luanda. Like FAPLA, they followed the Boers' retreat, then strung out in a strategic defence line across southern Angola, some way back from the border. Provincial capitals might have one Cuban house with room for 15 to 20 men, whose job was to liaise with the frontline and organize logistics. These houses became the centre of Cuban civilian assistance as the war was over, and Cuban doctors, nurses, engineers and construction workers battled for Angola's reconstruction.

When all Angola was liberated, Emergency Commissions, representing all the government departments, were appointed in the provincial capitals by the government in Luanda. After restoring water and electricity supplies in the capital (usually with Cuban aid), the Commissions attended to the reorganization of distribution, got emergency supplies into the shops, reported on manpower needs for the medical and education services and examined the question of workers' pay. (In the occupied zones workers were not paid for the 100 days of war.) In the central highlands towns the populations grew. By February 1977 country towns had more than doubled their pre-Independence size. The population of Bié city was over 20,000 by early 1977 (9,000 under the Portuguese); and in Camacupa it had increased to 21,000 as against 5,000.

Strains on the embryonic social services were evident. In Huambo province ten medical centres in country towns outside the capital were being put back into operation with 600 hospital beds. Peasants who had taken part in MPLA's pre-war Village Fronts organized co-operatives.

FNLA and UNITA had smashed windows, broken doors and furniture, and daubed public buildings and MPLA houses with slogans and human excrement. Voluntary groups of townspeople spent weekends weeding roads, clearing rubbish, repainting the town buildings. Paint sent from Luanda came in small quantities of different colours, and houses in Bié were bright with alternately blue and pink, and yellow and green walls.

The People's Palaces (former colonial government palaces in each province capital) soon had their wall-newspapers; telling of the occupation, the liberation, the speeches of Angola's leaders, poems, drawings by school-children, and quotations from Marx and Lenin, Samora Machel, Kwame Nkrumah.

The residences of the former governors now operated as improvised hotels for visiting government officials. People there debated local and national problems, compared the situation in other areas and assessed the difficulties ahead. Government Ministers often took their place on the long dining table with the rest. Looking back to those first 100 days, these former guerrillas, political prisoners and underground activists were distinguished by their simplicity.

On 18 November the first cabinet meeting took place. Ministerial salaries were slashed by 50%, and the thirteenth wage month, instituted by the Portuguese was cancelled. On 5 December, the Premier made a broad economic policy statement: there were to be no new exploiters.

The Council of the Revolution – the supreme state organ until the election of the National Assembly – took a series of measures including changing public transport fares in favour of poor workers. Neto's Battle for Production speech on 10 December launched a production offensive throughout the liberated areas, integrating the mass organizations into collective production work, and encouraging individual farmers to redouble their efforts for the 'resistance economy'. Ministry of Agriculture cadres went out to assess crops. Also in December a Labour Discipline law was passed to discourage absenteeism and sabotage; punishment was to be docking of pay. In January, the trade unions launched a first training seminar for shop stewards, on 6 February the first people's shops were opened in the capital, and towards the end of the month, the salaries of white-collar civil servants were brought closer in line to those of production workers, by government decreed statutory wage cuts. On 27 February the State Intervention Law defined the three sectors of the economy – state owned, co-operative and private – and made provision for legal nationalization and confiscation. The Education Ministry organized long vacation holiday camps for school-children and launched intensive planning for the next school year.

In March the oil industry started negotiations with Gulf Oil, and talks with Algeria's Sonatrach. The Transport Ministry requisitioned private hauliers' services to help in the national transport crisis. Cuban medical staff fanned out to hospitals in the liberated provinces, and Cuban agricultural and construction workers took on civilian tasks.

Counter Offensive South

The second Ebo victory by the joint Angolan and Cuban force was followed by another major battle at Kariango, which was reoccupied by the revolutionaries on 29 December. Heroic fighting in the Medunda mountains further affected the South African generals' confidence in their invincibility. In the east, FAPLA tenaciously held on to the vital stretch of the railway line, now cut off from Zaire and possible Mobutu reinforcements. Politicians in Pretoria were disconcerted by the absence of open support for their action.

In Luanda, the commanders reported that enemy morale seemed weak: they were failing to follow through their successful actions, and withdrawing whenever they met resistance. Santa Comba, near Cela was retaken on 16 January. The counter-offensive got underway immediately after the OAU summit on Angola with the counter-attack to liberate Ngunza on 25 January. South African ground forces had been pulled back towards Huambo, but their artillery was still stationed in the Ngunza mountains. As it began moving out, covered by armoured cars, it was attacked by two companies of FAPLA-FAR troops infiltrated behind their positions and equipped with 75mm anti-tank guns and RPG7 rockets. About 80 soldiers were killed and four Boer armoured cars destroyed. It had been hoped to surround and capture part of the South African force.

The advance from Kariango eastwards reached Mussende on 27 January. It was now a question of whether Huambo, or Benguela-Lobito would be liberated next.

The OAU summit that ended in deadlock on 12 January had been contemptuous of Vorster's ambitions to be hailed as the saviour of Black Africa from the rigours of communism. On the 27th, as the revolutionaries began sweeping south, the South African army was in full retreat. But Pretoria obstinately held on to the hope that it could continue to occupy the southernmost strip of Angola, along the Namibia border. Pieter Botha, the Defence Minister, declared that his country's troops would remain in the 'Angola frontier region' until it received guarantees on the border and on South African interests. The Angolans declared that not an inch of their land would remain in enemy hands.

On 1 February, Vorster appeared on television. Still covering up the extent of his army's commitment in Angola, he complained the 'US has misinterpreted the Angolan situation' and had refused to involve itself because of a 'Vietnam psychosis'. Washington, he said, should 'realize that a Marxist government in Luanda would have a domino effect in the rest of Southern Africa, notably in Zaire and Zambia'. Not to mention Namibia and South Africa itself.

In Luanda, on 2 February, the Afro-Asian Solidarity Conference was opened by Agostinho Neto. Statesmen from countries all over the world heard him reaffirm Angola's non-alignment and call for normal relations with Zaire and Zambia.

The following day, a small MPLA plane flew over Huambo, which had already been evacuated by the SADF, dropping leaflets calling on UNITA to lay down its weapons and join in reconstruction. Savimbi was already in Bié, where the retreat to Namibia was being planned. Nzau Puna left to join him in a four-engined plane.

Meanwhile the revolutionaries' main problem was crossing the rivers going south. South African forces and white mercenaries with UNITA ensured that hardly a single important bridge between Ngunza and the Namibia border was left standing. Hundreds of millions of dollars damage was done in the month of the South African retreat.

Aided by Cuban engineering units, FAPLA sappers were throwing up mud and culvert structures and resurrecting old ferries to get the armoured column, spearheaded by T-54 tanks, across the Queve. The first tanks in the advance were battered veterans from the siege of Leningrad, with internationalist Cuban crews. At Koroko experiments with the old ferry worked and the entire column crossed, and went through Amboiva – where it was welcomed by half a dozen UNITA soldiers who thought the heavy weapons to be South African reinforcements – and rejoined the tarmac highway. There was no resistance, apart from some mortar shots at Alto Hama, where UNITA soldiers were disarmed, and told to forget the war and return to their villages to work. The same message was now being broadcast on Angolan National Radio by Commander Iko Carreira, the Defence Minister.

Again the advancing column was slowed by a bridge, north of Huambo at Chipipa. On Friday 6 February the remaining UNITA ministers in Huambo, led by José Ndele, the 'Prime Minister', left for Bie. Huambo radio went off the air that night.

At 2 pm on 8 February FAPLA entered Huambo. There was no resistance. UNITA soldiers left in the town were milling about, leaderless. When they saw FAPLA's BTR troop transports they rushed up, convinced reinforcements were approaching. More than 200 were disarmed, given civilian clothes and sent home that first day. 'We addressed them, we told them UNITA was wrong, we would not kill them or hurt them. They should go back to their homes and start to work for free Angola.'

Three days later, the FAPLA-FAR column divided, some following the retreating South African force to Lubango, others going east, in the South Africans' footsteps, to Bié.

Meanwhile, UNITA was spreading calculated panic in the central highlands. The MPLA and the Communists were going to massacre every man, woman and child they could find, salvation lay south, in Namibia, or at best hiding out in the bush. No one should stay in the cities and towns, because, the people were told, Savimbi was going to come back with planes and bomb everything in the cities.

At around 10 am on 11 February Savimbi left Bié by plane for the south, and security behind the South African lines. South African armoured cars protected the UNITA withdrawal south. Bié had been a staging post over the last two weeks for a South African airlift of its eastern front back into Namibia, and the Runtu base. It was now to be the gateway south for thousands of misguided Angolans, deceived into believing their lives were at risk.

Some MPLA supporters, prisoners of UNITA, were forced to join the fleeing columns south towards Menongue. They saw the South African armoured cars south of Bié blowing the bridges on the main road after the last UNITA officers had gone through.

Bié was liberated on 11 February. The pretty hill town was empty, but a mile or so further on, at Bié Gare on the railway line, a small group of MPLA supporters waited for their comrades, banners unfurled. There were tears. A political meeting. Afterwards, leaving a small force to occupy the town, the column headed back towards Huambo and the road south to the border.

As MPLA supporters emerged from hiding, a desperate hunt began for the prisoners taken since August by UNITA. Political Bureau member Joaquim Kapango and other leading Umbundu cadres from the People's Movement were amongst those imprisoned all this time; they were executed on the eve of liberation. Their bodies, and those of hundreds of others, were found in mass graves. UNITA's fury had been turned on civilians, men and women and even children. The principal targets had been Umbundu leaders of the MPLA.

While Huambo and Bié were now free, the column from Ngunza was delayed by broken bridges. Lobito and Benguela, due to be liberated on 4 February, the 15th anniversary of the launching of armed struggle, were not reached until almost a week later, with again, almost no resistance. UNITA was laid up in ambush north of Lobito in the Canjala area. But on 9 February MPLA controlled the road into Lobito. The entry into the Atlantic port down the long steep hill through the townships, took place at midday on the

10th. Not a shot was fired. A second part of the column had taken a back road behind the city to emerge on the coast road south at Catumbela. It met a group of 20 UNITA infantrymen who silently handed in their guns. In Lobito city around 2,000 people welcomed the MPLA with placards and flags. There was quiet and calm. The column, in radio contact with Commander Sapu at Catumbela, decided to move on to Benguela.

At the outskirts of the red city on a metal rail and road bridge over the Cavaco river, standing to attention, rifles smartly in position, were the Benguela people's militias. Thousands swarmed around the tanks, clambering up, weeping, hugging and kissing their comrades. That night, there was dancing in the streets, singing and joy for the first time in a hundred days. The MPLA forces had arrived in time to prevent a massacre on 15 February of everyone who could read and write. Messages had been distributed explaining why they were UNITA's enemies.

In Lobito, the following day, a search party set out for the hills north of the Pundo crossroads. Men and women bent over the hillside scattered with decomposing bodies, looking all day for their relatives and friends. The Hill of Death: UNITA had begun summary executions there in the final weeks of its rule, under orders from Jorge Valentim. More than 500 were killed, children as well as adults, of all colours and all classes. On the 13th, when there was no longer any hope of recognizing the human remains still unclaimed, a small FAPLA squadron poured gasoline over the hillside and set it on fire. Throughout the night and for most of the following day flames and smoke continued to rise.

At Lobito docks, Commander Sapu called the workers together.

> I told them of the situation and said that we MPLA wanted everyone to go back to work . . . . The majority of workers agreed with me. I don't know how many dock-workers there are altogether, but around 1,000 turned up that day. They asked me if they had to have an MPLA membership card, like UNITA made them have. I told them no, it wasn't necessary. They were concerned they had no money to buy food, because they hadn't been paid for three or more months.

Liberation

Even at this stage, there seems to have been some effort in the Western camp to plan a military comeback. The French had apparently tried to mount a last minute salvage operation for UNITA on the southern front, much as, in January, the British had rushed their men into the north to bale out Holden. A plane load of French mercenaries had left Kinshasa for Huambo and Bié but finding them already occupied by FAPLA turned back. Landing in Kinshasa they reported that the South African army was defending Menongue and throwing up a defensive shield for the 'pro-Western forces'.

France's role with UNITA is still to be clarified: but French soldiers certainly entered Angola with the original invading Natal column, and were there at the end. In the next five years of destabilization of the People's Republic, and until the defeat of Valery Giscard d'Estaing at the 1981 French Presidential elections, France's military ties with its neo-colonies in Africa and with Zaire were used against MPLA, while it armed the SADF.

The French mercenary air lift from Kinshasa, coincided with a sortie by Zaire air force bombers into eastern Angola. In South Africa, the Air Force Public Relations Officer, Captain Robert Blake, said South Africa was prepared to use combat aircraft in southern Angola. On 12 February, Associated Press reported from Johannesburg,

> South Africa is openly seeking an accommodation with victorious communist-backed forces in Angola, but is also preparing for the possibility of a major war. [South Africa] is girding itself for war, with troop call-ups, increased military training schedules and a major build-up of forces along Angola's southern border. South Africans watch developments in Angola with a sense of foreboding and many fear an eventual confrontation with the People's Movement.

The South Africans were now dug in around 50 miles north of the Namibia border AP reported, with reasonable accuracy, and quoted Defence Minister Pieter Botha speaking that day:

> If the region is stabilized and the Ovambo interests and developments are not undermined by the Popular Movement – in other words if they restrain themselves in staying where they belong – doubtless discussions could be held with them regarding our interests in that area.

While racist South Africa licked its wounds, the liberation of southern Angola was raising revolutionary spirits all over the world. Lubango was freed on 10 February – by its own people, before the arrival of the FAPLA-FAR column. Around 20 January the news that MPLA was on the way had spread into the hills of the southern highlands round Lubango. Guerrilla groups had been active around the city and down the highway towards Moçamedes. Bases were strung out in the area, 17 men in Quipungo, who collected 142 weapons from successful ambushes, and 47 under the command of Farrusco, former commando in the colonial army, later to become one of FAPLA's top operational commanders in South Africa's undeclared six year war. A third group of 30 or so were in action west of Lubango and more than 20 other guerrillas were based southwest. Further afield, towards Moçamedes, on the edge of the desert, were Mocubal bases around Virei.

The Maconje base, where Farrusco and Afonso Maria set up their first guerrilla operation, was a perfect hideout on an abandoned farm, with plenty of food and water. Weapons and ammunition were acquired by ambushing military vehicles on the main Lubango-Moçamedes road. The first full-scale sabotage action was mounted on 26 December against a train on the

Moçamedes railway. Armed only with rifles, the guerrillas forced the train to turn back – which created panic at both ends of the line. Vila Ariaga, where the FNLA-UNITA and Portuguese ELP had massacred railway workers, all of whom were MPLA supporters, also contributed guerrillas. So frequently were enemy patrols attacked around Virei by Mocubal guerrillas armed with bows and arrows and old Mausers that it became a semi-liberated area. Caraculo and Santa Teresa guerrillas were engaged in mine-laying, and the Moçamedes-Lubango road was used only at night by enemy traffic. All bush shops in the area were closed to punish the people for supporting the guerrillas, and to prevent supplies leaking through to the bases, but the effect was nil. This was an area of cattle raising, and the principal diet is meat and milk. Closing the bush shops failed to close all supply routes to the guerrillas: Roman Catholic missionaries in the highlands, convinced by FNLA-UNITA's terrorism and their PIDE and South African allies that MPLA truly represented Angola's freedom, had been assisting the guerrillas for some weeks. Some were even lending out church garments to disguise the activists.

In Lubango itself, clandestine MPLA militants began psychological warfare units: children employed as bootblacks, workers and hotel employees began spreading the word that the Mocubals in the desert were preparing to attack the city.

Carlos Mangas, the air reconnaissance expert captured by the South Africans in their invasion of Lubango in October, had by now escaped from Lubango hospital, disguised as a monk, and was hiding in the city, in close contact with the guerrillas. He had been to the bases and returned on a fruit and vegetable cart. Also underground in Lubango was a former Benguela MPLA activist, who was trying to acquire a radio transmitter.

The people of Lubango were desperate for an end to the occupation. Like everybody in occupied Angola, they had been through the 100 days in fear for their lives. Sooner or later, you were liable to be accused of being MPLA, thrown into jail, your possessions stripped from you, your wife abused, and in Lubango, you could be taken up to the high clifftop behind the city, at Tundavala, and quietly dropped over the edge. The reign of terror was worst after UNITA took over the town centre on 10 January. UNITA's arrival signalled the start of a manhunt for all whites, coloureds and educated blacks, as it had in Benguela and Lobito. In the afternoon of 11 January, half the city had taken refuge at Lubango airport where the South African Defence Force was protecting them against the UNITA murderers.

At the airport a white woman was in labour. An Angolan doctor there went to her assistance, but the South African commanding officer would not allow him to attend the woman because he was coloured. There was an angry scene, and the officer eventually gave in. After the woman was delivered the officer asked that the baby be named for him. The birth drew people together, and some tried to draw out the South Africans on their aims. Their explanation was that:

> If MPLA ruled Angola, SWAPO would get support from MPLA; they,

> the South Africans, wanted to give Namibia independence, but their kind of independence. Whatever it cost them, they couldn't allow SWAPO to have Namibia. They began talking of dividing Angola at the Cuanza. The north could be for MPLA, and the south for their Angolan government that would not support SWAPO. They said they had not been able to take Luanda by November 11th as they had planned. But they weren't going to lose a second time.

Sometime near the end of the occupation Savimbi came to Lubango and held a big rally: it was a rally of despair. After that, UNITA went on a rampage, ransacking shops, looting and drinking. Jorge Valentim appeared from Lobito with his French mercenaries. He was overheard pleading with the mercenaries to stay on, but the French wanted to get out – fast.

A South African soldier, who witnessed the UNITA retreat said:

> Savimbi's command withdrew late one night, led by a senior UNITA officer; carload after carload of high officials redolent of power and authority, their vehicles well appointed Mercedes and Porsches instead of battered lorries or travel-stained Fiats. They were not mattress people like the refugees who had gone before. They were professors and senior bureaucrats and private secretaries, the backbone of the UNITA war machine.

The 'professors, senior bureaucrats and private secretaries' had nothing to show for the July-February administration in the central highlands. No policy statements, no administrative planning or action had been achieved. Chiwale, the Chief of Staff, had spent more time acting as associate Public Relations officer, alongside Savimbi, turning on the charisma to the Western press, than anywhere near the frontline of battle with his South African officer allies.

On the night of 8 February, Huambo's liberation day, the long-hoped for radio set was acquired. The first signals to the guerrillas were sent by Diogo, a former liaison officer in Benguela. He had been taken prisoner and tortured by the SADF, but had managed to escape through the hospital underground network in Lubango. From Miconje came Farrusco and Afonso Maria. In a dry river bed, beyond the tall, fragrant, eucalyptus tree-belt skirting the city centre, the attack was planned. On the 9th, however, orders were cancelled. UNITA soldiers had begun streaming into town and it was feared that the guerrillas' attack had been leaked to the enemy. But it was a false alarm; the soldiers were on their way south to Namibia and were hurrying to the railway station hoping to find a train, as road transport was by now non-existent.

At dawn on 10 February the guerrillas took Lubango. Quietly occupying strategic parts of the city, they allowed the UNITA train-load to pull out east. Some had wanted to attack the train but townspeople argued against it because civilians were also on board. But the engine driver, a longtime MPLA supporter, took matters into his own hands. He took the train almost to Matala, unhitched the locomotive and then steamed back to Lubango to join in the celebrations.

Radio Lubango, People's Radio, was back on the air. After a glorious rally in Lubango's main square, MPLA and Catholic missionaries and priests, who had assisted the MPLA underground, began distributing food. While church trucks piled high with maize and accompanied by priests and MPLA activists, fanned out through the suburbs and into the surrounding villages, people in the city set to work to organize rudimentary government, and guerrilla leaders at last managed to make radio contact with Luanda. 'Give us weapons' was their first request.

The FAPLA-FAR column never entered the city. The people of Lubango jammed Radio Popular's switchboard all day, asking when the column was expected, but it never arrived. Hearing the radio broadcasts, FAPLA-FAR saved time and went round the outskirts on south, chasing the invading column out. Only a few jeeps with FAPLA and Cuban officers drove into the town centre, met its revolutionary government and drew up plans for the emergency situation.

From Lubango, FAPLA-FAR were moving south to set up a strong defence line across the country from east to west and pressure the South Africans for a complete, unconditional withdrawal. In Luanda, Agostinho Neto was besieged with diplomatic initiatives from the West, designed to test the People's government and see what kind of concessions could be wrung from it at the eleventh hour. Ultimately, London became the venue for diplomatic contact. But the Angolan message was firm and clear: no conditions; no compromise. Complete withdrawal from Angolan territory.

In the field the political response was backed up by tank columns pressing down to the border. There was never any clash between the opposing armies' tanks: now equally matched, the South Africans had no inclination to fight. Advance parties of FAPLA and Cuban scouts and snipers closed in around the SADF camps. A few rounds of ammunition, reinforced by the sound of tanks in the distance, alarmed the South Africans, who hastily struck camp and moved south, further south, until eventually, on 27 March 1976, Kunene was emptied of them, they crossed back into Namibia. Standing near the border, surrounded by hot, dusty Angolan and Cuban soldiers, Lucio Lara, MPLA's veteran political organizer, hailed the victory. By his side, stood Oliver Tambo, President of the African National Congress of South Africa.

It was many weeks before the victorious revolutionary army extended along the whole length of the Angolan-Namibia border. Kunene had fast communications with the provincial capital, only 15 miles north of the border, and was linked to Luanda by air and good tarmac roads. But the huge, sparsely populated Kuando Kubango province, with its sandy marshland, criss-crossed by innumerable rivers and infested with tropical parasites, was only slowly covered by FAPLA. They finally reached Cuangar in mid-April. A truck with 30 FAPLA and a commanding officer went down to the border. On the Namibian side, despatched from the massive Air and Ground Forces base at nearby Runtu, were numerous AML90 armoured cars and hundreds of troops. FAPLA called for an officer from the SADF, and made a brief statement, informing the enemy troops that Cuangar was now liberated and belonged to the People's Republic of Angola. Clear assurances were given that Angola had no intention of violating the Namibia border.

The small Angolan force then withdrew to their camp, five kilometres north. The next day a FAPLA frontier patrol reported AML90s massed along the border. To emphasize Angola's intentions to defend every inch of its soil, FAPLA brought up the tanks – manoeuvring them in the bush with much noise and dust. The AMLs then turned round and moved off.

The South African Defence Force immediately began systematic border war. A squadron of PUMA helicopter gunships was sent into Angola to buzz the FAPLA positions. Many UNITA were still making their way through Kuando Kubango to the South African army camps in Namibia. The South Africans' fallback plan was already in operation: destabilization and continual undeclared border war in order to weaken the young revolutionary state's economic reconstruction and strike at SWAPO, which had seriously disappointed Pretoria. Failing to be deceived by Savimbi, SWAPO, strengthened by a new wave of refugees from Namibia, rallied to MPLA. The refugees told the full story of UNITA's alliance with the hated South African regime, and of the trainloads of Boer 'troopies', waving UNITA flags as they steamed to the battlefront. They also reported the triumphalist South African propaganda and arrogant self-assurance of its stooges in the Democratic Turnhalle Alliance who were tacking together an 'internal' programme for independence – South African style.

Angola had fought for its life, and won, against racist South Africa, armed by the NATO countries and supported by the considerable weight of imperialist diplomacy and economic power. Cuba and the Soviet Union had come to the rescue with men and weapons.

A new nation would be built upon this tremendous victory, a nation proud of its defiant stand for justice and freedom, and clearly understanding the causes of the war. For these reasons Angola is increasingly able to withstand the gradually escalating, bloody, military campaign to sabotage the revolution.

PART 2
The Coup from Within

5. Political Awakening

Politics after 50 Years of Fascism

The Armed Forces' coup on 25 April 1974 signalled the start of mass political action in Angola. New political groups sprang up. Among the white business community and the settler farmers on the Planalto highlands, in Benguela, Lubango, Luanda – wherever a sizeable white community prospered numerous small 'parties' were formed. The largest – MOPUA, based in Huambo – had discussed an alliance with UNITA.

Black groups also sprang up – black 'pacifists', black 'democrats'. More important was the organization of Angolans in association with and membership of the 'three movements': the People's Movement (MPLA), UPA-FNLA and UNITA. Between April 1974 and November 1975 polarization between these three groups took place. By Independence there were few who had not chosen their 'movement'. Many transferred their allegiance to MPLA after the UPA-FNLA and UNITA horror and chaos and their balkanization of the country.

The political work of the three movements was sharply differentiated. UPA-FNLA moved into an area with armed strength and forced membership cards on the local people. UNITA – apart from a brief initial period of addressing the white settlers – called exclusively on the Ovimbundu. MPLA appealed to all Angolans to take their destinies in their own hands, work for a better future, fight for real independence and organize for community improvements.

Written propaganda or political documents were minimal. All three organizations had their programmes printed, but this was of little use in a country with an 85% illiteracy rate. The national radio accorded equal time for political broadcasts. Television was experimental and served Luanda only until after Independence.

There was a dearth of political literature. The politically-minded literate minority thus lacked an important means of informing themselves, since in their reading matter they were subject to their own and their friends' private tastes. This was to be a source of confusion exploited by MPLA's enemies and contributing significantly to political tensions within the organization.

For most Angolans, Independence meant freedom from Portuguese oppression, better education, health, housing and job opportunities; these were the expectations. Unlike UPA-FNLA and UNITA, the MPLA's message was that hard work and sacrifice would be needed to achieve them. In the countryside, life went on much as usual, unless it was disrupted by the departure of the settlers or by the arrival of FNLA and UNITA troops. Only when their farm produce was stolen, their houses ransacked and sometimes their village burned down, did peasants understand what FNLA and UNITA rule meant.

In the towns, where there was more to loot, UPA-FNLA and UNITA troops intensified their activities. Petty criminals soon aligned themselves with the troops and took advantage of the increase in semi-legalized gun-carrying to feather their nests.

In 1974, Angola was still an overwhelmingly rural country, and the 15% or so of urbanized Angolans were still strongly linked to the countryside. Most of the 15% lived in towns with a population of under 2,500, and derived their livelihood at least in part from farming. In the major cities and especially Luanda, industrial production had been insignificant until after 1961, the skilled workforce was almost entirely white and Portuguese, many of the unskilled labourers were migrant contract workers, and the remainder relatively recent arrivals in the city.

Luanda was unique: the population of the city had mushroomed to over 650,000; in the shanty towns that sprawled around it, the Portuguese traders set up corner stores, mini-supermarkets and bottle stores, and often lived above the premises or nearby.

After the April coup, angry white settlers rampaged through the shanty *musseques*, killing, as they had done in the 1960s. The Africans reacted; and after the MPLA underground came into action, the people began organizing themselves into street militias to guard against white and UPA-FNLA, UNITA gangs. The settlers, and their black allies of FNLA and UNITA, dubbed the militias the '*poder popular*' – the people's power lot. MPLA's main mobilizing call was for people's power, the arming of the people in their own defence, and the people's struggle for their own government. Throughout the transition government, the Portuguese High Commissioner received complaints from FNLA and UNITA against the 'people's power' and demands that they be disarmed. The people drove reactionary whites out of the slums and set up co-operative shops to replace the traders.

Against the background of inter-racial tension and isolated violence, MPLA appealed for a non-racial Angola, and stressed that the exploitation Angolans had suffered was linked not to the white race but to the political regime. *Mestiços* (people of mixed race), said MPLA, were not necessarily exploiters: some had joined the guerrillas and been ready to sacrifice their lives for their people. Black, as well as white exploiters must be fought. With the influx of UPA-FNLA and their terror gangs from Zaire, and the later UNITA terror and exploitation of the peasants, the idea of black exploiters became a reality. MPLA's multi-racial allies from Cuba helped to prove that white skin was not intrinsically linked to oppression and plunder.

Inevitably the anti-racial platform was not an easy one to put forward in the early days after the fall of fascism. Too many *mestiços* had been linked to the system in privileged positions, too many whites – the overwhelming majority of the 350,000 white settlers – had behaved immorally towards their black workers. Racism against the whites and *mestiços* was difficult to eradicate until the FNLA-UNITA experience brought home MPLA's message, and meantime MPLA suffered tensions within its ranks, with consequences for its unity.

During the anti-colonial liberation struggle, the MPLA stressed the political education of its militants. In the external camps (such as those in Congo and Zambia) and in the guerrillas' liberated areas, political education guaranteed discussion of racial issues, regular criticism and self-criticism of comrades who held racial or tribal and regional prejudices, and analysis and debate on the Marxist content of the Angolan people's struggle. Unfortunately, little was provided by movement leaders by way of written political works. Neto's major speeches, in which he addressed topics such as racism, tribalism, and anti-imperialism, were printed in booklet form. Other leaders who had written political or creative works linked to the struggle all too often were not in print. Manuscripts, such as the head FAPLA Commissar Jika's book on the Angolan struggle, were not printed until after Independence. The text-book *History of Angola* was available, but this was merely a sketch of the country's past: not yet fleshed out with the people's living history and experience.

The MPLA had suffered a series of splinter movements in the past, and the most serious – Daniel Chipenda's Eastern Revolt, followed by Mario de Andrade's movement of intellectuals, the Active Revolt – had hit the movement at the crucial moment of the fall of fascism. In August 1974 a massive infiltration of an MPLA Congress in Lusaka, led to the organization repudiating the Congress and calling an alternative Inter-Regional Conference of Militants in the liberated areas in September. It had weeded out the infiltrated FNLA and UNITA men and eliminated the two 'Revolts'. Who was left?

There were the guerrillas of the MPLA Cabinda and Eastern fronts, who had been trained outside Angola, undergone intensive political education and were close to the movement's leaders who spent their time with the fighters at the front. (The majority of the political bureau were permanently fighting at the front.) There were members of the MPLA external organization, who with the same political training had been involved in solidarity work overseas, in logistics, and academic training. There were students who had been part of MPLA cells overseas, studying for their country's Independence.

Additionally, were those who had fought on the Northern Front, at the mercy not only of the Portuguese army, the bombings and napalm, but also hunted down by the UPA gangs, and cut off by hostile Zaire. Completely isolated from the external logistics bases and the leadership for long periods, they had survived alone.

In January 1974, Nito Alves, a political officer on the Northern Front, went to Luanda with another guerrilla from the Dembos area. For eight days he sought how to secure assistance for the Northern Front, discussed urban warfare with the Luanda underground, and the capture of weapons and ammunition. He returned to the bush. In May, after the April coup, he again returned clandestinely to Luanda, this time making contact with former political detainees who had been released. Among them were José Van Dunem, Valentim and Betinho, three young men who became part of the Alves circle and were involved in the 1977 Alves coup.

Links were forged at an emotional period – the dawn of freedom – between the northern, isolated fighters and the equally isolated Luanda underground. Clandestine work in the capital, was minimal. PIDE infiltration exceeded that in Lisbon. Informers were everywhere, the lack of a strong, urban working class with organizational and trade union experience was crippling to the task of setting up and maintaining an effective underground movement. The many secret MPLA supporters often limited their activity to listening to Brazzaville radio and vague talk of independence. In the ranks of the colonial army, political work was more effective. Angolan MPLA supporters met progressive anti-fascist Portuguese national servicemen, many of them university students and young officers; cells were organized in which they participated in debates and discussions, and organized avoiding action when the troops were sent to the front. As in Vietnam, units patrolled with their eyes shut, skirting guerrilla held areas. As the black and coloured intake increased, the combat effectiveness of the colonial army fell.

Finally, there was another isolated group – the political prisoners. Some had been part of underground cells, schooled in MPLA's politics, active in resistance work. Others, accused of MPLA sympathies had been sentenced without reason. Still others had been recruited by the PIDE while in gaol to act as informers.

At the Inter-Regional Conference, in 1974 the only recorded clash was provoked by the question of the eligibility of whites for Angolan nationality after Independence. Nito Alves' group, which included Van Dunem and Valentim, argued that whites born in Angola should not necessarily be accorded Angolan nationality, that only those who had taken part in the armed struggle should be eligible. Neto's non-racial argument won. But a new 35-member Central Committee elected at the Conference included Nito Alves and José Van Dunem.

The key to the Alves group's subsequent conduct was a sense of resentment on the part of some 'internal' MPLA activists against the leadership that was predominantly composed of members of the Cabinda and eastern guerrilla fronts.

Political Ferment

Early mass demonstrations in Luanda were severely repressed. The people were not to be deterred, however, and the white threat – when taxi drivers and settlers began murder in the *musséques* – stimulated the organization of People's Neighbourhood committees and self-defence groups. At first, lumpen petty criminal elements joined in forming street defence committees, but they were soon squeezed out by the working people, and the activists found MPLA responded to their thirst for political organization. The committees and defence groups soon became fervent MPLA supporters. The MPLA underground played an important part in this movement, and guerrillas filtering in from the Northern Front were soon drawn into the Luanda ferment.

In the countryside, the MPLA Action Groups emerged and began to organize their communities. After November 1974, when the MPLA became legal, it found committees and groups in areas where it never knew supporters had existed.

The key to the mass organizational thrust was community self-help. Reading rooms, literacy classes, creches, schools, health centres headed the list of priorities, and as the settlers fled, basic shops had to be improvised. The neighbourhood committees appointed secretaries to deal with each type of issue. All these structures became targets for arson and gun attacks by FNLA and UNITA neither of which attempted to emulate the MPLA activists' work and creativity.

Political committees had been formed among Luanda students for some years before the April coup, and the PIDE kept a close watch on them. A month before the coup a specially commissioned study of student attitudes was published, which showed medical students as particularly active, and attitudes generally favouring independence. After the coup, Portuguese students with Angolan links – even some without – were drawn to Luanda.

In Portugal the *Uniao Democratico do Povo* (UDP – a Maoist group) was linked to an Angolan students group called the *Comite Amilcar Cabral* (CAC). UDP was the only Maoist group in Portugal to win any worker following after the April coup; it participated in elections and had one member of parliament. The CAC was formed in July 1974 and publicly linked itself to the MPLA. Although only a small group, it became fairly influential among students and secondary school pupils in Luanda. Another leftist student organization, formed at around the same time called itself the Henda Committee, after Hoji Ya Henda (José Mendes de Carvalho), related to MPLA activist Mendes de Carvalho. Henda had joined the MPLA guerrillas, risen to a leading position in the youth, and been killed in 1968 when MPLA attacked Karipande garrison in the east. Cabral (assassinated in Conakry in 1973) and Henda were perceived as symbols of African resistance. The Henda Committees had links with Lisbon's most disruptive and flamboyant Maoist group, the Movement to Reorganize the Proletariat Party (MRPP), mainly comprising bourgeois youth, and whose bottomless treasury was a constant source of wonder to the serious left.

In Portugal, the UDP and MRPP were firmly pro-China, but their counterparts in Angola played down the China angle. The MPLA was the only left movement, and China was against it, so these fringe 'Maoist' groups kept quiet about their China sympathies. For similar reasons neither group seriously addressed the question of MPLA's Soviet support.

When the MPLA leadership arrived in Luanda and Lucio Lara opened the delegation, the MPLA's first rally had been the target of Portuguese police gunfire, with Lara narrowly missing death. Clearly, the people's power in Angola was with MPLA, so anyone seeking mass support there stayed close to the People's Movement.

By January 1975 CAC had its own journal, *Revoluçao Popular*. It began trying to influence the MPLA's own *Poder Popular* which was now brought out regularly by the co-ordinating committee of the People's Neighbourhood committees. The transition to independence had begun, and an all-party transition government was sworn in on 31 January. There are signs that jealousies emanating from the internal 'Luanda' group against the MPLA leadership were sharpening. The Political Bureau later stated that the group had tried to stop the leadership setting up MPLA's Luanda delegation in November. They had reported 'insecurity'; the guerrillas were not impressed and Lara advanced with his comrades as planned. Possibly, the Luanda group hoped to organize its own headquarters encouraged by the heady experience of the neighbourhood committees, and was unwilling to play second fiddle to the guerrillas.

A people's power week was declared to greet the new transition government. A final mass rally, held on 1 February in the huge Sao Paulo sports stadium, passed radical resolutions, clearly demonstrating political development towards universal socialist policies, with little regard for traditionalist or specifically African cultural issues. On 4 February, Agostinho Neto returned to a massive popular welcome.

The Eastern and Active revolts had been excised from the MPLA, but conscious of the weight of imperialist hostility and the crucial months ahead, Neto was anxious to cement the organization into close unity. His efforts to gather individuals from both the Revolt factions back into the MPLA fold were successful in a number of cases. Commander Mundo Real, a key guerrilla, was back as an operational commander on the Southern Front by the time of South Africa's invasion; Dr Eduardo dos Santos, after abandoning the Andrade Active Revolt group along with several others, became director of a Luanda hospital.

With the government – and consequently the ideological conflict between MPLA and FNLA and UNITA – concentrated in Luanda, internal political tensions and rivalries were also centred in the capital.

The Rival Camp

Alves had made contact with the MPLA underground in Luanda in early 1974, and a key Northern Front guerrilla commissar, Ernesto Eduardo Gomes da Silva 'Bakaloff' came to Luanda in July 1974 to spend a month in underground work. He had been astonished at the extent of penetration into the colonial army and had been smuggled into barracks for political meetings.

Bakaloff had been appointed commissar in 1972 for the whole first military region. Alves had first undertaken Northern Front political tasks in 1968 at a regional centre for revolutionary instruction. In 1971 he had joined others on the regional steering committee which had both military and political duties. He was not a leading guerrilla fighter, although during 1974 this was the description of him put about by his followers, and especially in Lisbon. In late 1974 the centre for revolutionary instruction '*Certeza*' (certain) was set up in the first region, and Alves subsequently staffed a number of MPLA structures with trainees from the school.

From the Luanda underground there was José Van Dunem whose prison term at Sao Nicolau prison, near Moçamedes, had cemented close ties with the other political inmates. There were two generations of political prisoners: those from the 1961 period – mostly working class and uneducated; and those from 1970 onwards, who like Van Dunem tended to be petty bourgeois in class origin, and with considerable culture and education.

Van Dunem also rose in the FAPLA commissariat. He was deputy to Gilberto Teixeira da Silva 'Jika', national commissar from September 1974 until he was killed by FNLA in Cabinda in June 1975. Van Dunem then acted as interim national commissar until Bakaloff's appointment a few months after Independence. Van Dunem had no military experience and was appointed commissar on the strength of his political work and status as a leading political prisoner.

The lack of political input into the isolated Northern Front made that group particularly vulnerable to the ferment of left-wing political theories imported into Luanda after the April coup. There were the Portuguese communists, who now faced the decision to become Angolan and join MPLA, or stay Portuguese and go home. There were the young Portuguese students affected by events in Portugal itself, the proliferating leftist parties in Lisbon, and the appearance of hitherto banned literature in Portuguese for the first time. Mao, Enver Hoxa, Stalin, Marx and Lenin were all new subjects for debate and reading groups. The MPLA, engaged in setting up responsible government and workers' mass organizations, lacked the time to arrange political study groups, direct cadres towards useful texts and send leading cadres to talk to the people. Men less deeply involved in practical movement work became the talkers. Alves and his fellow Northern Front men became influenced by such people before whom they were perhaps less diffident to confess their scanty political background.

Alves came under the influence of a Portuguese woman student, Sita Valles, with whom he lived. Previously linked to Portugal's Union of Communist Students, she came to Luanda in 1975. She brought Alves closer to other young Portuguese with similar political links and he left the Henda group by which he had been influenced previously. Bakaloff followed suit. The Alves group also broke with the CACs but kept street support alive for themselves, rather than campaign as part and parcel of the MPLA.

Just as both CACs and Hendas had projected themselves as 'a movement within a movement' so did the Alves group. But within a few months, they had persuaded themselves that they should wrest power from the organization and rule themselves.

From July to September 1975, the action of the people's power street committees grew in importance. FNLA had begun systematic murder in March when it killed over 50 unarmed MPLA supporters on their way to an MPLA training camp. From March to July, when the people of Luanda threw them out, the FNLA waged war on the capital street by street, moving in to one high-rise apartment block after another, setting up their mortars and bazookas and firing on the townships clustered below. The defence committees were armed by MPLA, the neighbourhood committees became increasingly popular and effective. Political discussion in the capital now began to centre around the neighbourhood committees – the *Comissoes Popular de Bairro*.

There were two lines: one that the committees should be tightly linked to the MPLA; another, minority view, that they should be 'non-party'. The minority view was strongly influenced by the Maoists and was the direct descendant of the 'movement within a movement' idea. It borrowed from the extreme leftist notion that links to MPLA would imply unacceptable 'control' which would be against mass interests. Those who argued this cause were soon pushed into holding a view of the neighbourhood committees as a more accurate manifestation of the people's will than the MPLA, which therefore was not entitled to be the people's vanguard. The problem articulated by members of this minority lay in the fact that they had not been guerrillas, or part of the small revolutionary band of tried and trusted militants who had risked their lives for the people. Perhaps, unconsciously, they sought a new legitimacy, and felt it could come from the mass of Luandans even less experienced than themselves in political and armed struggle.

Some neighbourhood committees firmly opposed this minority tendency. The CPB of Sambizanga, a workers' shanty-town north of Luanda near the docks, opposed the non-party line on the grounds 'this would mean spontaneous mass struggle without any leadership, which would lead to annihilation of the revolutionary forces'.

The second people's power week, held from 8 September 1975, dashed the hopes of the minority. The CPBs of Luanda came out en masse in support of close ties to the Liberation Movement, MPLA. A resolution adopted at its final rally condemned the non-party line as 'opportunist' and recognized MPLA as the 'only revolutionary vanguard' and FAPLA as the armed wing of the people. Henrique Santos 'Onambwe', a guerrilla commander from the south-east front who had been with Lara at the Luanda delegation opening, addressed the rally on the problem of defending Luanda. There had been debate whether FNLA units needed to be stationed in the capital or whether its defence could be left to the people's militias. Onambwe said defence had gone beyond the capability of pockets of home guard and that the capital's defence should now be undertaken by trained soldiers integrated into a regional defence plan and under an integrated command. At the same time, he called for greater development of organized militias under the People's

Defence Organization, ODP. From the same platform, Nito Alves identified MPLA as the only possible vanguard of the Angolan people, and mocked at 'super-revolutionaries' who played games while men were dying at the front. Alves urged that all co-ordinators of action committees should, in future, be recognized MPLA militants, and that members of the CPBs committees should be MPLA activists.

This was a signal for Alves supporters to find their way into key positions on the Luanda neighbourhood committees. It was a first indication of the future jostling for power. Ordinary men and women of goodwill, full-time workers, who had joined MPLA and its underground after the April Armed Forces coup – popular and respected in their neighbourhood – were now edged off the committees by young professional politicians allied to Alves. They spoke well, and they were not averse to using their education and superficial political reading to intimidate the rank and file.

One of these speakers, Betinho, an Alves man, had addressed the September people's power week rally, calling for a purge of left and right from MPLA. For Betinho, the right were reformists seeking to replace colonial power with state power; the left was falling into 'traps of idealism, voluntarism, adventurism and sectarianism'. Betinho warned that eventually opportunists of the left would emerge as reliable allies of those on the right. Betinho was a member of the week's '*grupo dinamizador*' (mobilizing group) and later held a senior post in the MPLA's Department of Information and Propaganda (DIP).

The people's power week was followed by a people's defence week, intended to improve the command structure of the militias and bring them under the Regional Committee for the Defence of Luanda and deal with undisciplined bands. The need for better weapons control had been highlighted by a tragedy in Bairro Lixeira, where six members of an informal '4th February' base had gone on the rampage and killed 11 civilians. Four days later a people's court sentenced the accused to death. They were shot by firing squad the same day and exemplified to the lumpen and criminal elements that MPLA would not tolerate lawlessness, even from those who claimed to be among its supporters.

The leftists who were influencing the Alves group were also criticizing MPLA for its trade union activities. MPLA had called on the people to work hard, to stay at work even during the FNLA terror, to increase production, and maintain output even after the settlers had abandoned their enterprises. Production, said MPLA, is resistance.

At the same time, the MPLA promised effective trade union organization and representation for the first time. With the fall of fascism, the right to strike was won. In Portugal it became a key tool in the hands of the working class, and many young, left Portuguese considered that it should serve the same purpose in Angola, ignoring the difference in conditions and future prospects.

In Malanje, Lopo do Nascimento, MPLA's Premier in the transition government, spoke on the issue at a September meeting of MPLA's regional steering committees. He argued that the anti-imperialist struggle and the military battle-front needed an organized economy behind them. Lopo had never left Angola, and had been instrumental in keeping alive the framework of an underground trade union structure during fascism. Those in favour of strike action soon agreed with MPLA's view, and this provoked criticism of the Movement overseas.

Alves did not quarrel with the anti-strike campaign and he addressed Luanda workers to explain why it was important that they should continue working. Pursuing the MPLA policy line in public, Alves was privately building a personal power base. He set up a Secretariat at *DOM Nacional* (the National Department of Organization of the Masses) – the most active MPLA section dealing with the organization of the movement's activists and mobilization of mass participation.

The Secretariat comprised trainees from '*CIR Certeza*', and Sita Valles. They gradually extended their work in the DOM and a number of militants were squeezed out, as had happened in the neighbourhood committees. In September 1975, around 50 regional cadres attended a DOM secretariat training course to learn about political organization and receive political instruction. By now the Alves DOM group were intent on removing political education from Lara's department; they were also preparing to replace steering committees appointed by the Political Bureau with 'zone committees' of their own choice. These were to be set up within 60 days, according to directives issued by the DOM group.

As Alves had distanced himself from both the Henda committee and CAC another leftist organization appeared: the *Organizaçao Comunista de Angola* (OCA) which claims to have held a conference in Angola in 1975 but neither a list of delegates nor the location was ever published. But these young ideologues had no place in Angola's future. OCA's platform according to the pamphlets it published was that MPLA was bourgeois and reactionary and stood in the way of people's war, which should be fought without Soviet aid. Significantly, OCA pamphlets were especially in evidence after August 1975 and the South African invasion.

In John Stockwell's *In Search of Enemies*: *a CIA Story*, he described a conversation with fellow CIA agents about the usefulness of a 'fourth liberation front which can call for a coalition of all the forces and denounce the Soviet arms shipments'. Probably OCA had no connection with the CIA but its activities certainly served CIA interests. Alves attacked OCA, ridiculing its foreign membership – particularly after he became Internal Administration Minister. Subsequently, a number of Portuguese were arrested and expelled for OCA anti-MPLA activities. Other Portuguese were treated in the same way for membership of a so-called 'Joseph Stalin Group'.

In the months before Independence, Nito Alves was the darling of the Portuguese press. Presented as a great guerrilla commander he was quoted as an MPLA leader, and his prominent position in the neighbourhood committees movement gave him a more frequent platform than other leaders concerned with less glamorous aspects of movement organization. In the first government after Independence, Alves seemed an unexceptionable choice for the Cabinet. He received the portfolio of Internal Administration with responsibilities for the neighbourhood committees and administration in the provinces, and he retained duties in the running of the movement. He had no responsibility for Police and Security; the Defence Ministry was responsible for the police, and a Security Service department was answerable to the President.

Alves' movement duties gave him influence in the media, and, with Lara and João Felipe Martins, he was a member of a co-ordinating committee for three important MPLA departments dealing with Political Organization, Information and Propaganda, and Mass Organization.

Warnings of Division

A month after Independence, MPLA celebrated the 19th anniversary of its foundation, and government leaders dispersed to attend public rallies in liberated Angola. In Luanda, Neto spoke of education, health and the prospects opening up with the creation of People's Angola. He also warned of divisive tendencies in the MPLA, speaking of those who objected to accepting weapons from the Soviet Union because they supported China in the Sino-Soviet dispute. He commented on revisionist agitation in Luanda and talk of a vanguard. Clearly, for Neto, the MPLA should continue a broad mass vanguard movement of national unity and any sectarianism or divisiveness could only favour the enemy. Celebrations of the anniversary were modest; in Luanda a football match saw MPLA leaders (mainly guerrillas) playing against a club team: Neto kicked off.

In sharp contrast to Angola's bitter fighting against the South African army, was the continuing ideological bickering in Luanda; it even reached the commissars at the frontline, thanks to José Van Dunem and the FAPLA commissariat. A popular radio programme '*Kudibanguela*' bemused its audience with talk of differentiation between anti- and multi-racism. Its young broadcasters were becoming involved in the hair-splitting of the Luanda debating societies. The MPLA warned the team of its responsibilities to spread the MPLA political message, but went ahead with plans to revive the old resistance programme, *Angola Combatente*.

Amongst the minority the wrangling continued. On 27 December at a meeting in Bairro Rangel 11 young men announced the formation of a 'General Council of the People's Neighbourhood Committees of Luanda', with themselves as its 'provisional secretariat'. Only five of the city's approximately 34 active committees were selected by the self-appointed secretariat to provide candidates. No senior MPLA or government leader was present at the Rangel meeting. The secretariat issued a manifesto, promising close links with the MPLA. Recalling leftist errors in the past, the secretariat Information Secretary indirectly criticized the CAC and Henda Committees, while its 'Secretary General' quoted Neto's warning against worrying about secondary issues when the essential struggle was for national reunification and against the invaders. Betinho was the secretariat's member responsible for guidance and mass organization, and since he was head of the MPLA information department, already had a large measure of control over the production and distribution of books being published by MPLA. One state-owned printing shop, Regral, was ordered to print Neto Alves' *A Dialęctica e a Guerrilha* (Dialectics and Guerrilla War) before Comandante Jika's *Reflexoes Sobre a Luta de Libertaçao Nacional* (Thoughts on the National Liberation Struggle). The Alves book as usual sought to divide. Its prime aim was to establish the northern front group as the MPLA's bravest and toughest fighters, and himself as an outstanding commander which he simply had not been. Jika's book, by contrast, was a thoughtful analysis of social conditions in Angola and the tasks of revolutionaries.

The Alves group came to dominate the evening newspaper *Diario de Luanda*. There was no way they could infiltrate the national daily, *Jornal de Angola* after the appointment in January 1976 of Costa de Andrade 'Ndunduma' as editor.

In mid February the Alves group responded by appointing a Portuguese, Vergilio Deniz Frutuoso, director of the *Diario de Luanda*. The media thus became the main battlefront between Nito Alves and the mainstream of MPLA. On 31 January, a further step was taken to silence the Alves 'ideologues': the government stopped all radio programmes that were not broadcast by full-time radio employees. This hit *Kudibanguela*, and a programme contributed by the trade union congress '*A voz do trabalhador*' (Worker's Voice). Both teams for these programmes were Alves supporters, dispensing a confusing mixture of ideological jargon and slogans that not only failed to clarify the political process but had a demobilizing effect on the mass of workers: politics seemed 'above our heads' because it apparently involved long words and foreign names. The war was still at its height, but Alves and his ideologues ignored the imperialist threat and concentrated on in-fighting.

Kudibanguela had been a popular MPLA radio programme during the transition government, and at that time had reflected mass opinion. It was closed down after UNITA complained that it publicized UNITA's collaboration with the Portuguese by quoting Marcello Caetano's memoirs. That the Alves group chose the most popular and essentially MPLA radio programme for infiltration and their own ends was typical, as was their manipulation of the neighbourhood committees. When *Kudibanguela* had been restored, after UNITA's flight from Luanda, Alves supporters Mbala and Rui Malaquias were on its staff. One of their first campaigns had been to support the 11-man Alves-dominated secretariat of the neighbourhood committees.

On 6 February 1976 the government palace in Luanda was chosen by Alves and his group for the first anti-government demonstration since Independence. Another, smaller demonstration was organized outside police headquarters. Around 200 young people, well-dressed in bright, modern clothes, paraded in front of the palace with placards calling for restoration of the *Kudibanguela* programme. No production workers or working-class women seemed to be among the demonstrators who had clearly been organized to appear. The small crowd mingled with foreign journalists who went to report the scene. They said they were there to support the 'correct political line of MPLA' and to demand the programme's return. Later, a counter demonstration by women activists from MPLA arrived. Inside the palace, government work went on as usual, and that evening Neto broadcast a stern rebuke to those who pretended to support the MPLA but sabotaged its policies.

The leadership was by now acutely conscious of the Alves campaign to outflank them on their left through populist and leftist agitation. Most of the group's activities were confined to Movement politics and what percolated through to the street was comparatively negligible. None the less, against the advice of several leading members of the Central Committee, Neto was determined not to single out Alves and Van Dunem for public criticism. He still considered them to be misguided but promising cadres to be won over for work with the mainstream.

On the afternoon after the demonstration, Neto went to the working-class suburb of Rangel – one of the first to organize MPLA militias – to meet Luanda grass-roots supporters at a closed working meeting, and to speak at a street rally. He spoke of unity of the Movement over class and racial divisions, and stressed the dangers of promoting movements 'parallel to the MPLA'. He announced that an investigation would be carried out into an incident that arose out of a 'very narrow group'. Perhaps if the MPLA leadership had made its opposition and analysis of the Alves campaign known in full to the public, the plot would have got no further. But the veiled references to parallel movements and narrow groups actually protected the plotters. Neto had no wish to risk confrontation with the war still raging.

Alves now entered a period of overt self-promotion and saw high stakes ahead. On 8 February he introduced the People's Power Law, passed by the Council of the Revolution and promulgated by Neto three days earlier.

The People's Power Law (Law 1/76) was intended to deal with the organization of elections to People's Power committees. Electoral commissions were to present candidates drawn from MPLA action committees, the trade unions and the women's organization. The only Angolans ineligible as candidates were minors (under 18), people guilty of crimes against the liberation struggle, and those who made financial profits from the labour of others. The aim of the people's power structures was to draw into direct participation in government men and women who were honest, hardworking citizens but not necessarily MPLA activitists.

Alves' line, once again, was opposed to the unifying principle of the MPLA mainstream. At the Town Hall, in patent contradiction to the law, he forcefully stressed that candidates must be MPLA militants and must be production workers.

Meanwhile Alves was working on the appointment of Provincial Commissioners favourable to his line, and he announced that some appointments were underway. This was a task for the Council of the Revolution, but Alves supporters in Malanje were agitating to create local demands for the Province to select its own Commisser. Alves went to Malanje to discuss this in January.

On 12 February the seven liberated provinces received their first Commissioners; six of whom were immediately sworn in by Neto. All the appointees were former political prisoners, three had been inmates (like José Van Dunem) of Sao Nicolau, and two had links with the First Military Region where Alves had worked.

That same month Alves was sent to represent the MPLA at the 25th Congress of the Communist Party of the Soviet Union; he was accompanied to Moscow by José Van Dunem. Alves addressed the Congress on 28 February and the two men remained in the Soviet Union a few more days to examine Soviet institutions.

They returned on 10 March and were met at Luanda Airport by Monstro Imortal and Pedro Fortunato, the latter newly appointed as Luanda Commissioner. Both were involved in the subsequent coup. There is no evidence that Alves was given any encouragement for his personal ambitions while in Moscow, but it seems safe to assume that he and Van Dunem must have siezed the opportunity to discuss their plans together. Their return signalled an intensified campaign in Luanda to project them, and Alves in particular, as leaders.

On 20 March Alves again went to the Town Hall, ostensibly to lecture on party structure in the Soviet Union. He also spoke about MPLA politics and said that while in Moscow he had received letters and telephone calls to say 'that there are revolutionary theorists, [and] renowned thinkers in Angola who describe as inopportune the publication of the People's Power Law'. There were campaigns in Luanda to set leaders one against the other he averred; and he announced people's power elections in Luanda would be held on 13 May.

The following week, Neto took him into his entourage to visit Uíje. On 28 March Alves was back in the Town Hall; again he used the platform to sow distrust and division. He had called the meeting in order to speak on measures agreed by the Political Bureau 'with the express recommendation' of Neto. In short this was simply a pretext to boost his own image as leading spokesman for the MPLA. What he actually concentrated on was denunciation of previously MPLA-affiliated splinter groups, the OCA and the Active Revolt. Possibly, by now, the Alves group's tactics were so clear that some militants were taking them to task, and the Town Hall speech was intended to reassure them that this was no splinter movement, but a loyal MPLA hard core. The effect on most people , however, was to understand that Alves considered himself to be a leading ideologue; but coupled with failure to grasp his line. It was an enormously lengthy, confusing speech, heavily larded with Marxist expressions and, despite being printed in full on three successive days in the *Diario*, failed to shed any light on his politics.

In a seminar of military commissars he did refer to ways of appointing key commanders. In the Soviet Union, he said, they could be appointed only after approval of the Politburo. He also again spoke of rigid control over those who might become involved in the People's Power institutions. Some observers felt these were veiled attacks on the Defence Minister Iko Carreira and the Premier Lopo do Nascimento. The speech had been preceded by the reading of two resolutions passed by Alves supporters in the People's Neighbourhood Committees 'General Council'. The first accused the media of a campaign against 'honest militants by opportunists' and sought a role in controlling the media for the council's 'Regional Council for Information and Propaganda'. The second called for official recognition of the 11 man Secretariat, pending establishment of a Luanda Town Council, not due until September at the earliest. The resolutions had been passed on 27 March, as the South African Defence Force retreated into Namibia. From now on, the Alves group complained they were under suspicion. OCA sympathizers in Lisbon commented on what they called a 'social fascist current led by Nito Alves and José Van Dunem inside MPLA'. It is interesting to speculate upon the possible effects of an alienation of Neto from Moscow at this stage.

FAPLA's Political Commissariat

José Van Dunem was now, with Bakaloff, in a key position to bring the national army political structures under the Alves group's control. The two most reliable and experienced Commissars, Jika and Kassanje had been killed in the war. Many of the new young Commissars trained and appointed through Van Dunem were underground militants with no experience of the guerrilla war. The second war of liberation had been brief – eight months – and many had been trained virtually on the job.

Military training courses were held in 1975 and 1976 at Centres for Revolutionary Instruction in and around Luanda. From the graduates came the first generation of officers and other ranks (there was no formal ranking system in the guerrilla army except for commanders and commissars). The CIRs were staffed by officers well known to Van Dunem although not all were involved in Alves group power politics.

The main question of concern to the MPLA leadership was political education in the armed forces. This had been neglected during the war, but the Political Bureau clearly understood that the South African threat remained. A large, strong national army was needed for the foreseeable future, and if the revolution were to proceed, it must be a politicized army. A conference for political cadres stationed in Luanda was held at the Defence Ministry from 20 to 27 March. Speakers included the Defence Minister, Iko Carreira, Monstro Imortal, and Dilolwa. Galiano, a young cadre, later a key figure in the coup played an important organizational role. The conference called for organization of MPLA cells in the units, an information bulletin and radio programme for the armed forces. There was an 'urgent need to set up MPLA structures within the armed forces'.

The next event around which Alves stirred up agitation against Neto and the government was the trial of foreign mercenaries. With the war over, the Minister of Justice Diogenes Boavida announced that British and American mercenaries captured on the Northern Front would be tried by a special court.

Key security officials were involved in preparing the trial and investigations. Neto was determined that the trial would be conducted freely and fairly; the accused were given every opportunity to bring their own defence lawyers. Neto did not want death sentences, but the Alves group campaigned for them, arguing that the indisciplined '4th February' Angolans had been shot by firing squad. The demand for death sentences, however, was not unanimous, and official Angolan defence lawyers were appointed; one, an Alves supporter Edgar Valles, declined to take on the task. A street demonstration, before the trial opened, calling for death sentences was thought to be further work by Alves agitators.

Bakaloff was one of the judges. Just before the trial opened he had become the centre of a political row connected with a statement he had issued as head FAPLA Commissar, entitled 'Political Declaration of the National Political Commissariat of FAPLA'. It dealt in considerable detail with lines of command and announced the Political Commissariat was to function as a 'section of the Central Committee' and not as a department of the Armed Forces General Staff. The implications were obvious. Instead of coming under the overall command of the Commander-in-Chief of the Armed Forces, Agostinho Neto, the Commissariat would seek to become a part of the Central Committee. This would give it a chance to gain support from sympathizers on the Central Committee, and provide support to the pro-Alves members. Voting patterns on the top policy-making body could then be influenced in a new way, advantageous to the group; and they hoped to bypass Neto's ultimate control.

The Bakaloff statement also outlined plans for political schools, reopening of the radio programme for FAPLA, and schools for ex-servicemen. A more controversial proposal concerned soldiers' political activities in civilian meetings, and for civilians to take part in meetings in military units within the limits of security.

The next day Neto issued a communiqué as C-in-C of FAPLA announcing 'the declaration was made precipitately and without my knowledge and to some extent goes against earlier decisions' and cancelled the declaration. Perhaps significantly, Neto had been out of town when Bakaloff issued his statement.

After the Bakaloff row, the mercenaries' trial went ahead as planned. Four mercenaries were shot by firing squad, the remainder received long prison sentences.

Alves now attacked the government's economic policy and tried to undermine the Premier's position. In a speech on 8 May Lopo do Nascimento explained government policy on the gradual path to socialism. He warned against exchanging the Portuguese or American bourgeoisie for an Angolan bourgeoisie. He spoke against the 'super-leftists' and the 'demagoguery of the super-revolutionaries'. He said there were opportunists both left and right of the MPLA who slandered its leadership as 'reformist' and he firmly reminded Angolans 'Our motto should be "Do not leave undone anything which can be done now, and do not start upon anything which cannot be done yet!" '

Alves favoured impetuous action to change Angola's economy. Although the Alves' group criticised the MPLA's economic strategy, they failed to provide any alternative thinking on this crucial issue. Indeed, the numerous Alves' underground pamphlets circulating in Luanda were silent on economic policy, nor had anyone been named for the Economics Ministry in Alves' coup government list.

Alves' Career at its Peak

On 22 May, immediately after Neto had countermanded Bakaloff's statement, Alves called a rally, in the small Cidadela sports stadium. This was solely for MPLA card carrying militants from the civil service, education and industry sectors; DOM workers checked their credentials as they arrived. The atmosphere was uncharacteristically tense; the stadium was ringed with armed guards on a scale that exceeded presidential security at that time. From the audience came the usual shouts of MPLA slogans and of 'Neto, Neto', but at least one insistent voice was countering with 'Nito, Nito'. This lone cry was not taken up by the crowd. Alves' rambling discourse equalled the incoherence of his Town Hall speech on 28 March. Members of the audience began to drift away but were stopped and the exits closed and guarded. Those on duty at the doors said they had received orders that no one should leave until Alves finished speaking; this was unprecedented. No account of the speech appeared in the newspapers the following day on the grounds that it was for MPLA militants alone.

Interest was mainly centred on the People's Power elections, which had been postponed until 27 June. On 2 June, a new list of those ineligible to participate in the elections was published. The numbers of those affected was minute.

The new regulations disqualified Eastern and Active Revolt, CAC and OCA members. Alves had begun something of a witch-hunt since his March Town Hall speech, and arrests had been made. Active Revolt was a special target for Alves, and he seems to have been particularly venomous because many of its 19 members were *mestiços*. On 10 January Joaquim Pinto de Andrade, brother of its leader Mario de Andrade, had been arrested, questioned and released after an incident when allegedly he had removed criticism of Active Revolt from a wall-newspaper at his place of work. Also arrested and held was Gentil Viana, a lawyer who signed the Brazzaville Active Revolt statement on 11 May 1974. In Lisbon there were suggestions of links between Active Revolt and OCA. They were taken up in *Jornal de Angola*. Most of the tiny membership of OCA and CAC were Portuguese and therefore ineligible to vote in any case. Alves' 'hard line' against former MPLA splinter groups was almost certainly designed to act as a red herring to cover his own tracks.

The leadership, however, was not deceived by these tactics. A list of Commissioners for eight provinces liberated from the FNLA and UNITA in the north and south included only three men who subsequently turned out to be

Alves supporters. The majority of the new appointees were MPLA militants who had won Neto's confidence. Some were former guerrillas (Ndembo in Moxico, Lukoki in Uíje); others were southerners who had fiercely opposed UNITA (Paihama in Kunene, Muteka in Bié). The appointments were widely discussed as proof that this time Alves had not been given a free hand.

The People's Power elections in Luanda went ahead as planned. After a well publicized campaign, conducted for three weeks before polling day, the turn-out was extraordinarily low – 10%. In the streets, some working people complained they had been kept away from the polls. To ensure that their candidates were elected Alves supporters had apparently resorted to intimidation. The new committees were presented at a mass rally on 4 July at which Alves, in jubilant mood, made the main speech. He chose to highlight the spontaneous element of people's committee work in the last days of Portuguese rule, playing down the role of the MPLA. He made no attempt to explain the low turn out. In Zone 10, *Bairro Operario* (Workers Neighbourhood) around 10,000 people were on the electoral roll, with 24 candidates of whom Beto Muanza, the leading one and an Alves supporter, polled only 929 votes. In Zone 7, *Patrice Lumumba Bairro*, Charulla, a marginal Alves supporter, was elected with only 386 votes. The Political Bureau later described these elections as farcical, but they were accepted at the time.

Typical of Alves' speech that day was populist rhetoric. He attacked racism, but continued 'on the day when, in Angola comrades, citizens sweeping the roads with the dignity of new moral and revolutionary consciousness are not only blacks but *mestiços* and whites, racism will disappear'.

These months of mid 1976 represented the peak of Alves' direct political influence and they coincided with an intensive public relations campaign on his behalf. In June 1976, a book of poems by Alves was taken to be published in Lisbon. In Luanda, the printing of his book on guerrilla warfare was put ahead of that of Jika, the dead FAPLA National Commissar. The Alves book *A Dialectica e a Guerrilha* carried a dedication to the commanders of the Northern Front and three Eastern Front commanders he had met in 1974, and a tribute from Bakaloff. The dedication seemed divisive. The test is of little interest except for the statement that 'the *coup d'état*, the putsch, is totally alien to socialism'.

There is some doubt whether the poems or the book were genuine products of Nito Alves' pen. At least one speech, the Poder Popular election address, was reportedly written by Edgar Valles, Sita Valles' brother.

On the second anniversary of the formation of FAPLA (1 August 1976), formal ranking was introduced into the armed forces. The commissioning lists were eagerly examined: there were 27 Commanders and 34 Majors, all chosen from the list of original signatories to the FAPLA proclamation of 1974. It was public recognition of the guerrillas, while the People's Power elections had brought a number of former political prisoners to the fore.

Alves headed the list of Majors; he may have believed he deserved better. By September, it was rumoured in Luanda that his Ministry of Internal Administration was to be abolished. In October there was to be what was generally regarded as a major Central Committee meeting.

The main Luanda bookshop, Lello, mounted a huge window display of Alves' poems *Memoria da Longa Resistência Popular*. Albertino de Almeida, in Lisbon, wrote a eulogy to Alves in the foreword to the 50 poems supposedly written over nine years. One of the coup criminals, Betinho, later said the promotion was part of a campaign to place Alves in power.

In late October, the Central Committee met in plenary session for the first time since Independence. It decided the transition to socialism would be attempted through formation of a vanguard working-class party. A Congress would have to be held to determine whether the vanguard could be formed at once, and how this was to be achieved. The Central Committee had responded to militants calls for ideological clarity and a commitment to scientific socialism. No mention was made of such formulas as 'African socialism' or 'humanism'. The general tone of the communiqué was elation but careful reading revealed that serious concern existed over the operation of the Central Committee, staffing of MPLA departments, inadequate control over the FAPLA political Commissariat and, ultimately, there was deep anxiety over a potential minority splinter group within the movement. Specific criticism was made of the FAPLA '*Povo em Armas*' radio programme whose staff was now to be changed. The Ministry of Defence was instructed to make an enquiry into the behaviour of those issuing distorted propaganda, and army headquarters was told to exercise greater control over the political commissariat.

A resolution on unity was passed to combat divisiveness, sectarianism and opportunism'. On 30 October, Neto spoke to a large crowd that was demonstrating support for the resolutions:

> There is no division among us. It is simply a question of detecting where the elements are who can make it appear that there are divisions among us. There are not two MPLAs. There is only one. And, comrades, if anyone talks of another MPLA, carry him off to DISA [security] so we may know who he is, and where he comes from, if he is from this country or from another.

The Ministries of Internal Administration and Information were abolished; the duties of the first were assigned to the Prime Minister and of the second to an MPLA department. The Ministers continued in office until administrative steps had been completed for transfer of their functions. With the 20 November issue the *Diario de Luanda*, the pro-Alves evening paper, ceased publication.

That the Central Committee had ordered an enquiry, headed by José Eduardo dos Santos, into how the organization had apparently been split into two wings by Alves and Van Dunem, was not disclosed at the time. Sita Valles was removed from the DOM Secretariat and Portuguese influence minimized by a ruling that only Angolan citizens could be active in MPLA.

Far from heeding the warning of the Central Committee, the evidence shows that after this crucial October meeting Alves and Van Dunem increased their factionalist politics and began preparations for a take-over. The prospects of a Congress became a deadline for their efforts; those who stood in their way would somehow have to be swept aside. Over the next few months many innocent people would be accused of sabotage and thrown into gaol by Alves and his supporters.

6. The Alves Coup

The Central Committee Inquiry

The decision to keep the inquiry secret reflected Neto's conviction that the Alves-Van Dunem problem could be solved discreetly and that the two men were open to reason and discussion. Some members of the Central Committee disagreed and tragically several of those who fought most strongly for early public expulsion of the two men were subsequently murdered by their squads.

In 1977, the clandestine activity of the Alves faction was intensified. An open challenge to Neto's authority at the next Central Committee meeting headed the list of their priorities. Even the MPLA Youth organization became a platform for the faction. In February, at a youth central committee meeting in Malanje – where an Alves supporter was Commissioner – veiled attacks were made against the MPLA leadership. The youth meeting's resolutions were not ratified by the political bureau.

New civil and military appointments were made by the Movement to re-establish MPLA control. Four new Commanders were announced by the military, three of whom were Eastern Front veterans. Dino Matrosse was made Deputy National Political Commissar as part of strengthened control over the FAPLA Commissariat. The Port of Luanda was placed under Commander Ciel da Conceiçao 'Gato'. An inquiry was opened into the rule of Emilio Braz, the Huila Province Commissioner replaced a Neto man. The Alves faction was busy preparing an 'answer' to the Central Committee inquiry. In January 1977 a meeting was held in a farmhouse near Luanda to discuss the Alves defence statement. Bakaloff, Monstro Imortal, José Van Dunem, Juka Valentim, Mbala, Betinho, Luis Kitumba, Pedro Fortunato were amongst those attending. Monstro was on the Central Committee board of inquiry and thus able to keep Alves informed of the direction the inquiry was taking. With the aid of his counsellors Alves prepared '13 Theses in My Defence', which along with other Alves faction pamphlets was passed around Luanda 'underground'.

The Huila inquiry was revealing disturbing evidence of a faction running government there, elbowing out MPLA militants who opposed their autocratic rule, and sanctioning racist attacks on whites and *mestiços*. In Luanda severe shortages of food and essential goods were causing hardship and lengthy queues in spite of enormous sums in foreign exchange paid by the government to guarantee imports. Where were the goods going?

The Minister for Internal Trade, David Aires Machado 'Minerva' denounced corruption in the state retail chain EMPA, closed it down in February 1977 and gaoled leading members of the administration. To justify his actions he published an inspector's report which said administrators had embezzled money and goods and allowed supplies to rot. The 'scandal' had been perpetrated by whites and *mestiços*. They were later exonerated as it became clear this was part of the preparations for the coup and the 'evidence' was fake. One of the coup plotters later testified that Minerva had arranged the report to discredit the government.

The Central Committee inquiry should have been ready at the end of March, but Neto made state visits to Yugoslavia and Poland and the Central Committee did not meet to discuss the report until May. Every day provided further evidence of the attitude of the faction leaders. Ndunduma, at the *Jornal de Angola*, wrote an editorial – 'When criticism is not enough' – hostile to those 'who scatter verbose pamphlets, spread rumours, incite racism and tribalism, attribute to MPLA and some of its leaders all of the difficulties we are experiencing'. By May Day and the big annual parade Alves was fairly isolated; he was almost surrounded by empty chairs on the platform. But clandestine copies of the '13 Theses' were still circulating even though the official inquiry was supposedly secret.

It is difficult to identify a coherent ideology in the Alves campaign. He tried to mobilize street support with racist appeals against whites and *mestiços*, and had edged out both from those MPLA structures he was determined to control – white and *mestico* union officials were forced to resign, and others were filtered out of DOM. Yet it was Portuguese and a handful of Angolan whites who contributed to his 'study groups' and built up his image.

Alves' government list (drawn up in the event of the coup's success) named members of all racial groups for his first cabinet. The conspiracy's ringleaders, obviously, were awarded key portfolios. In Luanda, the Alves faction was composed of individuals who were personally ambitious and disaffected with the MPLA. In the provinces, it included individuals appointed by Alves and Van Dunem in their roles as Minister of Internal Administration and Deputy National Political Commissar. Alves had recruited key individuals in the security services to cover his tracks.

According to those who read them, Alves '13 Theses' consisted of a mumbo-jumbo of Marxist catch-phrases with no clear line. Alves attacked the CAC and OCA groups, but made use of their language and drew on some of their former supporters. He accused MPLA leaders of being anti-Soviet, and some, such as Lucio Lara, were labelled 'Maoists' and others 'social democrats'. The implication was that the only repository of true socialist ideology was Alves. Once again Alves sowed division and distrust.

There was considerable evidence that the faction leaders were vigorously attempting to interest socialist country diplomats, including those of the Soviet Union. Alves' political ambitions were clear to Soviet diplomats. Conceivably Alves was presenting himself as a more legitimate ally than Neto who was pursuing a firmly non-aligned course.

Meanwhile the government's search for arms caches, notably in Sambizanga where the faction had been active, revealed both weapons and ammunition. Alves agitators launched a campaign suggesting that search parties had conducted fascist-style intimidation and arrests. Neto responded by ordering an inquiry, to which all residents were asked to contribute; the search parties were completely exonerated. Undeterred, the Alves group called meetings in Neighbourhoods where their men held key posts on the Neighbourhood committees.

On 19 May the MPLA Steering Committee for Luanda held a meeting with militants from all the city's Neighbourhood Committees. It condemned 'demagoguery and calumny'. But the tension continued.

The Central Committee finally met to hear the result of the inquiry on the 20 and 21 May. At the last minute, it was decided to hold the Fifth Plenary at Futungo de Belas, instead of at the Museum in the city centre as expected. The change of venue was not notified to members until the morning of the 20th, minutes before the meeting was due to start. Alves request for a three day adjournment to allow him to study the commission's findings was turned down. Probably his aim was to give the group time to organize a demonstration at Futungo. They had planned to hold one outside the Museum to demand the dismissal of the Central Committee and government, support Alves and Van Dunem and isolate the President. Armoured cars and military units were to have been ordered up on the pretext of protecting the crowd. Alves already knew the contents of the inquiry report, thanks to Monstro Imortal.

To dismiss a member the Central Committee required an absolute majority of two thirds of its members (Article 13 of the Statutes). The Committee, elected after the 1974 Inter-Regional Conference of Militants, had 32 of the original 35 members (three had been killed in the war). In the debate a clear majority favoured dismissing the ring-leaders but there was disagreement regarding whether or not they should be arrested and brought to trial; Saydi Mingas, Dangeureux and Onambwe were among those who opted for this measure. The five or six members reliably reported not to have supported the condemnation were presumably in sympathy with the Alves group.

Alves and Van Dunem declined the opportunity to retract. At the resumed discussion on the second day a resolution was passed confirming the existence of factionalism aiming to divide MPLA, and expelling Nito Alves and José Van Dunem from the committee. They left the meeting free men, and immediately went underground.

Thousands of MPLA militants waited in the Cidadela Sports Stadium to hear the results of the meeting. Neto announced that factionalism had been condemned and its leaders expelled, and warned of other possible expulsions in the run-up to the Congress due to be held later in the year. He rejected

Alves' attacks on senior colleagues, and warned against confusing race with class: 'there is no immediate logical connection between skin colour and membership of a class'. Neto called for MPLA activists to 'wage a genuine and serious struggle against all factionalists . . . .' The situation in Luanda was uneasy. Public buildings were under unusually heavy guard, police patrolled the city, and radio patrol cars were deployed by the Ministry of Defence in the expectation of some action by the two expelled ringleaders.

In the ranks of Alves supporters there was some confusion. Eleven members of the group had been arrested in the weeks preceding the Central Committee meeting, and the disappearance of the two leaders was now being circulated as evidence of their arrest.

On 26 May the Luanda Provincial Commissioner, Pedro Fortunato, was dismissed, and the Political Bureau issued a lengthy statement disclosing the extent and the recruiting methods of the Alves network. The statement, recorded by Lucio Lara, was broadcast over the national radio on 26 and 27 May, and was published in the *Jornal de Angola* on 27 May.

Coup

The Alves network extended to every sector of Luanda, from industry to residential neighbourhoods; individuals in certain provinces, mass organizations and the armed forces had been recruited by Alves. The Political Bureau's statement was intended to alert the people to the gravity of the situation, and provide militants with the tools to analyse it and act in accordance with Neto's call for 'serious struggle against all factionalists'. The parallel DOM Secretariat and the role of Sita Valles, that the faction had sought the support of foreign embassies, and been the instigator of the *Kudibanguela* agitation were all disclosed in the statement. Militants were called upon to concern themselves with production and ensure normal distribution of goods. It was a call to action: but underplayed the danger.

The two ringleaders, having gone underground on 21 May, engaged in feverish plans for a coup on 25 May. It was to have been an essentially military operation. A final planning meeting in Palanca Bairro, attended by Alves, Van Dunem, Bakaloff, Betinho, Mbala and Second-Lieutenant Manuel José Veloso was held on 24 May. The proposal was to take the prisons, the national radio and *Jornal de Angola*, and eliminate Lara, Iko Carreira and Onambwe. Alves and Bakaloff were in hiding near the industrial suburb of Viana on 25 May. When no reports of military action came in, they began another round of meetings that day to devise further plans. Alves met Major Borges 'Van Troy', Second-Lieutenant Pombal, Commander Sihanouk and officers from the Anti-Aircraft Defence, in Bairro Cuca. He rebuked the soldiers for failing to carry out the coup plan and then held discussions with Monstro Imortal (kept in the background for security reasons and attending only highest level meetings) and Van Dunem, followed that afternoon, by more talks with the same military group, plus six others including Captain

Faisca, Major Baje, Betinho and Luis Kitumba, in Bairro Cuca.

Extra military planning meetings were held in Major Van Troy's home, and by Luis dos Passos at the political Commissariat of FAPLA, with death squads formed to capture and kill specified members of the MPLA political and military leadership. On the evening of 25 May, Alves again withdrew, this time to a house at the Mabubas dam, 50 kilometres north-east of Luanda.

Van Dunem, with two other members of the inner circle, Nado and Valentim, continued working into the night; preparations went on during 26 May. Van Dunem had three meetings, mainly with military officers, a co-ordination meeting to examine the role of the military units involved, and a meeting with the civilians. A military operational command was formed, and the death squads' role clarified: in this way lumpen proletariat elements, including criminals and gangsters, were involved as active participants.

Alves relied on mobilizing mass civilian support, and wildly overestimated his personal standing with the population of Luanda, where the backbone of the coup would be. Two schemes were being discussed within the Alves and Van Dunem circles: one proposal was for a military action for 27 May, and the other was for a more civilian-based action on 28 May. The latter had been proposed by Betinho and associates in the Neighbourhood Committees network who suggested that it should start in Sambizanga Bairro, while the death squads under João Ribeiro 'Kiferro' would capture the MPLA leaders; Commander Sihanouk would head the related military action.

The Betinho plan was presented to Alves at Mabubas and he agreed to return to Luanda on the evening of 26 May to carry it out. In the event, and late on the night of 26 May, the military action was accepted to be put into effect in the early hours of the morning of 27 May. At a late stage Alves and Van Dunem again met in Cuca Bairro and prepared to execute the military coup. Military support for the coup was feeble in fact. Veloso later reported: 'Each unit ought to have sent a representative to the operational central command, but we didn't have enough people – it would have meant there was nobody left inside the units'.

The plan had at least one major weakness: it depended on the ability of Alves faction officers to convince their troops that there was a spontaneous civilian uprising; and on the Alves rabble rousers to suddenly convince the working people of Luanda that the army was out in force to support 'popular demands'. The civilians and military were each sceptical about the other's ability to carry out their assigned tasks. The military raised the possibility of Cuban intervention against the coup and Alves assured them that the Cubans would stand by as neutrals. Alves told the officers that 'the masses' were ready and trusted the soldiers. The plotters' aim to overthrow Neto and seize power was concealed from the people throughout the planning.

According to the plan, at 4 am officers in the plot would go to the units involved to encourage the troops to be ready to protect a mass demonstration against economic sabotage by some members of the government and against the 'unjust arrest' of some 'worthy militants'. The demonstrators would call for Alves and Van Dunem to be reintegrated into the government and for changes in the government and MPLA leadership. The Sao Paulo prison would be attacked with an armoured car and the prisoners freed. The national radio station would be occupied and pro-coup broadcasting would start at once. Death squads would kill leaders and officers who supported Neto; civilian agitators would persuade workers to gather at the Government Palace and requisition buses and trucks to carry demonstrators. During the demonstration, Monstro Imortal – on stand-by at the Defence Ministry – Sihanouk and Bakaloff would call on Neto to resign and to dismiss the government and Political Bureau. Demonstrators would then be told that Alves was about to read a proclamation over the radio as President of the Republic. If Neto rejected the demands he would be killed. But Alves and Van Dunem had not disclosed this decision even to the inner circle of plotters, many of whom thought Neto would simply be exiled.

The only member of Neto's government to be retained was Minerva. Some individuals named had never been involved in the conspiracy. The proposed new government list named Nito Alves as President, Monstro Imortal as Defence Minister, Fortunato as co-ordinator of Provincial Commissioners; the Labour Portfolio was for Aristides Van Dunem, Juka Valentim was named for Information, and Betinho as Minister of Education. The economics ministry was not mentioned. Sihanouk, according to Fortunato's evidence, would have headed the security services and Bakaloff was to have been army Chief-of-Staff. The 'Proclamation to the Angolan People' was found with Sita Valles in her handwriting and said:

> The Government has just been overthrown. In a brave action, the mass of the people of Luanda together with our glorious FAPLA have risen in arms against the present situation in our country – hunger, misery and repression over the great majority of our people, luxury and corruption for a minority. The mass of the people and the glorious FAPLA proclaim Armed Popular Insurrection to the whole country. The people are rising throughout the country against the reactionaries and opportunists who had taken over the leadership of our glorious MPLA and who, while proclaiming socialism as their objective, aimed at consolidating a petty bourgeoisie in the climb to power, at the cost of oppressing the workers, peasants, revolutionary intellectuals and patriotic petty bourgeoisie they claimed to defend and represent. A state of emergency is decreed in the country.

The proclamation was never broadcast. The attempted coup began at dawn on 27 May with gunfire around Sao Paulo and near the docks. The first attacks were made against the Sao Paulo prison where an armoured car blasted open the gates according to plan. Alerted by the gunfire, loyal army commanders rushed to the Defence Ministry to co-ordinate response. The prison guard resisted the attack, but the insurgents succeeded in freeing many prisoners, and Helder Neto, in charge of prison security, was killed. The prisoners included the 11 Alves supporters, around 30 FNLA and UNITA officers and officials, and 100 common law prisoners. British and American mercenaries and Portuguese prisoners elected to stay in prison for safety.

At the Defence Ministry, the loyal officers were sent out to reconnoitre the situation in various military units. It was not known that the crucial 9th Brigade, the first conventional fighting brigade in FAPLA, whose regular commanding officer was on a training course overseas, had come under Alves' control. The crew of an armoured car lured several vehicles into the Dragoons' compound at 9th Brigade headquarters, including Commander Bula, the deputy Chief-of-Staff, and Commander Dangeureux from FAPLA Headquarters. Chief-of-Staff Commander Xietu nearly fell into the trap but turned tail with his vehicle at the last moment, threatening the rebels with a hand grenade. The 9th Brigade reconnaissance battalion became a temporary prison for these and others rounded up by the shock units or intercepted at special check-points. Several of the Defence Ministry's radio patrol cars had come under the factionalists' control.

The national radio station was the next target. Between 6 and 7 am small arms fire could be heard around the radio station and a solitary armoured car patrolled the nearby Catete highway out of the city. Civilians began making their way to work and at 7 am the regular news broadcast was heard as usual. A threatening phone call instructing the news reader not to broadcast the news bulletin or run the recording of Lara reading the Political Bureau communiqué, was ignored; staff members assumed that the extra forces were a security measure.

Shortly afterwards a young reporter, Rui Malaquias, entered the announcing booth and ordered the broadcaster off the air, 'in the name of the revolution'. She complied only when Malaquias, was accompanied by an armed soldier. The studio control and technical centres, announcers' booths and switchboard were taken over and soldiers moved in. Shortly after 8 am improvised broadcasting began.

The people were told to demonstrate at the Government Palace. Initially, that this was an anti-government broadcast was not clear, but after a few minutes of incoherent and contradictory phrases associated with the splinter faction, listeners did not need to be told that the Alves group had taken over the broadcasting station. The plan for a demonstration, however, was frustrated. The Palace area was swiftly blocked off by loyal FAPLA, and in the suburbs, the people evaded attempts to herd them into trucks at gunpoint.

At 8.15 am the radio said: 'This is Angolan National Radio under the control of the MPLA Action Committee, for the defence of the fundamental interests of the masses, everyone to the demonstration in front of the palace.' Veloso, the chief of operations, later recalled:

> According to the plan the masses were to go in front. The masses were the decisive factor. So we asked, 'Mbala, you said the masses were going to come out and so far they have not.' Mbala replied 'The masses are soon going to come out but where were you?' I said we were there, we were waiting but the masses had not materialized.

Shortly after 9 am the radio was broadcasting specific attacks against the government, based on the resolutions passed by Alves' supporters in some of the Luanda neighbourhoods in the previous fortnight. The first prepared statement was presented as a resolution from the Sambizanga neighbourhood and its themes were: repression by the security department, the need to restructure the *Jornal de Angola*, an alleged alliance of right-wing and Maoist forces against the revolutionary victories of the people, and freedom for Alves and Van Dunem to defend themselves against charges of factionalism. Then a new appeal, in more demagogic tones, was broadcast for people to go to a demonstration at the Palace.

Although the rebels controlled the broadcasting, the city's telephone system was working normally and presidential staff were in their offices at the Palace. Loyal officers were able to co-ordinate counter-action in consultation with Neto: the main coup-makers were on the outskirts of the city and receiving reports from subordinates sent in to reconnoitre. By 10 am it was clear to the factionalists that they did not have the civilian or military backing to reach the government Palace, and without any explanation their broadcasters announced that, to avoid confrontation, 'popular' demonstration was now to be in front of the national radio station.

Inside the radio station at this time the atmosphere remained calm as the majority of the staff had become idle spectators of what the Alves group were doing. Several members of staff who were refusing to co-operate with the factionalists went to a basement cafeteria to make coffee for themselves and prepared to wait out the rising. They could hear bizarre statements booming out over the internal loudspeakers. A civilian crowd of 2-300 did gather outside the radio station, but this was a mixture of sympathizers and the merely curious; some of the crowd, at least, showed that they were there to protest against the factionalists' transmissions.

Soon, the Ministry of Defence team was able to mobilize loyal armoured units in a counter-operation by the presidential guard and a headquarters unit. Tanks and armoured cars began rolling towards the radio station. The factionalists realized that many of the soldiers were remaining loyal to Neto and the leadership. An Alves sympathizer from the FAPLA Political Commissariat broadcast an appeal to soldiers to allow civilians to go to the demonstration. An announcer said that Alves had passed in front of the studios – although this was probably incorrect – and later that some 'corrupt' Ministers had been arrested. While the factionalists continued to broadcast their political declarations, other members of the staff were already noting a significant build-up of fresh armed forces and several armoured cars being driven cautiously along the side of the perimeter fence.

Eventually the loyalists entered the radio station by moving a substantial ground force through a small back gate, sweeping through the building, ordering out everyone in sight. These infantry troops made no attempt to sort out which members of the radio staff were Alves supporters and which were not. One of the factionalists tried to give instructions to the soldiers who were arriving, not realizing that they had come to support Neto.

The main gate was still in rebel hands and after the sweep some 50 or more radio workers found themselves exposed on a terrace between the main entrance to the building and the perimeter gate; behind were the newly-arrived loyalists, in front were the armoured cars and guards of the factionalists. The civilian workers sat or lay full length on the ground and waited for the firing to begin, but suddenly a loyalist officer signalled that they could go back into the building for safety. A writhing, human carpet formed as people crawled on elbows and bellies towards a half-open glass door.

As the loyalist forces arrived, the factionalists had taken a small boy into the announcers' booth and pushed into his hand a script to read about Alves. He was reading this when a handful of loyalist soldiers, including a couple of Cubans, burst into the cabin and interrupted. A Cuban soldier asked one of the radio technicians to broadcast an announcement that the radio was back under loyalist control. The technician was too nervous to speak, so the Cuban soldier made the announcement himself. This announcement led some observers to believe that the rescue was an entirely Cuban operation. In fact, Cuban representatives in Angola offered assistance to Neto, and Cuban personnel joined in the Angolan counter-measures, but the immediate response was led and carried out by Angolan forces. Later in the day, Cuban soldiers in uniform, with white cotton tabs tied to their epaulettes, could be seen driving about Luanda in small cars and keeping a friendly watch on security operations.

After 20 minutes engagement at the radio station the Alves forces were dispersed and broadcasting staff were allowed to leave. Alves supporters simply walked away, though the key figures were later arrested. Shortly after noon loyalist troops escorted senior radio staff back to their posts and broadcasting was resumed.

The combined force of army, police and security that had taken the radio station now moved towards the 9th Brigade Dragoon camp nearby. The rebels were given 20 minutes to offer unconditional surrender as a fullscale attack would have endangered scores of prisoners held by the factionalists. While the camp was being encircled the Alves group removed their most important hostages. Around 100 of their prisoners remained in the camp and were freed but the seven MPLA leaders captured earlier that day had been taken to an unknown destination.

At 1.30 pm the Political Bureau announced the situation was under control. FAPLA combatants were instructed to return to their units and people to stay at home 'so that the counter-revolutionaries can be more easily deiected'.

Many of them were by now on the run. Bakaloff made his getaway when he heard the national anthem on the radio. Van Dunem and Galiano fled from the Grafanil camp to a farmhouse owned by one of the group, Kindanda. Alves, Van Dunem and Sita Valles met there and then separated with Alves, Bakaloff and several others making for the First Military Region they had known as guerrillas.

Still unaware of the scale of the day's events, Neto broadcast at 3 pm and spoke only of a 'certain disturbance'. By 9 pm, as more information flowed in, he broadcast in a more sombre tone. He now knew of the kidnapping of some of the Movement's most trusted leaders, of the collaboration of individual military and security officers and of at least some incidents in the provinces. He said:

> Some of our comrades have still not been found. We do not know if they are dead or if they are still alive. They are comrades who devoted their lifetime to the independence of our country, who devoted their lifetime to the freedom of the Angolan people.

The hostages had been taken to the Sambizanga Neighbourhood Committee offices, then moved to a private house belonging to Kiferro, the shock unit commander. Here they were mocked by gun-toting civilians and put into an outhouse. They had already been bound tightly with nylon rope, except for Commander Nzaji who was bleeding from barbed wire bonds. Commander Gato, the Port Director, survived to tell the story of their last hours.

They were sitting on the floor of the outhouse when men opened fire on them from outside with machine guns. Bula received fatal wounds immediately, Eurico, stomach wounds, Gato himself twisted sharply and received only flesh wounds. Mingas, Garcia Neto, Dangeureux and Nzaji were badly hit Gato lay for several hours with his comrades dying around him. A young boy came to watch and tried to point out to the killers that Gato was still alive, but he successfully feigned death and was driven away with the other bodies to a rubbish dumping ground. By chance, Gato was in a diesel fuelled vehicle which did not burst into flame when set on fire, as did the other, petrol fuelled vehicle. Under cover of smoke and darkness, Gato dragged himself from beneath the bodies and, uncertain of the situation in the city, made for Cuban workers at the docks whom he knew would recognize and assist him. Gato's information led government forces to the bodies of the leaders. Two other victims were found: the bodies of João Rodrigues, a loyal soldier, and Cristino Santos, a loyal member of the Sambizanga action group who had stood up to the factionalists. On a beach near Luanda the bodies of 12 other victims, including children, were found.

The murdered leaders were a cross section of the MPLA. Helder Neto from Luanda, killed at the prison, was arrested whilst a student, in 1959; Dangeureux from Moxico had been a peasant primary school teacher, joined the guerrillas and led the eastern resistance to the South African army. Nzaji from Luanda had fought on the Cabinda guerrilla front; Eurico, deserted from the colonial army to join the guerrillas. Bula, from Zaire province, had fought on many fronts since joining the armed struggle in 1961. Mingas had abandoned a comfortable and privileged life to join the guerrillas and had been one of the first MPLA cadres to study in Cuba, and had served as Secretary of State for Finance in the first government, Minister of Planning and Finance in the transitional government and as Finance Minister in the second government of independent Angola. Garcia Neto had organized students in Portugal for the MPLA and had worked in MPLA's international relations department.

MPLA and the People Close Ranks

The news stunned the people. There was strong popular support to find the ringleaders. Veloso and several others were picked up before they were able to organize a place to hide. A few weeks later Van Dunem and Sita Valles were found in a barn in a manioc field in nearby Cuanza Norte province. On 7 July, Alves was arrested by villagers in his home area, near Piri. Bakaloff was not found until 9 November, and his arrest in Bairro Palanca, was announced on 21 November.

Confessions, and written answers by Nito Alves, followed the arrests of ringleaders and conspirators enabling an almost complete picture of events to be pieced together. Alves wrote that he, Van Dunem and Sita Valles, jointly decided to murder Mingas, Bula, Dangeureux and Nzaji.

The attempted coup of 27 May had essentially been a Luanda operation, on a limited scale. But related action in Malanje had been discussed, and Alves supporters in certain key positions around the country had been active. Of 16 Province Commissioners, six were dismissed after the coup, all from provinces around Luanda; a seventh, Fortunato of Luanda, had been dismissed just before the coup.

On 6 June the Political Bureau suspended the steering committees of Luanda, Malanje, Benguela and Cuanza Sul provinces, and appointed Provisional committees to replace them. Several steering committee members were retained, including Mendes de Carvalho, Beto Van Dunem and Coelho da Cruz in Luanda.

Malanje had been the second area for Alves activity, but his supporters were baulked by local MPLA militants. The province was a cross road leading to the land-locked eastern provinces of Lunda and Moxico, and also linked the eastern part of the central highlands to the capital. Factionalists had organized sabotage of the distribution network in Malanje to deny vital supplies to revolutionary Moxico province, seat of the MPLA guerrilla front. A handful of junior FAPLA officers in Moxico tried to provoke a rising of the local garrison, but failed and were crushed by the troops and loyal leaders. When news of Commander Dangeureux's murder came through, the people of Luena were so incensed by what was seen as a 'Luanda revolt' against the MPLA, that they shot a number of government delegates from Luanda whom they regarded as suspect.

In Bié the province leadership, under Faustino Muteka, prevented a bid by two military officials to occupy the local radio station and Commission office. In Benguela, where the factionalists had actively attempted for some months to discredit MPLA mainstream activists and agitate against the government, swift preventive action was taken by loyal activists and military from the

FAPLA training college. The provinces were quiet, and indications were that had Alves succeeded in taking the capital he would have faced a challenge from MPLA in the interior. A senior commander in the provinces stated, 'We should have marched on Luanda and crushed it.' Security and defence in Luanda was for months after the coup undertaken by military units from other provinces – especially Kunene and the south.

South African military attacks increased sharply in the wake of the coup. How much information had been leaked to enemy forces by those involved in the coup was not known. Bakaloff's involvement was no surprise, but the implications of Monstro Imortal's complicity were deeply disturbing. Monstro had joined the northern guerrilla front early in 1961 and was in the first batch of trainees sent for military training. He had survived an FNLA ambush in 1963 and in 1966 he led the Cienfuegos column to relieve the first region, remained there as commander for five years. Later he led operations in Cabinda and was MPLA's nominee on the transition government National Defence Commission.

In Luanda, the political and military set up an operations centre inside the Defence Ministry and began investigations into the coup. Within three days hundreds of people had been arrested in Luanda and other arrests were made in the provinces. The first concrete evidence uncovered was of action to cause wide scale disaffection against the government. Food supplies had been withheld and stored for distribution after the coup. Military units' pay and stores were withheld in order to foster discontent. Foreign involvement was detected. A three member board of inquiry: Manuel Rui Monteiro director of the MPLA Guidance Department, Ndunduma from the *Jornal de Angola*, and Pepetela Deputy Minister of Education and like Ndunduma a revolutionary writer and guerrilla, conducted an investigation into the involvement of a group of Portuguese intellectuals. In the light of the overall investigation, nine Portuguese were officially expelled on 20 June; they included the former director of the *Diario de Luanda*, the sales manager of the Lello bookshop and several doctors and students. Rui Coelho, a member of Sita Valles' circle, testified that: 'We acquired the idea that the MPLA should be tied to the Soviet Union, (to the Communist Party of the Soviet Union), in a bond similar to that which unites the Portuguese Communist Party to that Party.'

As a result of the investigations, the members of seven out of the twenty Luanda Neighbourhood Committees, two leading members of the women's movement, were dismissed, as was a member of the President's personal staff Maria da Costa Veloso. Sita Valles had tried to send a message through her to the Soviet Embassy asking their help for herself and Van Dunem to flee the country. Minerva was dismissed on 7 June, and on 10 June the arrest was announced of Major Costa Martins, his personal adviser at the Ministry of Internal Trade. Martins, a Portuguese Air Force officer, had been Minister of Labour in the Portuguese government from July 1974 and, along with several other Portuguese left-wing military, took refuge in Angola after the right-wing coup of 25 November in Portugal. In Angola he was alleged to have had connections with the French secret service SDECE. He was later reported to have returned to Lisbon in June 1978 and to have been arrested by the Portuguese on his arrival.

Foreign delegations came to Luanda to express their support for Neto and the MPLA and messages of sympathy poured in from around the world. On 31 May Neto received a delegation from the People's Republic of the Congo, and the Soviet Ambassador, Boris Vorobiev. Mozambique, Sao Tomé and Cape Verde also sent delegations. Cuban support was strongly reaffirmed by Raul Castro, second secretary of the Cuban Communist Party and Vice-President of Cuba's Council of State. Cuban solidarity had never been in doubt; it was a mark of the political insensitivity of Alves and Sita Valles that they had assumed that the Cubans in Angola would remain neutral in the face of an attack against the MPLA.

On 11 June the MPLA buried their dead at a state funeral. The formal protocol was unable to contain the outpouring of grief. Neto and other leaders led the mourners to the gravesides and Neto delivered a stark oration. To the shrieking and wailing of the bereaved women, Angolan children covered the graves with great sprays of tropical flowers; a lone police bugler silhouetted against the dying light of day, played a final salute. For the thousands who had followed the coffins through the streets, the funeral relieved some of the stunned quality of the grief. The next day Neto returned to the Cidadela stadium, where he had denounced the faction, and at a mass rally in the football field, pressed home the message that, almost inevitably, factions joined reactionary forces. He described the agents of the Alves conspiracy as 'mainly individuals from Luanda, intellectuals of bourgeois or petty bourgeois origin. Some were compatriots, others foreigners; foreigners who were not capable of making a revolution in their own country came to make a revolution in Angola.'

The investigations continued and a special court martial was convened to try those accused of treason. Thirteen FAPLA officers were stripped of their rank by the Ministry of Defence. They ranged from the three Commanders involved in the coup (Monstro, Bakaloff and Sihanouk), through five majors led by Alves, one captain and four lieutenants. No official statements were made on the sentences handed down on guilty soldiers or civilians. The general assumption that the ring-leaders were executed by firing squad was confirmed by Neto in a terse comment at the FAPLA anniversary ceremonies on 1 August. Neto said 'Once assassinations were begun, particularly here in Luanda, of comrades who were killed for clear tactical objectives, those individuals were also shot.' No list of those executed was published, and this fuelled speculation in Angola and abroad, encouraging rumours such as that Alves was living in exile. Relatives of those arrested were in doubt for some time, although some soldiers' families received direct information from the Defence Ministry. As family visits were made to the prisons information was spread. Neto announced in a speech on 15 September 1978, just over a year later, that 'many hundreds' who had collaborated with the factionalists would shortly be released. Within two years, Angolans who had served prison terms were freed and the Portuguese had been returned to Portugal.

When the Central Committee met again in mid-August at a further plenary session, two more of its members were suspended for failing to disclose foreknowledge of the factionalists' intentions. They were Aristides Van Dunem, a former trades union secretary general, and Armando Xi-Cota. Both men pleaded mitigating circumstances and made sincere self-criticisms. They had taken part earlier in the campaign to explain the coup and how Alves had tried to undermine the MPLA.

The Central Committee was now reduced by around one-third of its pre-coup membership: three members had been murdered by the factionalists, five had been named in the conspiracy, and two suspended.

The main lesson of the coup for MPLA's foreign opponents was that by mid-1977 the extent of mass support for the Movement was such that dissidents were unable to present a convincing case for a popular uprising. After the coup, the people actively assisted in tracking down the conspirators. In the northern region, where the guerrilla conspirators came from, the peasants joined MPLA search parties for Alves; one family had recognized him when he approached their farm for food. 'We decided not to cook bananas, that would not have taken enough time, but to cook something that would take longer to prepare. But while we sent people to warn the militias and FAPLA he escaped.' Finally, a young boy picking coffee noticed Alves in his father's plantation. Carrying their machetes, the family and neighbours quietly closed in on him, and sent messages to the FAPLA and militias to come. A wild buffalo hampered the peasants but eventually they arrested Alves up a tree and escorted him to the military.

If the Alves group was secretly backed by the imperialist camp (Costa Martins was identified as a possible Western agent) the governments involved had misunderstood the nature of MPLA's power. A successful coup would obviously have played into imperialist hands, weakening Angola at a critical moment when Zaire and South Africa were both intent on overthrowing the progressive government. An Alves victory in Luanda would undoubtedly have prompted massive response from the several hundred thousand loyal MPLA military units and the militias, with fighting and uprisings against any attempt by Alves to impose his men in the provinces. Neto clearly understood that the coalition of Portuguese extremists, foreign spies and Angolan petty bourgeois elements was objectively a pro-imperialist alliance, and said imperialism was using the factionalists 'to destroy everything we have done since independence and during the liberation struggle and to destroy everything we have planned for national reconstruction'. He also pointed out the alliance had been deliberately built up, certainly from the Portuguese side. The factionalist group had used the language of the extreme left 'because in Angola today you can't attack MPLA saying you are a fascist or a capitalist'. Operation Cobra, a joint US-Zaire-South African invasion, was due to be launched in September 1977. There was an increase in frontier attacks east and south after the coup.

For the majority of Angolans in the countryside, the coup was a remote event in the capital. But in the larger towns, where individuals from the Alves group had been at work, the long term effect of the coup was to sow doubt about the wisdom of 'getting involved in politics'.

Perhaps the student body was the most affected by this trauma. A number of leading students had been won into the Alves camp, and after the coup it became even more difficult to mobilize for politically committed action youth at the University and in the higher classes at secondary school, the majority of whom, essentially, were still petty bourgeois.

The Alves faction had appointed itself the repository of true socialist ideology, an arrogant assumption that led them to discard the 19 years of MPLA's experience as an anti-imperialist liberation front, and eventually to seek to overthrow MPLA's tried and trusted leaders.

Blinded to their own inadequacy and reaction, the factionalists blithely approached Socialists to present their case. By the time of the coup, Alves had revealed himself – not least through his incoherent Town Hall addresses – as an ambitious young man intent on manoeuvring to divide Angolans one against the other, with the single objective of seizing power. He was able to shut out all considerations of unity faced with apartheid and imperialist aggression. Had the group contained any serious Marxist-Leninists, this alone could not have occurred. In addition, the group's criticisms of economic policy would have been backed by their own option, spelled out in pamphlet form at least.

Most damaging, potentially, was the faction leaders' attempt to involve Socialist embassies on their side. Were the MPLA leadership not endowed with a firm understanding, and had not strong bonds already been forged with the Socialist countries, the Faction might have sowed distrust between MPLA and its only reliable allies at this crucial moment. The consequences for the defence of Angola's revolution would have been clearly disastrous.

The factionalists had made one positive contribution, in that the MPLA and working people were now deeply aware that after Independence, past conduct was less important than present commitment to build independence and a just society. The principle of maintaining revolutionary commitment, and not resting on old laurels, was thus an extremely lively and hotly defended issue at a time when the Movement began studying its transformation into a vanguard Marxist-Leninist Party.

PART 3
Revolution and Counter-Revolution on the Frontline

7. Building the New Society

Portugal's Civilizing Mission in Angola

Angola spans tropical, sub-tropical and savannah country. 85% of its people are peasant farmers. There is plenty of good farming land and no lack of water. In the centre and south are high grassy plateaux, strewn with great boulders left by prehistoric glaciers. To the south-west lies the blazing Moçamedes desert. East are the great rivers, the headwaters of the Zambezi, the Cuango, Kuando and Kubango into which flow hundreds of streams, criss-crossing the rolling eastern hills. The long Kunene arises in the central uplands and flows south, bends sharply into the Atlantic, marking along this final stretch of its course the frontier between Angola and South African-occupied Namibia. In tropical Cabinda, nearest the equator, is the dark Mayombe rain-forest that sheltered the MPLA's guerrillas.

The resistance against the Portuguese and, since independence, the MPLA's nation-building policies have united what were seven central African kingdoms. When the Portuguese first dropped anchor here in the 16th Century they found the Kongo kingdom along the great Congo river. Northwards lay Cabinda and the Loango kingdom, southwards the Ndongo kingdom of the Kimbundus. To the east lived the Lundas in the grasslands of the upper Congo river basin; they founded kingships to the south-west in Angola and south-east in Zambia.

By the 17th Century, central Angola was the home of many small Ovimbundu kingdoms, south were the Kwanyamas and Ovambos and south-east the Ganguelas and Mukuankalas, descendants of southern Africa's Khoisan. Each kingdom had its distinctive economy, culture and history.

The 1884-5 Berlin conference and ensuing scramble for Africa led Portugal for the first time to try to 'pacify' the entire area it called Angola, (from Ngola, the chief of the Kimbundus' Ndongo kingdom). Expeditionary forces were sent to overturn African rulers and establish garrisons at strategic points. Their role was to protect and support traders and settlers whose task was to utilize the African economy for Portugal's needs. Angola's people would no longer be sold as slaves overseas but indentured as slave labour at home. African social organization and culture were targets for extermination by the colonial state; they represented independence, when servitude was the goal.

Until these wars of 1890-1920 the white army had been small; drawn from career officers and transported convicts who formed most of the rank and file. The '*guerra preta*' (black army) was mustered through collaborating chiefs, though a few may have been freebooting mercenaries.

Other 'special forces' could also be mobilized in times of need. In 1895 a Captain Trigo Teixeira marched 72 convicts from Luanda prison 950 miles east to 'take Moxico' before the British got there from Zambia. Later the Moxico people rose against them, fighting with traditional spears and bows and home-made shotguns, '*canhangulos*'.

Throughout the country the people rose up and fought for their independence and traditions. The coastal kingdoms had for many years been subjected and millions of slaves had been shipped to Brazil and Cuba. The first to suffer now were the Ovimbundu. By the end of the 18th Century these kingdoms of central Angola were thriving merchant communities trading with the Portuguese merchants centred at Catumbela on the coast, in beeswax, honey, slaves and ivory. This pattern changed after Portugal built a fort at Caconda in 1769; in the Benguela highlands, it opened a trading route east to foreign traders and their coastal African middlemen. It also strengthened the Ovimbundu monopoly, since the traders had to pass through their kingdoms. The Ovimbundu's economic strength grew, they organized caravans that plied south as far as the Kalahari, east to Katanga and occasionally even to Mozambique in search of merchandise. Gum arabic became the prize and dominated the trade from 1874. The 'time of the rubber' lasted until around 1900 when Brazil entered, and soon cornered the market. For 30 years rubber brought unprecedented wealth and power to the Ovimbundu. Their greatest king was Ndunduma, and it was he whom the Portuguese set out to destroy first.

In 1890 Ndunduma was defeated and his kingdom broken. In 1896 Numa, king of Bailundo rose with his people against the Caconda garrison, he was crushed, with heavy losses. Finally from 1902-3 the Ovimbundu rose together against the Portuguese. Older people still remember the Bailundo wars. They began as a mass military offensive and developed into a guerrilla war against the urban enclaves and trading posts, staffed with a new and rapacious breed of exploiter, swarming over the highlands from the coast. The guerrillas attacked traders and their liquor stills, symbol of the white man's corruption and power. Guerrilla bands set fire to the stills and salvaged the rivets for bullets. Expeditionary forces were sent against them and they holed up with their families in the mountains and caves where they held out close to starvation for another two years before being overrun by army reinforcements.

As the Portuguese army advanced, the missionaries followed. From 1911 the Benguela Railway Company, a British venture owned by Tanganyika Concessions, began building its trans-Angola railroad. The colonial administration was not far behind.

To the south, the Kwanyamas on the border with Namibia were the last victims of Portuguese occupation. They fought courageously for over ten years under their fearless leader, Mandume, who was finally captured and beheaded. Xangongo 'island of tears' fiercely resisted building of a fort there in 1906. The Portuguese history books tell of a 'general uprising' in Kunene the following year. More troops were sent in and were met by an army of 20,000 who fought them from July till September. In 1909 the people of Dombondola (to the south-west) rose up. A fort had to be built there to quell them. In 1915 fresh troops went from Lisbon to deal with troublesome Kunene. The main actions were fought at Mongua and Ngiva. Mongua fell on 20 August 1915 after three days of fierce fighting. Ngiva was overrun by the colonial troops on 4 September.

Once resistance was crushed, the way was open for the planters; they first settled between Luanda and the Congo basin – coffee land. North-east the diamond mining company began carving out its huge capitalist 'kingdom', building up what was to become the largest labour force in the country, (over 20,000 workers at its peak). The railway crossed Angola from Katanga to the coast. Chain-gangs of weary men cleared the bushland, hewed the sleepers as earlier slaves had paved the road east from Benguela to Bié with their bones. By 1921 the railway was completed.

Only in the furthest east and south were Angolans still relatively free of settlers. In the late 1920s they totalled around 30,000. By 1950 they had grown to over 78,000.

Families near the coast, on the coffee land, were worst affected. The influx of settlers changed peasant life. Large scale land grabbing became the order of the day. One old man told how:

> When they got here they were given control of everything we needed. They found coffee, rice, potatoes, garlic, onions all in our hands. They told lies. They said Angolan blacks don't work. Those of us who worked our own lands were bandits they said. Whereas those who worked the Portuguese lands, oh, they said, those blacks know how to work. They came from Lisbon with guns and knives to kill us. At my age I've seen a lot. The men went off to contract labour and the women stayed behind at home. But later they came to get the women too, to work for the state. The children were left alone on the ground.

Most contract workers came from the central highlands. Ovimbundu communities had by now been torn apart by settlement and exploitation. The Portuguese war against them had coincided with the decline of their rubber trade. Some new commodity seemed the way out of their sudden poverty and subjection; they grew maize which was what the settlers wanted, but without any crop rotation the land became exhausted and families had to move on to fresh ground. A period of migration and back-breaking toil followed. When the settlers began planting on a large scale the young men went as wage labourers on their farms. Those who did not go voluntarily were forced by legislation and government recruitment.

By the mid-1950s there were few Umbundu villages with adult able-bodied men to work their fields and provide for the children. In 1955, an anthropologist, C.E. Edwards, reported

> a network of roads covers the Benguela highland with the result that all villages are at most only a few miles from a track which is usable by motor vehicles. A truck seen on one of those roads will most likely belong to a trader, though it might belong to an official on one of his rare local trips, to a missionary or to a labour recruiter. Men can go out to work in three ways. By going to look for work in a city or on a plantation, by being recruited in their village by a travelling labour recruiter (angariador) or by being recruited through the District Officer (posto) for military service or for contract labour (a period of a year's non voluntary work). The 'natives' are, unlike the 'civilized' subject to the Labour Code (which essentially provides for the forced contract labour). There is no Native Legal Code nor does Portuguese law apply to 'natives'. Administrative Officers may apply Portuguese law, or native custom known to them, or their own judgment.

Maize, still the central crop, was 'grown by the Ovimbundu and sold by the traders to the official boards which have storehouses along the railway line'. He said nothing about prices paid by the traders to the black farmer – or more likely his wife, left to till the land, draw the water and hew the wood, while her husband was away on contract.

Anarchy had succeeded the ordered and prosperous communities of the 'rubber days'. A German agronomist working in the central highlands from 1970-73 noted that society, clan structures and family life itself were:

> disintegrating while the men were away working on white settler plantations of economically dubious quality . . . . Men normally visit their families once a year, for a few weeks, or even for a few days. Under such circumstances it is no wonder that many families are disintegrating.

Further west in Cuanza Sul, Cuanza Norte and Malanje, the peasants were massively expropriated by the settlers. The men tended to flee the appalling contract work and make for Luanda, leaving their families to fend as best they could. To replace them, more and more Ovimbundu workers were shipped in. Luanda's shanty towns began to spread at the same time as the 1960 industrial expansion, and more urban jobs. Middle-aged peasants became cane-cutters, sugar mill porters, dockworkers, construction navvies and factory sweepers and hauliers (the lowliest work with no prospect of advancement) and were completely illiterate, until 1975, when the MPLA began adult literacy classes. They were isolated and afraid: the PIDE might find out they had fled from the local Senhor's contract force and deliver them back to their planter master.

Others went to Benguela and Lobito, which were also expanding as the railway company provided a growing number of jobs and the Lobito docks expanded. In the far south, the port of Moçamedes became a contract labour centre and the fishing industry and fishmeal factories employed around 10,000 workers. Inland lay the Moçamedes desert and as it grew greener towards Kunene and the Lubango uplands, the Mocubal roving cattle farmers and Mhuila subsistence farmers were the new victims of settler expansion. The Mhuila were turned off their land and either forced back to less fertile ground in the hills, or indentured as labourers. Fiercely independent Mocubal ranchers were partly tamed by the Portuguese merchants with alcohol. Some agreed to trade their cattle for cheap wine. Others refused and were hounded by administrators and traders. A rash of court cases followed in the late 1960s when Mocubals rebelled against local corruption and malpractices and sought redress by legal means. There were areas where traders feared to penetrate because the people began meting out their own justice against the Portuguese when the courts failed them.

Kunene province, hived off from Huila after 1970, was the last to be settled. Ambitious Portuguese fenced off huge tracts of the people's grazing land to build their own ranches. The Kwanyama cattle farmers, were forced to break the law – and the fences – to survive. When PIDE tracked them down they fled to the mines of Namibia and South Africa.

Kuando-Kubango remained the 'end of the earth' in settler talk. Only the army knew the lowlying, tsetse fly infested south-east. Serpa Pinto, the capital, was mainly renowned for its nearby political prison camp. The inmates, MPLA activists, were used as convict labour to build a handful of administration buildings and homes. Hunting lodges were scattered in the bushland where big game could be taken.

North of Luanda, the 1961 settler terror had forced thousands of families to flee into Zaire. Those who stayed behind held on to their small plots of land and grew coffee, gradually withdrawing their labour from the settler farms. The settlers responded by shipping in more Ovimbundu contract labourers. A deeply divided black community resulted, exactly what the settlers wanted. Local people despised the Ovimbundu, and felt if they too refused to work, the settlers could be defeated. A few of them found friends in the local people and intermarried. The basis was laid for tribal distrust that the FNLA and UNITA were to exploit for recruiting in 1974 and 1975.

Planters built high concrete walls around their farm settlements topped with barbed wire and watchtowers. The local villagers were closely watched, workers and farmers who aroused suspicion were dragged off to plantation prisons to await interrogation by PIDE, who wanted information about the guerrillas. In 1963 when the Cabinda front was opened, the PIDE set up the Cabinda special black forces and an army of informers. Then came the MPLA's work on the eastern front from 1966.

The people of Lunda, Moxico, and northern Kuando Kubango, who joined the MPLA guerrillas soon became the main force of the liberation movement's armed resistance. They marched into Zambia and brought back weapons and ammunition; built collectives, and farmed under the cover of trees to prevent Portuguese air reconnaissance from mapping the guerrillas liberated areas, and went into villages and towns recruiting for the guerrilla force.

From the first guerrilla actions in May 1966 MPLA had swept to the north and south and was pushing westwards towards Bié.

There was incipient unrest throughout the countryside, and it was increasingly difficult to prevent it spreading to the towns. Recruiting blacks and coloureds into the army to fight their own people was vigorously in progress. But the guerrillas continued to gain ground; an underground movement was active in the towns.

In a July 1966 seminar on military 'psycho-social action' – part of the counter-subversion Portugal deployed against the liberation movement – agit-prop military staff were reminded that an important part of their programme was directed 'at our own troops, to combat enemy propaganda so that this should no longer have any effect on them'. By 1969, the Angolan Information, Co-ordination and Centralization Service (SCCIA) had been set up to link the administration with PIDE and military intelligence in the battle for the hearts and minds of the people. One official Ramiro Monteiro in a lengthy tactical analysis stressed that it 'is easier to prevent subversion than to fight it' and argued the political counter-subversion programme should 'raise the economic, social, and political level of the community'. He also pressed for more economic opportunities for blacks: 'the percentage of Africans in trade is very small. Trade would settle the African down and given the interests he would have to defend, make him less vulnerable to subversion'. Health services, 'one of the most important factors in conquering the support of the rural people' should be extended and industrial training courses set up for Africans. Monteiro's advice went unheeded by the settlers, who were very much in control of Angola. In sharp contrast to Mozambique, where the colonial administration sent its officers from Lisbon, many leading administrative positions in Angola were filled by immigrants.

A Dr Afonso Mendes from the Institute of Labour and Social Action of Angola,was the signatory of a secret colonial document devoted to analysis of 'aspects relative to counter-subversion'. 'The degree of receptivity of these populations to subversion is very great'. He listed some of the reasons why 'the white man is presented as an evil human being, greedy, and the sole cause of the horrors of the past, perhaps even the traditional enemy of the black man' as:

> slavery, the wars of pacification, abuse of power, physical violence exerted by the administrative authorities, forced labour, administrative measures, expropriation of land, removals of the population, forced cropping – the practice of forcing cultivation of certain crops by Angolan farmers – countless violation of traditional laws and African values.

Dr Mendes also referred to the racist behaviour of some 'small whites' but his main indictment was against officials, who should attempt 'to treat Africans as Portuguese citizens, respecting their dignity and their rights'.

He also noted that 'the average monthly salary of an African rural worker was 600 escudos [about £8 a month] whereas the European worker in the city gets six times as much' and called for 'narrowing the gap' and establishing a minimum monthly wage. Mendes also spoke against the settlers' use of the military and para-military against their workers. He noted that: 'cases of extreme physical violence against workers are not infrequent' despite forced labour being theoretically illegal and punishable with a two year prison sentence. Often workers were not paid and were subjected to 'other grave irregularities by employers', which created an impression that 'the white man continues to do as he likes with impunity'.

The provinces that lost their men to the contract work were the most densely populated. By 1971 Huambo and Bié were together providing over 95,000 registered contract workers. Huila and Kunene in the south were sending around 10,000 to the coast and fishing industry and 12,000 or so mineworkers to Namibia and South Africa.

The absence of the men, the lack of medical and educational services to help the women and their children intensified the already acutely low population growth. By 1970 it had sunk to 0.66% compared with an average 3% for most developing countries. Enforced resettlement schemes in areas affected by armed struggle also took their toll.

The MPLA's Record Before Independence

The MPLA's programme, approved at the September 1974 Inter-Regional Conference of Militants, aimed to change all this. No more exploitation but minimum guaranteed wages and equal pay for equal work; an end to discrimination on the grounds of race, ethnic origin, sex or age, and free public health and education. These positions were already identified with MPLA. Its *Angola Combatente* radio programme had featured them widely; also many Angolans had concrete experience of MPLA's stand. Among the exile community in Zaire, the social, health and education work of MPLA was so well organized that when Zairean officials heard of their expulsion they complained to their central administration that their own people would now be left without social support. In the liberated areas, the SAM (military health services), bush schools, and literacy courses provided more practical evidence of MPLA policy. Literacy manuals and a first ever *History of Angola* had been distributed in the bush. After the April coup, as clandestine militants came out of hiding they initiated MPLA committees which took on some of these tasks.

Neither FNLA nor UNITA had any similar record. Although during 1974 and 1975 UNITA frequently promised to take correspondents to its bush camps to see the schools and medical posts it claimed to have set up, these visits never took place.

By 1974, the FNLA's record in Zaire was so poor that clearly, it had little if any mass support. The PDA, and its President, who had been appointed to the Social Affairs portfolio by Holden, unable to gain access to money or the levers of power, had not the means to initiate community work.

The differences between the three rival organizations were to be seen more clearly in Luanda than elsewhere. The FNLA's record of murder and intimidation, the UNITA's tribal appeal and dearth of organization or programme contrasted sharply with the MPLA's militant self-help. As the *Comissões Popular de Bairro* (People's Neighbourhood Committees) sprang up all over the city under the MPLA flag, residents were at first impressed and then enthusiastic. FNLA's attacks and armed robbery prompted citizens to set up barricades in the townships. When FNLA and UNITA banded together to attack the 'M', the people rose up against them throughout Luanda.

Independence and Building a Nation

FNLA's strategy for power was one of simple domination by one tribe, the Kikongo. That domination would be facilitated by American arms and support. After independence a capitalist economy was planned, run by the multinationals with ample rewards for those Angolan leaders who would be signing the contracts.

UNITA's strategy was based on Ovimbundu tribalism, and a return to the halcyon days of Ovimbundu prosperity. The key to UNITA's capitalism was the multinationals, which, again, would provide economic input – and peace with racist South Africa. The US, the EEC and South Africa would provide the arms and the support.

MPLA alone, sought real independence and non-alignment, and thus needed to build a strongly united nation. Only the MPLA was committed to resolving tribal and racial problems, with working-class and peasant interests a priority.

The MPLA leadership was under no illusions regarding FNLA and UNITA followers. As creatures of imperialism their grass-roots support came from working men and women swept along by demagogy and tribalism. The number of committed militants in both organizations could hardly exceed a few hundred. MPLA's priority was to integrate all six million Angolans at home and 350,000 in exile, into the tasks of national reconstruction and the building of socialism. There was no question, as yet, of forming a Party. The broad movement and mobilization of more support must continue.

Neto set the issue of class in the forefront of independence politics. Kikongo and Ovimbundu would receive equal treatment, despite FNLA and UNITA tribalism. The cold-blooded massacre of the movement's Ovimbundu members by UNITA had led to public mourning for the Ovimbundu victims of the UNITA rule, and campaigns emphasizing the support given by many Ovimbundu to MPLA before the war. Constantly stressed was that those who had supported UNITA had been tricked and they were not to be blamed for supporting the wrong organization.

Kikongo from FNLA's much vaunted northern stronghold, present at the British mercenaries' trial, testified to their sacrifices and sufferings at the hands of FNLA and its allies.

FNLA and UNITA troops were disarmed, their uniforms exchanged for civilian clothes, and they were told to return to their homes and join the battle for reconstruction. The only prisoners taken were officials denounced by the local people as responsible for murders, or officers and NCOs of the organizations to whom specific war crimes could be attributed. There was no discrimination. Only former proven officeholders, (not rank and file) could neither run for Party membership nor vote in the first round of elections for the people's power structures. Prisoners were taken to Prison Farms to do agricultural work, and attend political education classes.

In the meantime, Neto worked for the return of the 300,000 exiles in Zaire and the 30,000 or so in Zambia. Those in Namibia – though told they would be welcome – could not be formally assisted to return, since the MPLA refused to negotiate with South Africa. Leading ex-FNLA officials returned to Luanda in response to Neto's amnesty and they broadcast appeals for others to follow suit.

By 1980 more than 250,000 exiles had returned. Former FNLA and UNITA members, including former officials and army officers, were holding civil service, industrial and agricultural jobs, had joined the army and the people's militias, were studying in technical college and at the University and playing in football teams.

The pressing needs for more cadres and skilled workers to carry out the government's policy of balanced regional development and growth in social and community services meant that each region was called upon to make the effort to produce its own cadres.

Mass Health

During the guerrilla war, MPLA had organized health care in the liberated areas. The new 1975 Constitution established health care as a right for everyone. How could it be made one in practice, when of the 200 doctors recorded in 1973 only 50 had stayed on, and the bulk of the skilled health technicians and ward sisters had gone home to Portugal? When the colonial health system had serviced a minority of 350,000 whites instead of six million Angolans, and when it had been a curative system instead of a preventive community service?

Rural Angolans had lived miles from a doctor or even a nurse. Their extreme poverty meant that endemic parasitic diseases had debilitated hundreds of thousands of working people. Education and health were equally important for improving production and productivity and raising basic living standards.

Unlike many other African countries at Independence, Angola possessed a hospital in each provincial capital, and to restore them to working order was a relatively simple objective. More complex was to utilize the provincial hospitals as preventive medicine centres turning their trained staff to train others and to begin seeking support for the undertaking from local community officials and mass organizations.

Also fundamental to the MPLA's attitude towards health was an appreciation of the contribution that traditional midwives and *curandeiros* (curers, as opposed to fetish priests who practised sorcery) could continue to make. Efforts were made to draw traditional medical workers into contact with the national health service, with the aim of progessively incorporating them into scientific medical practices, and analysing their remedies – especially those based on herbs – in the laboratories.

Cuba was asked to provide the bulk of hospital doctors and technicians until enough Angolans had been trained. The GDR, the Soviet Union, Yugoslavia, Bulgaria and the Holland Medical Committee also sent volunteers. (Algeria sent a war-time team to the Luanda hospitals.) As FAPLA liberated the provinces, Angolan and Cuban staff moved into the hospitals, and repaired the damage while providing a skeleton medical service. In many cases equipment had been sabotaged, and furniture and mattresses destroyed. A year after independence all 16 provincial hospitals were functioning again; in December 1977 Neto reported that 14 of them were staffed by Cubans. 418 Cuban doctors, nurses and health technicians had performed 16,000 surgical operations, delivered 6,000 babies (another 9,000 had been delivered in hospital by Angolans) and had examined over a million patients.

In December 1975 a National Health Service had been created, providing free medical services and medicines for everyone, but private practice had been allowed to continue in parallel until May 1977 when private practice was abolished by law. 1977 also marked the launching of mass vaccination campaigns for the first time. In a national polio vaccination campaign 1.6 million children took Soviet made sweets. More than 40,000 volunteers carried out the job from schools, clinics, and under the shade of trees, on street corners in the cities and in village market places. Mobile units toured the hamlets. Angola won an award from the World Health Organization, which had supported the campaign.

Regular vaccination of children and adults has since been established, with special emphasis on mother and child care.

In the capital, problems due to class confrontations among the health workers initially beset the reorganization of the health service. The Portuguese had eliminated most of the revolutionary nurses, either by killing them or transporting them to the political prisons. Consequently many of those left in the nursing service at Independence tended towards petty bourgeois élitism and, being some of the more skilled Angolans, perhaps felt that they should now be promoted to a higher status in the medical profession, instead of working under highly trained Portuguese professionals. Encouraged by leftists and factionalists active in 1976 and early 1977, they pressed for privileges and promotions. But by contrast, the majority of doctors by 1977 were commited to the revolution. They had endured the danger and exhaustion of war, worked endless hours to compensate for the inadequate number of doctors, and many were now engaged in training programmes and community health experiments. Hospital conditions had sharply deteriorated owing to the exodus of the senior nursing staff and technicians. Many

Angolan nurses wanted promotion without the hard work. The petty bourgeois camp also resented criticism from the patients, swarming in from the townships who by now strongly defended their rights in the hospitals when they received high handed treatment from the nurses. Workers' assemblies were held to examine the situation. Finally, the Health Minister, MPLA guerrilla doctor Kassessa, resigned, and a former nurse, Coelho da Cruz, was named as his successor. This apparently appeased the petty bourgeois camp. The accent now was on training new recruits. Coelho da Cruz launched a new 'health promoters' campaign.

> In each village we want a basic health worker who will know about hygiene, nutrition, how to keep house and obtain stable ecological conditions. We are only used to swallowing pills and having injections. We want to change this mentality and work for preventive medicine. We also have to change the attitudes of our health workers.

In Luanda, by December 1979, 500 women were active in the townships after a 3 month course including hospital work. A promoter is a volunteer who works in her free time, to improve health conditions and channel the sick towards expert medical care. In the countryside, far from medical help, promoters also dispense free basic medicines such as aspirin and anti-malarial prophylactics. They also accompany the sick to the nearest health post.

A national training scheme for paramedical staff was launched at the same time. Over 1,600 Angolans were trained in the first batch of students who attended 17 Technical Colleges of Health linked to the provincial hospitals.

The structure of the National Health Service is, therefore: the volunteer health promoter; health posts, staffed by a nurse; a health centre with an out-patients surgery, pharmacy, and a 15-20 bed cottage hospital. If necessary patients from the health centre are sent to the provincial hospital where the specialists work. In 1979 133 health posts and 62 health centres had been set up. By 1980, there were 800 health posts and 180 health centres. More than 200 First Aid posts had also been set up in factories and state-owned farms.

Before Independence, 600 paramedical staff had been trained annually. In 1980 2,395 were undergoing first year training and 943 were into their second cycle of theoretical studies. Between 30-35 doctors graduated from the Faculty of Medicine annually, and intake into the first year course rose to over 200. In 1981, 60 students began their course at a second Medical Faculty founded in Huambo.

Although a national pharmaceuticals industry was planned, the Ministry still had to import all medicines, and foreign exchange shortages also affected its budget. In 1979 the total value of imports was four times that spent in 1973, over US $1,600 million. But the authorities needed twice as much.

The growth of Angola's National Health Service may be indicated by the following figures: the number of doctors in 1973 was 211, in 1979, over 500 and in 1981 700 (150 Angolans); paramedical staff numbered 1,593 in 1973; 4,000 in 1979 and 7,000, plus 2,000 in training, in 1981. The number of hospital beds increased from 9,477 in 1973, to 14,374 in 1981. One million out-patients were recorded in 1973; five million in 1979 – the figure for 1981 is not available.

Education for Everyone

The MPLA's 1974 programme called for a 'swift attack on illiteracy' and 'free compulsory primary education for a minimum period of six years'. Before independence, from 20 October to 4 November 1975 a national conference on education was held in Luanda, and in December, education was nationalized. Church schools were allowed to continue in operation provided they charged no fee and taught the national curriculum. The religious staff were paid as normal school teachers. Religious instruction was not to form part of the school course, but priests and the churches could provide this outside school time in separate classes to volunteers. The training of priests, preachers and nuns, continued in seminaries and convents.

For centuries Africans had been excluded from learning, and for decades only the petty bourgeoisie of *assimilados* had learned how to read and write, therefore, education for all was an important issue for the working and peasant classes. The MPLA taught that self-help was the ideal to pursue, and supported this with exercise books, pencils, chalk and as many school manuals as could be printed.

There was no other way. The number of schools in colonial Angola, built to cater for children of the 350,000 settlers, was pitifully small. In 1973, primary school intake was half a million, 33⅓% of whom were Portuguese, and in secondary school, 72,000 of whom 80% were Portuguese. By 1977 there were over one million primary school children and 105,000 secondary school students, and the Ministry of Education received hundreds of new requests for materials and teachers.

In the depths of Kunene province, 'Drive with care! Maputa School!' announced a notice nailed to a wooden stick along the dirt track. Ten yards further on was a new log cabin with thatch roof. Not a house was to be seen. The school was crowded with children from the *makondas*, family kraals, scattered in the savannah. The parents had built it, MPLA had found the teacher. In Bié city, in one of the brick house suburbs, the colonial administration had built a single small concrete schoolroom. Now there are two shifts for the single room and outside, under a large shady tree a third teacher is at work, his blackboard propped up against a trunk. Later, the peasants returning from work in their fields take their places on the same benches for their literacy class. In a brick factory in another Bié suburb, the workers sit down by the kilns for their literacy class every afternoon. Amongst them is a white-haired weather-beaten Portuguese brickmaker. Portugal never taught him to read or write.

At the Benguela Railway Company a worker said: 'The English never did anything to help us to read or write. Now we are on lesson 14. We know a little about our struggle against colonialism. And later we shall learn things to help us with our special work on the railways.'

Housewives with their babies on their backs or playing outside study in their neighbour's house, in porches, or community buildings, mainly during the afternoons.

More than 102,000 adults learned to read and write from November 1976, when the official literacy campaign was launched, to November 1977. It cost the state $10 for each student. 'The low cost is thanks to the revolutionary spirit of our literacy teachers who have perfectly understood that teaching literacy is a political act and are not asking to be paid for their work' said the Literacy Director. In the first year, 21,000 classes had been held across the country, organized under 150 municipal literacy centres. The original target of 20,000 literate adults in one year had been overtaken five times. Although material conditions are often better in the cities, it was the countryside that advanced the most. The Literacy Director, Guilherme de Sousa, explained: 'the peasants are more demanding. They were the most exploited under colonialism and they see the need to make up for lost time'. By 1980 more than one million adults had learned to read and write.

When the MPLA met for its First Congress, in December 1977, work had begun on restructuring the entire education system. The guiding principles were to build manual labour, and respect for it, into the system, to integrate production by students into their education, and to provide education for all from the very young to the old. The revolution must give everyone a chance to become the 'new man'.

Changing the syllabus was one priority. In the liberated zones during the guerrilla war, MPLA had introduced revolutionary new texts for literacy teaching, and had begun producing the first *History of Angola* with the help of its scholars in Algiers. Now there was a need for new science books, and to teach world history, particularly world social history, to help Angolans identify their place in the broad spectrum of human progress and enlightenment. Obviously, African history would be an important theme.

The 1977 Congress heard

> from the ideological and scientific viewpoint, in spite of certain changes in structure and syllabus over the past two years, we still see the adverse effects of colonialism in our educational system and amongst our teachers. School today still does not match the needs of our people and the structures still do not conform to Marxism-Leninism, and this is in itself a serious danger for the continuity of our revolution.

The Congress rectified this state of affairs by approving an entirely new structure.

Three education sub-systems were designed. Normal schooling is now eight years of basic education, which is free and compulsory. Children then go on to middle school, technical colleges or the University, which are also free, but not compulsory. A second sub-system meets the needs of just-literate adults, of whom the majority had four years of primary school under colonial rule. They now receive a 'crash' primary education course, telescoping eight years into four, and then join the others in middle school. Finally, completely illiterate adults must first pass a basic literacy examination and then join the special adult primary school programme, where eight years primary schooling is condensed into six years. A special category of 'Provisional Colleges' was set up for older illiterate children, but since this problem will now be diminishing the colleges will be converted to other uses.

Since 1976 night classes have been held in secondary schools round the country, while night literacy courses supplemented afternoon classes for farm and factory workers. The acute shortage of teachers led the government to launch an appeal for part-time teachers, seconded by their places of work. The Ministry of Education launched a worker-student scheme which allows workers to spend half their working day studying, but still receive a full salary. 90% of University students are part-time workers, and, according to the Trades Union Congress, UNTA, 60% of unionized workers are in some form of part-time education.

Most teachers training is being undertaken locally while the teachers continue with their work. Over 25,000 primary school teachers are still needed before primary schooling can be extended to everyone. At Independence most teachers were under-qualified and after a national survey the Ministry announced that only 7% were adequately trained. UNESCO has helped organize the on-the-job teachers' training programme.

Primary teaching is solely in the charge of Angolans. In the secondary schools help has been brought in from Portugal and Cuba. In 1976 Cuba offered 500 secondary school places for Angolans, and this scholarship programme was expanded the following year. In 1978, Brigades of Cuban teachers were sent to Angola.

Although the shortage of teachers and the need to re-train the existing ones probably resulted in a lowering of standards in the first few years after Independence, a significant start was made to broaden the social base of education. Students learned something of their own country, and of world history, especially world social history. Marxism-Leninism was situated in its historical context but there were too few cadres adequately trained in its principles to mount specific political education courses.

The Mass Organizations

The Portuguese coup in April 1974 signalled the start of street politics. MPLA had to work underground until, in November, it signed an official ceasefire with Portugal, nevertheless its supporters immediately began organizing mass actions. A first demonstration left the Luanda townships on 1 May, carrying placards: 'Peace and Work', 'Viva Spinola' 'We would be grateful for the freeing of our political prisoners'. But according to a Portuguese journalist 'the police clubbed them till they dispersed. And the people of the townships understood their time had not yet come'.

On 26 May a large, well organized demonstration demanding complete, unconditional and immediate independence gathered in front of the Governor's Palace. The MPLA banner was flourished for the first time. Later that day a counter-demonstration of about 100 whites called for the return of PIDE and shouted 'Vivas' to Caetano. The first signs of mass African political commitment threw the white community into disarray. A few days later in Sao Paulo a white bar owner shot dead a black MPLA supporter. The victim had simply stated that he supported Spinola. More murders of blacks by white settlers followed and a repeat of the 1961 slaughters, when white settlers tore through the townships with their guns, seemed likely.

Silvino Silvério Marques, a known fascist who had been arrested on 25 April because he was not a member of the Armed Forces' Movement, was named by Lisbon as Angola's new governor. He had been Governor of Angola from 1962-5 and responsible for hounding the small, black cultural groups which were the only form of African organization then permitted.

On 15 July 1974, more than 10,000 Angolan troops in the colonial army, marched through the capital in uniform and pledged to stop the killings. It was a demonstration of the MPLA's strength: its clandestine militants in Luanda had succeeded in penetrating the colonial army following the mass recruitment of blacks and coloureds. When MPLA guerrillas secretly visited the capital at this time, they were amazed to discover the underground movement's organizational strength.

MPLA's mass organizations had all been founded in exile and had been active among the exiled community in Zaire, Congo and Zambia, and the liberated areas of Angola. On 9 February 1975, a Central Committee meeting called on the movement's mass organizations to mobilize the people for the anti-imperialist struggle and national independence. The first task was to resist the army.

The strength of grass-roots participation in the organizations, became the basis for the People's Neighbourhood Committees that administered Luanda in the transition and threw out the marauding bands of FNLA and UNITA. During the second war of liberation, these structures received and helped refugees, assisted with combat duties, and organized dangerous supply runs to stranded comrades. The area between Cangola and Tango, where 60,000 MPLA supporters gathered behind FNLA lines, was supplied from Luanda by truck and porter through the Mass Organizations Department of the MPLA.

But DOM's principle task was to stimulate production through the mass organizations. '. . . during the first war [we learned] : we must consolidate production. We cannot mobilize the masses without a concrete response to their immediate needs . . . . No political work can be done unless these problems can begin to be solved' said Pinto João, head of DOM in the aftermath of the war. Activists began to encourage the co-operative movement in the countryside, and trade unions began to organize work in factories and offices. The mass organizations launched voluntary work campaigns, often on 'Red Saturdays' to cut cane, pick coffee, clean the streets and cities or paint houses and buildings that had been sabotaged and partially destroyed.

The enthusiasm workers exhibited in the campaign needed to be channelled into ordinary working hours. After a special week's voluntary work drive the DOM director commented: 'this loses all meaning if the spirit behind it – of thinking about consolidating our economy – is not put into practice every day in every place of work by everyone'.

Building the Trade Union Movement

UNTA's most challenging task was to build a genuine, active trade union movement in the town and countryside. Colonial *sindicatos* were not empowered to negotiate or pressure management if this would affect output, they functioned solely as a white, social security association.

Now, unions were to carry out entirely different tasks. Social services were provided by the government; wages and output were to be determined by the Planning Ministry and other appropriate government departments. Many people had difficulty in understanding what the unions were for. This included some of the young, inexperienced cadres recruited from the work-force to start building union committees.

UNTA's function is to represent the work-force in a dimension not fully covered either by Party or Government, even though each broadly represents working-class interests. UNTA reports on specific work problems and exerts pressure in defence of workers' interests. Union officials need not be Party members, leading UNTA secretariat officials are, but many shop stewards are not.

Initially UNTA was a failure. Although the Union Congress called for better working and welfare conditions it undertook little or no positive action. A first National Conference in October 1975 had elected a secretariat and Neto had spoken of the need for workers' committees at all work places. The Secretariat stated that it faced 'an absence of class consciousness and previously sketchy trades union organization'. This was not an underestimation of the Luanda, Lubango, Huambo and Lobito work-force, but a reflection of the fact that the liberation struggle had been largely advanced by the peasantry, while the urban workers who began to grow into a significant community only after 1961, had been a repressed, disorganized group lacking class ideology, or a working-class tradition.

Now the Secretariat had to build a movement from scratch. Elections for officials were out of the question, the workers often barely knew each other after the disruptions of the war. Organizers – mainly young people – were thus appointed by the Secretariat. Their advantage over older, experienced men was that they could read and write; also, they were keen to take an active part in their new society and were full of confidence. Some older and illiterate workers were cowed and too diffident after years of fascist and racist repression.

The Alves factionalists saw their chance with some of these inexperienced young shop stewards, and the May 1977 coup brought reversals to the unionization drive. Factionalist cadres engaged in extensive political agitation on economic and management issues. Their endless meetings were resented by the workers since no action ever resulted from them; older men objected to being harangued by these young 'politicians', and when the coup was explained, workers felt their mistrust of the union cadres was fully justified.

The new Secretary General (appointed after Aristides Van Dunem's dismissal) Pascoal Luvualo, was an old campaigner and member of the Political Bureau, who understood what the organization needed for its revitalization. He began with an examination of workers' participation in management. The factionalists, by provoking conflict between workers' structures, MPLA committees in the factories and management, had created significant political and economic damage. Nobody knew what their responsibilities were, workers were uncertain who was supposed to be representing them.

The law on State Intervention, passed in March 1976, had established a control system over management for state owned economic units. Management teams were to comprise: one delegate to represent the government, and two delegations of workers – one elected from the shop-floor, the other nominated by the government. This management committee, would have collective responsibility for the unit concerned. In addition, there was to be a separate general Workers' Assembly, to be convened by management once a month to inform the entire workforce of the economic unit's record and plans and to answer questions from the floor.

This law was amended in October 1977. Collective management had failed; it was replaced by personal management. A Director, not necessarily a Party member was appointed by the relevant Ministry as its representative and had full responsibility for running the firm, in line with planning directives from the central planning authority. A new style management committee would include more representatives of the management, as well as workers, but its task was limited to problem solving; the Assembly of Workers would continue. UNTA and MPLA structures were to work independently; neither had any powers to intervene against management but should report to the relevant officials outside the factory.

Cuban shop stewards and union administrators trained their Angolan counterparts and a major recruiting drive began both in the city working community and in rural Angola. The recruiting campaign was linked to a campaign of workers' self-help projects.

Many workers were still unclear about UNTA's working relationship with the MPLA, but they did see that UNTA action brought concrete results. Support for the union structures – organized vertically to include all workers in one branch of activity – increased. When UNTA began organizing emulation campaigns, in which factories competed for the best production and productivity record, and individual workers won prizes for model productivity, there was widespread support, with positive results for economic output. Voluntary work also improved. Only the civil service – and particularly education – remained largely outside the union movement, clearly indicating the petty bourgeois majority in those sectors. In the rural areas, by mid 1980, agricultural workers' unions had been built up and UNTA reported that the state owned sector – with 80% of all unionized labour – led the way.

The largest unions were the five provincial branches of the Coffee Workers Union with 112,000 members; the 12 provincial branches of the Agricultural and Livestock Workers Union with 43,000 members and the five branches of the Heavy Industrial Workers Union with 49,000. The Transport and Communications Workers Union had 30,000 members, the Construction and Housing Workers Union 35,000, and the Light Industrial Workers Union 12,500 members. There were 50,000 members of the Health and Public Administration Workers Union, 28% of whom were women, and 42,000 members of the Food and Hotel Workers Union.

For May Day 1980, the UNTA headquarters drew up a militant statement severely critical of management and, by implication, the government and state for failing to implement genuine worker participation in monitoring production. The statement pointed out that UNTA had active branches in 7,061 factories, but very few of these factories were calling the monthly workers' assemblies, required by law. Of 84,000 workers assemblies in the state owned sector, only 2.4% had actually met between May 1979 and 1980. Only 186 out of 3,805 state owned firms had set up the management committees established by the 1977 amendment. The responsibility lay with management since only they had the power to convene the assemblies and management committees.

UNTA's statement also included figures for voluntary work: 200,000 volunteers had performed 65 million hours of work during the same period, and more than 4,000 permanent voluntary work brigades had been formed around the country. A three month campaign against absenteeism had reduced it to 5% in most work places.

Decreases in production, breakdowns in public services, factory stoppages, often blamed on the workers, were largely the result of inefficient management. UNTA demonstrated how output problems were usually due to shortages of raw material and spare parts, or badly drawn up production plans, and that output had been higher than the original target figure. In some instances workers had not been regularly paid. UNTA went on

> our working class has not yet gained the degree of political awareness needed for it to carry out its historic leading role. But in no way can our workers be held responsible for widespread breakdowns in stocks of raw materials and spare parts, for the lack of planning and economic co-ordination between different organizations, for damage to equipment and other goods in our ports and airports, and for the shortcomings in the proper use of our foreign technical assistants.

The reactionary petty bourgeoisie, UNTA said

> are sometimes ensconced in leading positions in the state machine and are trying to convince our leaders that it is the workers who are

> responsible for the failure to carry out their economic programme. They are doing this to justify their own incompetence, their bureaucratic ways and their lack of authority, initiative and drive, as well as their failure to account for their own activities.

These, UNTA continued, are the main reasons why full production capacity had not been used and the working day not properly accounted for. And it added 'voluntary work should not be made to cover up slack or unproductive periods caused by management's mistakes and shortcomings'. In order to achieve genuine worker participation in management, which UNTA saw as the key to improving economic efficiency, fierce struggle must ensue.

In 1982, however, Party leaders were still calling on the government to implement the 1977 worker participation clauses more fully. As we shall see, the petty bourgeois élite fought hard against the rise of worker cadres. Because of the economic crisis and evidence of mismanagement, President José Eduardo dos Santos and the Central Committee took the decision to replace some of Neto's political appointments of Party members to key production posts, by competent technicians. This was interpreted by the petty bourgeoisie as the offer of another opportunity to seize the levers of power.

The Role of the People's Militias

The militias are rooted amongst the peasants who lived with the guerrillas in the liberated areas. MPLA armed the people to defend themselves, their crops and homesteads, against the Portuguese army and the settlers. The militias were separate from the guerrilla force whose job was to carry out specific attacks against the enemy.

Around April 1975 in response to FNLA's terror campaign, and UNITA marauders, the MPLA began to organize people's defence groups in the cities and countryside. In August 1975, the People's Defence Organization (ODP) was created, to organize the militias on a nationwide scale.

Members of the militias need not be members of the MPLA Workers' Party, or even to have been supporters of the MPLA during its broad liberation movement days. With well over one million working men and women ODP members, compared to about 30,000 Party members, the militias represent a broad cross section of the people, armed in defence of their interests.

The militias have their own national command and political commissariat, separate from the Defence Ministry. Recruiting is organized through places of work or residence. Only rarely is militia duty a full-time occupation, for example, around 1978, a full-time militia force was mustered in Kunene province, to defend against South Africa's constant invasions. Militias undergo basic military training, and then take sentry duty on a roster basis, in place of normal production work. New recruits attend political classes prior to military training to discuss the aims and role of the militias in the community.

Overall the largest numbers of militias are concentrated in Huambo, Bié and Moxico provinces, in central and eastern Angola. Tens of thousands joined up after the defeat of UNITA, whose stragglers were threatening crops and demanding food, and thousands of defenceless civilians were forced into the bush to follow the UNITA bands.

ODP also fulfils needs arising out of the gradual decline of traditional authority. ODP helps to solve community problems: a husband beating his wife, tales of witchcraft. Additionally because literacy is seen as a first step in the battle against the black marketeers and speculators who dominate the people's lives, much time is devoted to learning to read and write.

The Campaign Against Tribalism

Since the African community had never had the opportunity to achieve literacy the skilled population in Luanda at Independence was no more plentiful than elsewhere in the country; at least 30% of its factory workers were unable to read or write. The petty bourgeoisie were reluctant to leave Luanda, thus the provinces had generally to rely on local manpower, with training carried out locally, despite very low level skills. This, however, did help build regional self-sufficiency and eliminate the possibility of cadres from Luanda moving in to take up the best jobs.

At Independence, there were numerous detribalized Luandans in the cities, unlike in the countryside where, because the Portuguese administration had prevented mobility of the African population, people rarely left their region, except on contract labour. Members of different tribes, with different languages, customs, social history and family structures were virtually alien to each other. Intermarriage was extremely rare, and after Independence, when young FAPLA conscripts contemplated marriage with girls near their garrison, the girls' parents opposed such matches whereas the young people dismissed their objections as outmoded.

Long before Independence, the MPLA had warned its guerrillas to guard against tribalism, and by open criticism encourage all Angolans to put national, before tribal loyalties. The FNLA and UNITA fostered tribalism – particularly Savimbi who called all Ovimbundu back to 'the homelands' in the central highlands.

In Angola, equality of opportunity for all ethnic groups was enshrined in the Constitution and, by way of provincial training projects, became a reality after Independence. Since the MPLA had mobilized guerrillas from the coast, from Cabinda, from the eastern-most hinterland and as far south as the Namibian border, no tribal balancing act was necessary when senior officials were to be appointed to Party or government posts. The Party-building process was carried out in all the provinces, irrespective of whether or not they had been liberated under the MPLA guerrillas. Determined to give lie to the UNITA slanders regarding the punishment to be meted out to former UNITA supporters, Huambo and Bié, where the UNITA war effort had centred, were made priority areas for national reconstruction, job creation, food distribution and government trading.

Those Angolans who returned from exile in Zaire – 250,000 in 1980, of the 300,000 there in 1974 – had difficulty integrating into revolutionary Angola. The older generation had known Angola in their youth, but thousands of those in their teens and early twenties had no memories of the country, and no knowledge of either Portuguese or national languages. Most had turned to petty trading, black marketeering and marginal activities on the edge of Kinshasa.

Angola was a country of subsistence farmers and urban peasants, where the Portuguese monopolized trading; its urban working class had been created only ten years earlier. The returned exiles missed the gaudy squalor of Zairean urban slum life. Some of them formed street gangs and lived in the shanty towns, and by 1978 were at the centre of a rising tide of armed robberies; some peddled fake degrees and certificates which, because skilled labour was scarce easily enabled them to find administrative and white collar jobs. The majority, however, found the black market more attractive. Others courageously set out to integrate themselves into Angolan society. The most positive contribution to the national economy made by the exiles from Zaire came from the artisans, some of whom had worked as shoemakers, tailors assistants and hairdressers, and in Angola's townships, even downtown Luanda their shops provided a useful service, though at grossly inflated prices.

The Party was closed to them. But by 1982 their trading activities and their fellows who were in fairly senior government jobs, gave them a power base which enabled them to put pressure on weak Party cadres and probably extract from the Party whatever amenities and sanctions they needed. Obviously tensions resulted at times, especially when black market food prices soared, but there has been no vendetta. Unfortunately until the government can offer an alternative market, the people are dependent on these traders, and thus they provoke national animosity.

Cultural Liberation

While the MPLA and its supporters, from intellectuals to subsistence farming peasants, began the long journey in search of their cultural roots, they also looked ahead and wondered about the future.

> I am sprung from contradictions of fascist colonialism. I am not the new man. I struggle to become seed, seed sown in our land, watered by the blood of our people. I am sprung from contradictions, I am life evolving, with unconquered vices full of longing to conquer them. I am not the new man. I am only seed, seed sown in our land for the collective harvest of tomorrow.

In his book on the MPLA's guerrilla war, Jorge Morais addressed the problem of communicating ideas under fascist rule.

> Angola in the fifties was the undeveloped colony of an underdeveloped Portugal – successive Portuguese governments since the 18th Century had tirelessly fought against each and every new idea. The repression meant it was almost impossible to communicate ideas. Not just ideas from outside the colony but ideas within the colony, sometimes even within the same city or even village.

The growing organization of the resistance was portrayed as 'sporadic acts of senseless violence and revenge'.

Angola's people were now free to exchange ideas, and discuss their lives, their families and the future.

New editions of Angolan authors were published and eagerly bought by the public; 'pop' and traditional music and dance performers flourished everywhere.

One of the new writers stressed the novelist's and poet's role as a teacher:

> I believe national literature is . . . essential . . . in consolidating our independence. [It] helps to forge national unity, it is a vehicle for people to come to know situations, ways of life and ways of thinking in our country. Perhaps not all of our potential writers have understood this and so not all are making efforts to write . . . . Literature . . . as a part of a cultural whole creates . . . national consciousness . . . . I don't think a country can become really independent without its own national literature. It shows the people what they have always sensed: that we have our own identity.

Six years after Independence, some landmarks in this new Angolan literature ranged from Luandino Vieira's portrayals of township life and death under the Portuguese, to Pepetela's sensitive discussion of liberation – political, cultural and sexual – set in the Mayombe guerrilla camps he had known, and Manuel Rui's wry novel about a Luanda family and its precious pig in the heady but hungry days of Independence. All these writers worked as revolutionary cadres: Vieira in the budding national cinema industry, Pepetela as Deputy Minister for Education, Manuel Rui as lawyer and administrator. Poets, such as Antonio Jacinto and Ndunduma, also worked, but found time to write.

These writings were in Portuguese, but there was great interest in reviving the main Angolan languages. The Party set up a National Languages Institute to compile vocabularies, dictionaries and grammars; a task that only interested missionaries had previously attempted. Adult literacy classes were conducted in the relevant Angolan language, where Portuguese was poorly understood. But because of the regional diversity of languages, Portuguese remained Angola's *lingua franca*.

Women and the Women's Movement

Lucio Lara, married to one of Angola's leading women party cadres, set the tone for Party policy on the women's movement:

> What is needed is to define the current role for women. Not just to mobilize them around . . . the literacy campaign and the battle for production, but to define their lasting role in national reconstruction. We must fight the preconceived ideas about women at the fireside, because we have many comrades who are truly good comrades and militants but who still do not look kindly on the militant woman. This creates delicate problems we have got to overcome. But at the same time, we should not try to achieve everything at once.

It is difficult to assess the progress of women in Angolan terms, because debate on the woman question is largely conducted privately. There is no confrontation, and the women's organization, OMA, seems very passive, only rarely is the subject of women *per se* discussed in the press.

The Party and government have abolished sex discrimination at work, in training schemes, and in pay packets. These three acts, made easier by the fact that the state is the country's largest employer, have given women unprecedented opportunities for their own liberation.

For most Angolans the women's right to work is not at issue. The majority of peasants have for years relied on the women to work the fields the year round, and they became the principal source of agricultural production in subsistence farming areas where the men went off to contract labour. In the towns, women went out to work to increase family income, and children were left with relatives. Since independence, inflation has increased the need for urban women to work, and the organization of creches and private play groups by women who must work, means that the concept of a working mother is increasingly accepted.

Women now are employed in all spheres, from road sweepers, air traffic controllers, and doctors, to Ministers, nuns and shop stewards. Almost all are mothers, and OMA has concentrated much of its pressure group work on improving working women's lives: creches, improved maternity benefits (including a three month rest and the employer obliged to keep her job open), and campaigning for family allowances for all Angolans, which was granted by the government early on.

Equal pay for equal work is accepted without question and in most factories men and women do the same kinds of work. Women have been keen to join the union movement and several leading union organizers are women. The state has encouraged domestic workers – all women in Angola – to join a union and press employers for proper social security contributions and to observe the minimum wage scale.

Women are studying at all levels of the national education system. Pregnancy is no obstacle; if it were the status of women could not advance, since the birth rate is very high. Students will often miss two weeks classes, have their baby and be back writing examinations. Although the women's desire to train for more skilled jobs is creating tensions with the men, there are no indications that the women are significantly intimidated by male attitudes.

Sex related issues: polygamy and concubinage; contraception and abortion; love and marriage are, however, still a source of problems. Arranged marriages still continue; bride price still changes hands, in spite of opposition by both sexes – particularly the young men who often do not have the necessary cash. OMA prefer to avoid open opposition to the bride price: this would invoke hostility from many traditionalists and towards modern women.

Most men are strongly opposed to the practice of contraception, feeling that their virility is at stake. Many justify this attitude on the grounds that Angola needs to increase its population. Medical and social workers counter this by pointing out that the infant mortality rate should be reduced before the birth rate is increased; also that the average woman's health is generally at risk due to over-frequent pregnancies. Statistics are scanty but informal urban samples show a high fertility rate, and it has also increased in rural areas since the end of contract labour. Although there is no legislation against contraception (the MPLA took a firm stand against those in favour of a ban) contraception is not yet available on a national scale and there is no family planning service. City women can buy contraceptives from private pharmacies and they can be prescribed by doctors for those women medically unfit for further pregnancies. Most women employ their own methods but are unused to public discussion of these; many resort to experienced midwives for abortions, even though the Portuguese anti-abortion law has not been repealed.

The Women's Organization first national congress, due in 1983, may take up some of these aspects. Doubtless the growing immorality in the cities will be debated. The revolution eliminated prostitution, but concubinage took its place. Men of all social strata are involved and many working mothers are left to fend for their children with neither material nor emotional support from the father. The Party took a clear line, but so far it has not been strictly implemented and thus has little effect.

Younger Party members practise monogamy, which will be the rule in the future. It is impractical to ban from Party membership all peasants who traditionally practise polygamy and already have several wives.

Divorce (illegal under Portuguese rule) was instituted by the People's Republic but this affected only a minority of Angolans as most of them were married by customary law, and not by either civil or church ceremonies.

Leading Angolan women in the Party (four are on the Central Committee) are often deeply irritated by the attitudes of their male colleagues, but hope that the effect women will make upon traditional mores by their work, which will also increase their economic independence, will, in time, solve this problem. According to Rodeth Gil, for most women, health care and education is a major priority.

Angolan women have far to go before they are truly liberated, but they have begun. Burdened with the tasks of production, home-making, child-bearing, drawing water, carrying firewood, and now learning as well as teaching, Angolan women's lives are still shorter than men's, like those of all Third World women.

Deolinda Rodrigues, founder of the Angolan women's movement, some time before she was murdered by FNLA wrote: 'I grew up, stunted, but still I grew up passing through youth, fleet as a shooting star. Today I am a woman; I don't know really if I am a woman or already an old lady'.

Building the National Army

Building a strong national army to defend the anti-imperialist revolution was necessarily the country's top national priority.

The People's Liberation Army of Angola (EPLA) was formed in December 1962, after the start of armed struggle. During the succeeding 12 years of fighting it grew to include military communications experts, gunners, infantry and sappers. FAPLA, the People's Armed Forces for the Liberation of Angola, was proclaimed on 1 August 1974; its commanders were leading guerrillas from the various fronts. Those who had joined Daniel Chipenda's Eastern Revolt were, of course, excluded. Politically the new armed forces leaders had passed scrutiny during both the 1972 Readjustment Movement on the Eastern Front and the 1973 Readjustment Movement on the Northern Front. General mobilization proclaimed on 26 July 1975, did not swell the ranks of FAPLA until August. But in the months between, hundreds of young Angolans joined the MPLA's armed wing, where they first received political training, and then weapons and basic military training. Cubans arrived to staff new CIRs spread out through the provinces in October 1975.

War against the South Africans gave FAPLA its most intensive combat training. Though the war officially ended in March 1976, the South African covert war of attrition began at once. In addition to mopping up operations FAPLA had to organize a strong defence along Angola's 2,000 kilometre border with hostile Zaire and almost the same extent with Namibia. Political education was again seen by military leaders as a priority particularly as Defence Minister Commander Iko Carreira said, in May 1976, that:

> The general and rapid mobilization we were forced to decree to confront the invasion of our country . . . and our own shortage of political cadres and of structures for political and general education has led to a drop in our Armed Forces' political level. In some parts of the country [because] we had to recruit very quickly . . . patriotism had to be enough . . . . [This brought] us some problems. We were also forced to do a lot of quick recruiting in the cities without regard for whether they were MPLA militants or what their class origin was . . . we even had lumpen proletariat . . . . [who] also caused problems. Now we are in a period of consolidation. We can distinguish the kinds of problems

> we face. There is a degree of élitism in FAPLA. Some comrades have an intellectual training or military skills from the colonial army which leads them to demand a level of organization and material support . . . we are not yet in a position to provide. Sometimes these same comrades demand positions of responsibility in the army which we feel should be awarded on political rather than technical competence. They don't always understand this.

Iko also spoke of 'a degree of anarchy in the army'. A fundamental political problem had to be solved:

> When we came out of the underground, MPLA structures were not introduced into the FAPLA. Although our combatants took part in MPLA Action Committees, there were no Action Committees specifically linked to the armed forces different units . . . . This carelessness has brought us problems.

A seminar for political commissars was held in Luanda in May 1976, and followed up by seminars for commissars round the country. Greater support for the political education of army commissars was requested from the Movement and the Political Bureau.

The militias were seen as fundamental to national defence

> ODP will be the largest armed force in the country . . . . We do not make weapons; we are given weapons and we buy them. As far as possible, all workers in the town and countryside who are not in the armed forces will eventually be armed as members of the militias to defend places of work . . . .

The Defence Minister pledged that the Angolan navy would be expanded and soon able to take on elementary coastguard duties. The Air Force with its MiGs was superior to those of many African countries.

On 1 August 1976, FAPLA's second anniversary, the ratification of an agreement between Cuba and Angola was announced, whereby Cuba would continue to help train the Angola armed forces.

At the Luanda waterfront there was a march-past by the army, navy and police, to commemorate the anniversary. Later, the first Angolan parachute regiment organized a display, and a fly-past of reconnaissance aircraft, with Angolan crews, a MiG 17 and a MiG 21.

Military staff colleges were set up, and serious training began at all levels. Senior officers – Commanders and Majors – attended short and long training courses under Soviet and Cuban instruction. NCOs were being turned out for the first time, and basic training now included a two hour daily literacy class for illiterate peasant and working-class recruits; political instruction was also given daily.

The May 1977 coup led by Nito Alves, and in which the FAPLA

commissariat had played a leading role underlined the extent of the political problems in the army. On FAPLA's third anniversary, Lucio Lara, addressing a fresh national seminar of army commissars said:

> In the days of guerrilla war, the Commander sat down with his soldiers and [held] a session of criticism and self-criticism . . . everyone was a militant. Today . . . not all soldiers, sergeants and officers are yet militants . . . . [such] confrontation would bring indiscipline, disrespect, and loss [or excess] of authority . . . . So . . . this face to face [session] between different ranks, should be carried out by militants within militants assemblies.

The militant in these armed forces assemblies is on equal footing with his superior officer.

The close of the first PT-76 amphibious tracked vehicles course, under Soviet and Cuban instructors, also marked the anniversary with a spectacular exercise in the countryside north of the capital. The same year, Cuban instructors had trained militia leaders and rank and file.

During 1977 and 1978 South Africa stepped up its aggression, with major incursions by motorized columns into the south and south-east, and the first large scale bombing raids. SADF was not yet on permanent operations inside Angola, but the hit and run ground and air raids were becoming more frequent. FAPLA was anxious to build up its fighting strength. Defence Minister Carreira reported in November 1978 'we are going through a phase which, we are convinced, is preliminary to fresh aggression by troops in the pay of international imperialism . . . . Our soldiers, sergeants and officers must be trained so they are able to destroy racist South Africa's plan to destroy our People's Republic'.

In September 1979, South African airborne commando units bombed strategic roads and railways linking the Angolan south and south-east to the Atlantic and northwards to the rest of the country. Bombs fell on the southernmost major industrial city of Lubango and many workers were killed or injured by shrapnel or buried under falling masonry. Angolan anti-aircraft defence had proved to be powerless to stop the SADF, which had penetrated the radar barrier and flown across hundreds of kilometres of bush to strike behind the radar line.

The air war intensified, signalling the start of a new phase, precipitated by FAPLA's increasing ground capability. Trained conventional army units of infantry, motorized units and anti-aircraft defence systems had been transferred south. SADF was reluctant to confront this new style FAPLA, and instead mounted daily attacks from the air.

Iko explained: 'we are still unable to dominate our skies because it involves a fairly advanced technology and a long period of training. But . . . in a short time we shall also be on a level with the South African force in the skies!' Iko spoke of FAPLA's small frontier garrisons, which operated in isolated areas in difficult terrain, and 'mark out our sovereignty and they are facing aggressive South Africa. They are not able to resist large scale operations. We are creating conditions to replace them with well trained units'.

Angola and Cuba had planned to reduce substantially the number of Cuban troops in Angola by 1979. The FAPLA training programme was going well, and it seemed that conventional Cuban infantry was no longer necessary to defend the border with Namibia to stop aggression into Angola. But these escalating South African hit and run raids into the south made a re-evaluation of the plan necessary. Troop withdrawals were halted.

In August 1981, when FAPLA's 7th anniversary was commemorated, South African troops had again invaded Kunene province in an operation described by the Pretoria High Command as SADF's largest combined operation since World War II. The invasion culminated in the permanent occupation of a huge swathe of Kunene, and the loss of hundreds of lives. Refugees poured northwards out of the fighting zone, and found refuge near Lubango. In autumn 1982 permanent refugee camps had been set up to house the women and children of Kunene province, where the SADF still held almost half the province, more than 50 miles inside the Namibia border. FAPLA units were pinned down by massive air attacks from the SADF which continued to dominate the skies of Kunene. Instead of demanding SADF withdrawal, Western propaganda continued to raise the spectre of large numbers of communist troops occupying Angola. On 9 September 1981, President José Eduardo dos Santos told British correspondents:

> There are no soldiers from the German Democratic Republic in Angola. There are also no troops here from the Soviet Union. We have never hidden the presence of the Cuban internationalists. We stated recently in Lagos that since 1975 there has been a decreasing number of Cubans here, as the defensive capacity of our own Angolan army has increased. We also stated that we have established co-operation agreements with the Soviet Union and that through these agreements we have Soviet instructors here who are helping us train our cadres and organize our fighting forces.

In six years, Angola had built a national army, strong enough on the ground to withstand the SADF – Africa's best NATO equipped army. The unpalatable truth for the West was that this achievement was due to the efforts of Soviet and Cuban instructors. Angola's army was not only independent of Western technology but quite capable of fighting Western weapons, which continued to find their way into the hands of white, racist South Africa.

8. Foundations for Socialism

Destroying the Old Order

'We are going to build socialism in Angola. How we do this is an exclusively Angolan affair.' At Independence, Neto faced economic chaos. Agricultural and industrial production, transport and distribution, finance and banking had all been controlled by foreigners – multinationals, Portuguese entrepreneurs and white settlers. Suddenly almost all of them had gone. What was to be done?

MPLA's founding Manifesto stood for broad national economic control and workers' rights. At the September 1974 MPLA Inter-Regional Conference of Militants a Programme was approved, which also stressed production for national needs: state control of foreign trade and banking, and a national currency; a role for foreign enterprises beneficial to the Angolan people, and a continuing private sector. Development of modern mechanized agricultural production was seen as the overall key to the development of the economy.

In September 1974 the main problem was how to restructure the ownership of the means of production, which was essential for the fulfilment of MPLA's promise to build prosperity for all Angolans. The existing colonial system had first to be destroyed; a task facilitated by the Portuguese settlers themselves.

All but 10% of the 350,000 whites had fled, taking with them whatever plant they could. A soft drinks factory found its way to Brazil; two thirds of the nation's trucks had gone; tractors were found in ditches, their engines wrecked and vital parts missing; the Luanda public water and electricity plans had been smuggled to Lisbon, and teachers even went off with the school records.

The construction firms left first, by the end of 1974 work had stopped in the midst of a building boom. Throughout 1975 Portuguese entrepreneurs left with what assets they could, and the organized Lisbon airlift from July to October 1975 evacuated settlers and their families to Zaire or Namibia, with whatever they could salvage.

The transition government enacted legislation for state intervention in firms abandoned by their owners, and workers in urban areas formed committees to maintain production in response to MPLA's call to 'produce to resist'. But until Independence no organized action could begin. MPLA's first, token nationalization – of the Caxito sugar plantation and mill in August 1975 was ineffective until the FNLA's defeat.

Angola's new Constitution incorporated a socialist economic policy: state ownership of national resources, development of the public sector and co-operatives, and the fostering of 'just social relations in all sectors of production'. It specifically guaranteed 'private activities and property, even those of foreigners, so long as they are useful to the country's economy and to the interests of the Angolan people'. Agriculture was defined as the cornerstone of development, and industry as the 'decisive factor'. Progressive taxation would replace the flat colonial head tax on Africans.

When Neto proclaimed Independence he called for rapid growth of heavy industry; referring to foreign aid he said it was acceptable provided that no conditions were attached. Lopo do Nascimento defined the government's economic task as conversion of the colonial economy into a 'resistance economy' and later a planned economy.

The Colonial Record

Since the outbreak of armed struggle in 1961 and the arrival of large numbers of troops, Angola had seen unprecedented economic growth. The guerrillas' effect on Salazar's fascists was comparable to the Treaty of Berlin: white settlement of this huge land was again a priority. Whites would prevent black unrest, develop the land, and work in the factories, which would have to be built with foreign capital. The army would provide support to the settlers as occasion arose.

But the subsequent influx of semi-literate peasants and industrial workers into Angola largely gathered in urban areas and in service jobs, as truckers, traders, shopkeepers, waiters. Despite a marked development of agriculture, especially in the Malanje area and on the central and southern plateaux, less than 3% of arable land was being farmed at Independence. Modern, mechanized farming remained the exception, even among the settlers.

Cash crop production increased substantially, particularly of coffee, cotton and sisal. There was considerable foreign investment in an import substitution manufacturing industry (from Escudos 8 million in 1967 to 50 million in 1970); but predictably most foreign capital flooded into the mining sector. In 1972, exports were of raw materials: 45% from mining, and 43% from agriculture and livestock; only 12% were manufactures. All skilled and semi-skilled jobs both in town and country were held by whites, which, plus the low level of agricultural technology meant that any spin-off of new techniques to Angolan farmers was negligible.

Angolan businessmen were scarce. There were artisans and petty traders in the towns, and land-owning farmers (whose acreage was too small to attract the settlers' envy) in the countryside. The most lasting achievement of the war boom was to create the embryo of an African urban working class, and build up the numbers of migrant wage labourers, created by earlier forced and contract labour laws to service the coffee plantations. By 1973, migrant workers were employed in the fishing and fish-meal industry, in the docks, on the railways, and on the plantations that had spread from the northern coffee lands through central Angola to the ranches near the Namibia border.

Caetano's 'open door' investment policy of 1965 encouraged Gulf Oil which struck the huge Cabinda offshore fields in 1966. Significant in the long term were the numerous small and medium investments in manufacturing by Western multinationals, thus rendering Angolan industry dependent on Western technology for the foreseeable future.

Industrial production was dominated by the food industry. An agricultural machinery and bicycle plant, car assembly lines, a steel-from-scrap mill, two cement factories and a paper mill were also in operation. The textile industry, and the fish processing and fishing industry were expanding, and there were ship repair yards in Luanda and Lobito.

In response to the rapidly expanding settler population came substantial government spending on infrastructure: schools, hospitals, tarmac roads were built wherever the white community was large enough. Communications substantially improved, particularly as a result of the war, but also of settler maintained bush air strips and radio.

State Intervention

Strategy for changing ownership of the means of production was defined in the State Intervention Law, passed in February 1976 when the South African Defence Force still occupied the south. There were to be three sectors in a planned economy: 1) state economic units (*Unidades Economicas Estatais* – UEE) comprising the state owned sector; 2) co-operatives; and 3) private enterprise. The state took control over all strategic interests including defence, press and publishing, and foreign trade. It was also empowered to take over monopolies. Those companies liable for state intervention could be either confiscated or nationalized. Nationalization might bring compensation.

At a mass rally of industrial and office workers, on 1 May 1976, Neto announced the first nationalizations. Breweries, sugar plantations and mills, a cement plant and a textile factory, employing altogether around 5,000 workers, became state property. By May 1979 71% of all production companies had been nationalized, and a further 7% were jointly owned by state and private interests. On the land, an insignificant number of farms remained in the hands of settlers who had stayed on. Over 1,500 formerly white owned plantations had been nationalized and were in production. Private, foreign ownership of the means of modern mass production was a minority; there were no Angolan entrepreneurs.

The state sector has continued to grow. By the end of 1981 the Ministry of Industry reported that 64% of the manufacturing sector's production was from state owned companies, compared with 58% the previous year. Of the remaining 36% of manufacturing production, 11% came from joint ventures, and 25% from wholly privately owned firms. Private enterprise production was, therefore, still diminishing. In 1980 it had totalled 30%. The Ministry also reported that 75% of the industrial workforce was employed by the state sector, 8% by the joint ventures and 17% by private firms.

The powerful multinationals – Gulf Oil and the Diamang diamond mining company, upon which Angola largely depended for its livelihood – were the last to be nationalized. Among the first were Portuguese fascist interests and the absentee settlers, who were given three months to return to Angola or be dispossessed; few returned.

Oil and Independence

Petrofina had operated small oilfields south of the Zaire estuary and in the Kwanza basin since 1956. It remained astride the northern front throughout the war but paid royalties only to MPLA. Gulf Oil was in a more difficult position. On 20 December 1975 the US State Department, under instruction from Henry Kissinger, ordered the company to end operations, withdraw all staff from Cabinda and cease royalty payments to MPLA. Cabinda was firmly in MPLA territory and by this time Cuban troops were protecting the province and Gulf installations, from potential, new attacks by Zaire and mercenary forces.

Despite the deprivation of desperately needed foreign exchange ($1.5 million a day), Angola did not retaliate against Gulf Oil but instead repeatedly asked the company to reopen production as early as possible. Advice from Algeria, Nigeria and Libya confirmed MPLA's view that nationalization would be disastrous.

Gulf's offshore technology, with equipment manufactured to Gulf patented specifications, was unique. If its technology was withdrawn, the entire Cabinda offshore oil production would have to be scrapped; Angola's economy would be destroyed overnight. The opinions of African oil producers on nationalization were shared by Soviet and Cuban oil experts. They could have provided alternative technology but it would take time to install and in the interim, MPLA would need millions of dollars of aid in order to survive. This would have resulted in dramatic international political repercussions, and have also prejudiced Angola's chances of selling its crude on the international market. This alone was a powerful reason for maintaining capitalist multinationals in the Angolan oil industry.

Secret contacts between MPLA and Gulf Oil were maintained in Lagos and London while the State Department enforced its embargo. Gulf technicians were back on the job on 29 April 1976, and director Charles Smith announced in Luanda, that a major investments programme was to be launched during the year, with exploration of new Cabinda offshore wells that would mean a 'very significant increase' in crude exports by mid-1979. Gulf sources said that relations with MPLA were 'pretty excellent' and that output would quickly regain the 135,000 barrels a day pre-war figure.

Gulf's US $125 million royalties, that had been paid into escrow during the freeze, were now transferred to the Luanda government.

Negotiations with Gulf took over two years before Angola gained a majority 51% state share in the Cabinda operations. In the meantime oil was bringing in vital foreign exchange, Angolan workers were being trained, and fresh investments were being made. The oil company was to become an important lobbyist in Washington for diplomatic relations with Angola, and a key element in preventing a repeal of the Clark Amendment which would have allowed the Reagan administration a free hand to subvert the People's Republic.

Legal experts, with assistance from other African oil producers were drafting the Oil Law, promulgated in August 1978. The Angolan state now has a monopoly on ownership of all natural hydro-carbon resources, including crude oil and natural gas, and may enter into agreements with competent foreign companies for exploitation of these resources. Gas found in association with crude may no longer be burnt off but must be rationally exploited.

The state's oil company, SONANGOL, formed in June 1976, now enters into production sharing agreements with the international oil companies. This places foreign firms in the role of contracted companies who must pay all investments and take on all risks. Physical assets become state property. All crude produced is divided into cost recovery, and profit oil, shared according to ratios negotiated between contractor and Angola. Offshore blocks have been lined up along the coast, and both Total (*Compagnie Francaise des Petroles*) and ELF have joined Gulf, Texaco and Petrofina, as foreign oil companies engaged in production sharing agreements with SONANGOL. Angola also applies a price cap clause to these agreements, which gives SONANGOL all extra profits derived from upwards fluctuations in the international oil price.

Gulf/SONANGOL negotiations were carried out against this background, from 1976 until September 1978, when the Angolan state company finally acquired its 51% stake in Cabinda Gulf. The agreement is not identical with the production sharing accords signed with newcomers, in that it recognizes Gulf's previous investments, and Angola paid fully for its stake. Thereafter, a fixed margin agreement on operations of the joint venture means that Gulf's 49% earns it a previously agreed profit, worked out as a fixed profit per barrel of crude.

In 1981, CABGOC (Cabinda Gulf Oil Company) was still the largest single producer of Angolan crude, with responsibility for about half the 500,000 barrel daily output planned by Angola for 1985, for which altogther, foreign companies are laying out over US $1,000 million in investments; but 51% of the CABGOC output is now state property. Gulf's share of national oil production has been cut back to 25% compared to 70% in colonial times. Gulf has also continued to invest in and increase crude output. The 25% of national output going to Gulf will continue to decrease as the new offshore wells yield their crude.

There are good prospects for significant production increases. No complete seismic survey of the offshore area existed at Independence, and only 15 offshore wells had been drilled along the 1,000 kilometre Atlantic coastline. The seismic survey is now complete and two French oil companies have both struck promising fields. Within a few years, diversification, away from reliance on US partners towards a more balanced spread, is planned. City Services, and a number of other smaller US firms, as well as Italian firms are involved in new contracts. No socialist countries have so far become involved in Angola's oil production. Angolan crude is freely available on the world market, except to Israel and South Africa; stringent clauses ensure that tankers may not even refit in South African ports.

SONANGOL's long term task is to operate all levels of the national oil industry with Angolan oil technologists and managers. In 1979, an Oil School was set up at Ngunza to train skilled workers and laboratory assistants, and there are plans to extend the school to cover higher grade technical training. Before independence MPLA members received training overseas in oil technology. Graduates still train overseas, while Ministry and company staff have attended numerous in-house training schemes organized by the multinational oil companies at their headquarters in Europe and America. Within Angola international oil seminars are regularly held to improve Angolans' knowledge of all international aspects of the industry.

By 1982, SONANGOL had acquired valuable experience marketing its share of crude on the international market. Nationally, it almost completely monopolized the distribution of gasoline, diesel fuel and domestic gas, and was increasing its stake in aviation fuel distribution. From February 1977, owing to nationalization of Portuguese interests, SONANGOL became a minority shareholder in the Angolan oil refinery outside Luanda – Petrangol. Belgium's Petrofina retained control but Cuban oil technicians had to be called in to guarantee day to day running of the refinery, since apparently Belgian and Portuguese technicians were reluctant to help the People's Republic.

The refinery is now the centre of a major investment programme designed by the Party both to guarantee future national supplies of most refined products, and to supply those Southern African countries still relying on imports from South Africa. When these plans became known and were studied by the Southern Africa Development Co-ordination Conference, of which Angola is co-ordinator of energy policy, Pretoria sent a commando unit to attack the refinery. They failed to destroy the production and refining area, but blew up storage facilities causing a three month fall in output. The investment plan, however, is going ahead.

Many foreign advisers considered that for SONANGOL to attempt to sell crude on the world market was absurd, yet today the national oil company sells over half the national production. Studies for refinery expansion were extensively revised by Angolan technicians, and contrary to outside advice, the Ministry favoured a hydro-cracking unit to utilize fuel oil residues from the Angolan refinery, and eventually from Tanzania, Mozambique and possibly Zimbabwe in order to decrease oil industry links with South Africa.

Diamonds and De Beers

The oil industry boom came almost on the eve of independence and had affected few Angolans. Diamond mining, however, exemplified colonial exploitation. Since 1921, Diamang virtually monopolized the north-east alluvial diamond deposits and ruled over $50{,}000^2$ kilometres. A state within a state, with its own army, police force and intelligence service, equipped with helicopters, armoured cars and infantry it controlled over 18,000 workers who had little if any choice but to work for the company.

Diamang also owned all the agricultural land in its huge concession, and employed peasants to fatten the company's pedigree herds and farm the company's fields. Before Independence, no Angolan was allowed to go into the diamond selecting room at the mines or had any experience of sorting or valuing the stones. Cutting and polishing took place in Lisbon, at Dialap, a subsidiary of Diamang.

After Independence the only immediate change was a sharp fall in production. Most of the Portuguese work-force had fled, and the management in Lisbon was in no hurry to replace them, or make any changes. Consequently the government in Luanda took action to raise the wages of the work-force, and to satisfy company creditors. In an effort to reassure management, and encourage a new start government funds were injected into this 100% privately owned company. But unlike Gulf Oil or De Beers, Diamang did not co-operate, and minimal production continued for the next two years. It became clear that the De Beers company, involved in marketing the stones through its worldwide monopoly, Central Selling Organization, was more interested in nurturing future relations with MPLA than were the Portuguese.

In August 1977, the government nationalized all Portuguese small shareholders' capital in Diamang, retaining 60.85% for the state. European and US bank holdings, and De Beers' 2% stake were left untouched. In 1980 the assets of Portuguese institutional investors were nationalized, giving Angola 77% control. Lisbon retaliated by nationalizing Angola's share in Dialap's Lisbon polishing and cutting industry.

MPLA's failure to act earlier lost the country valuable foreign exchange and capital assets. In October 1977 when Neto visited the mines following the first nationalization of small shareholders, he was told of an 80% output drop, a 70% loss of equipment, 30% idleness of the work-force due to management sabotage, and that the company's debts were approximately £10 million.

During its first year of operations as a state controlled firm, the company doubled production from 352,793 carats in 1977 to 712,837 in 1978. Output has continued to grow, although in 1982 low, world diamond prices affected national revenues. Plans for expanding the diamond mining industry in Angola include setting up a cutting and polishing operation under state control, and making a start on mining Kimberlite diamonds. Several pipes are known to exist and the generally high quality of Angolan stones (70% are gemstones) makes capital intensive investment worthwhile.

Angola's relationship with the Central Selling Organization has continued. While the government's intention is to develop a national diamond industry, initially it has concentrated on plans for cutting the stones. The Oppenheimer family, like the Gulf Oil bosses, find it at least expedient to work with the political and economic realities of Angola.

Diamang workers began to organize literacy classes immediately after independence. Special part-time primary and secondary education courses are held for these workers with basic literacy but no schooling. Technical training has been extended to include engineering, and repair and maintenance courses. By 1981 the company needed fewer foreign technicians than it had under colonial rule. Housing is the subject of research and planning and a model workers' town is being built at Lucapa, the diamond province capital.

An important effect of the Portuguese management's attitude was to provide a spur to trade union organization. Workers' committees sprang up in response to MPLA activists work after Independence and these have evolved into unions both for mine and agricultural workers. Traditional support for MPLA has always been strong in the east of Angola. Many guerrillas who fought on the Eastern Front were recruited from these areas, and FAPLA drew many recruits from the east after Independence. The people's militias were then armed, and now this local People's Defence Organization of mineworkers and peasants guarantees security at the mines.

Change on the Land

Independence for the overwhelming majority of Angolans meant freedom to work their own land in their own way. White settlers could no longer expropriate family farms, order the abandonment of villages, move farmers to sites selected by bureaucrats. With the end of the forced and contract labour system, men are free to live with their families and cultivate their land.

This freedom, however, also meant that acres of cash crops would be left uncultivated. Food cropping too suffered from the Portuguese exodus. Portuguese traders had acted as middle men between town consumers and countryside producers; creditors and purchasers to numerous Angolan small farmers in the bush. Their absence called for urgent replacement. The MPLA constantly stressed the need for unity and interdependence between urban workers and peasants, but six years after independence, there was a serious scarcity of food and cash crop production had decreased to a mere fraction of former output. A rural exodus was steadily in progress, and by the end of 1981 the situation in the countryside was bleaker than ever before.

Mechanization as the key?

Large scale, sophisticated mechanization seemed to some people the key to the problem; others argued fiercely in favour of co-operatives with simple mechanization. Co-operatives would involve peasants in the national economy on a voluntary basis; land reform, modern technical skills, complex administrative machinery would be unnecessary. The flexibility of co-operatives would enable the very different realities in different parts of the country to be accommodated.

In 1976 pilot co-operative schemes were set up by the pro-cooperative cadres in Malanje and Cuanza Norte. A previous experiment by MPLA political activists, in 1975, in Huambo province had been highly successful. The 'Kimbo Fronts' (village fronts) were organized by villagers using their own lands, and peasants farmed small plots for subsistence and produced some surplus – mainly potatoes and maize – to sell.

The Malanje and Cuanza Norte scheme was different. In these areas large scale expropriation of land had taken place. In 1976 the pilot co-operatives used abandoned settler farms and left the peasants' own small-holdings to be farmed individually. This became a pattern all over the country.

Large, mechanized settler plantations were taken over for state farming. Malanje, and after complete liberation, the southern plateau around Lubango, became areas for intensive pilot projects using Soviet, Bulgarian and GDR aid and technical assistance. South of Lubango, at Humpata State Cereals and Fruit Farm, a group of former settler farms has been combined, and Angolans are being trained in its management and cultivation by Soviet farm workers and managers. During 1977 this, and other state farms, concentrated on recruiting workers, importing equipment and surveying and planning for 1978, declared as the 'year of agriculture'.

At Humpata, before Independence, local peasants who had fled into the barren hills after settlers had taken their land provided farm labour, often for as little as two or three escudos a day, returning to the hills at night. In 1978 the new Humpata farm management allocated part of the state farm land to the peasants and drew up plans for a new village after the future inhabitants had chosen the site. A school and medical post were built as the village grew. Soviet and Angolan workers turned a former settler farmhouse into a literacy centre and exhibition hall. Combine harvesters, tractors, and harrows were imported from the Soviet Union and Angolan workers are being trained as drivers, mechanics and managers. The area has several dams, and large scale irrigation schemes are under study By 1979 wheat and maize production had returned to pre-Independence levels.

The Humpata farm was successful because the Soviet group was able to organize input efficiently, and local conditions facilitated the availability of a work-force. But in general, and especially in areas where the settler farming population was small and land expropriation minimal, it has been difficult to find a work-force for state farms.

The 1980 Special Congress thus, once again selected development and support for the co-operative movement in the countryside as a government priority.

The Co-operative Movement

At the Second Conference of Angolan Trades Unions in 1977, Neto said:

> Thousands of Angolans are owners of the means of production. They have their plot of land. We know very well how difficult it is in rural areas to transform these small-holdings into co-operative or state farms. Under colonialism this property was fictional. Our peasants were violently dispossessed to make way for the settlers' plantations. They were wrenched off their land to work as contract labourers. Only today, with the People's Republic of Angola, is this right to property real and inviolate. The infamous contract system under which our people suffered for years is over for ever. And if we now, in the name of socialism, of the government of the People's Republic, start expropriating our peasants, our people will feel at once that socialism only means making more sacrifices. The way to transform the peasants' private property into a special kind of property is through production co-operatives. But this will only happen with the will of our peasants. It is a task that will take years of organizing and educating.

Announcing the 'year of agriculture' on 1 January 1978, Neto returned to the problem when he said, 'massive constitution of co-operatives is essential. But these will co-exist alongside small-holdings. We do not disdain small-holdings and appropriate state support will be given to them'. Between 1976 and 1977 the Ministry had registered over 92,000 peasants who had voluntarily come forward to form associations. During 1978 the movement grew further.

Already in February 1978 a seminar held in Moxico, birthplace of the co-operative movement during the guerrilla war, had recognized that peasant 'associations' would preserve individual property. Members of an association that was based entirely on individual property would all contribute towards purchasing association equipment. There would then be 'first degree co-operatives' described as 'semi-socialist' and second degree co-operatives, that would be 'socialist'. Most of the so-called co-operatives functioning today are, in fact, associations based on collective farming of settler land.

Individual land is farmed outside the co-operative. This 'middle road' does not conflict with the peasants' traditional desire for their own property, because they themselves draw up their statutes and decide how many hours work they will contribute to the collectively farmed settler land.

A significant advantage of the 'middle road' element is that it enabled the complex and explosive issue of land reform to be bypassed. In Angola, where countless families were expropriated, by settlers – often 50 or 60 years ago – and tribalism had been deliberately fostered by the colonial authorities, any sweeping land reform designed to reallocate private property would be not only divisive, but foreign to socialist principles. Through these associations, expropriated land is reverting to the peasants on a massive scale, but collectively.

In 1979, the government estimated that about 12% of urban food needs had been met by state farms, this demonstrated that the field was open to individual, small farmers and peasant associations. It also indicated that government should adopt an even more flexible attitude to the types of co-operatives and associations to be encouraged. At the end of 1980, 2,542 peasants' associations and 304 production co-operatives were recorded in the countryside.

The MPLA had initially asked the Ministry to train technicians to visit villages and explain the advantages of the association system. The response was mediocre. Remembering the success of the Kimbo village fronts, political organizers suggested that villagers should themselves be given the task of promoting association. From 1977 'rural dynamizers' were taken from numerous villages to the nearest market town and involved in a short course on organizing production associations. A booklet of guidelines was produced by the government, and flexibility was the key. After returning to their home areas the 'dynamizers' travelled to neighbouring hamlets on request to hold teach-ins on the movement.

Mobilization was no longer a problem; the critical issue became material support. The government had promised that peasant associations would receive land, seeds, fertilizer and basic agricultural equipment, mainly hand operated ploughs and hoes and cutlasses. An added incentive was the Ministry of Internal Trade's promise to set up small, local shops where the association could exchange goods for basic consumer items.

Associations of many different kinds grew up across the country. Around the big towns, where the men work in factories and offices, women set up agricultural co-operatives. After the isolation of heavy manual work on individual plots, women have been especially receptive to the idea of co-operatives.

Resettlement co-operatives were also formed – mainly in the southernmost parts of Kunene and Kuando Kubango – by peasants forced to flee South African and UNITA attacks. They have been resettled on good agricultural land and given state aid. Similar co-operatives have been formed by Angolans returning to the north after years of exile in Zaire.

The material support promised by the government, however, was not provided. Equipment, seeds and food were not forthcoming, water pumps were not mended, or repeatedly broke down. 1978 appeared to have been prematurely appointed as the 'year of agriculture': the means and organization were not available for its success.

Provincial towns and capitals were far better stocked with food and clothing than Luanda – owing to the efforts of the revolutionaries – but most Angolans lived far from the towns; they needed support in their villages. Transport, administration and organization were too haphazard to provide this. Inevitably enthusiasm for the associations began to wane; people drifted away from work on the co-operative and to farm their own plots.

Some practical assistance began to filter through on a national scale in 1979. By the December 1980 Special Congress, the Central Committee was able to report that 10,000 hectares of cotton had been grown in the 1979/80 season, with 30,00 hectares planned for the next five years, while 25,000 hectares of maize had been reactivated. Banana production was also being restored. Since 1978, 2,214 tractors had been imported and distributed to state farms and peasant associations, as well as ploughs and other machinery, and 203,400 tons of mineral fertilizers.

All kinds of unforeseeable problems beset efforts to modernize the associations. Party cadres working closely with the peasants were exasperated by Government's bureaucratic attitudes. The men in the Ministries failed to grasp rural realities. Refrigerators were sent to areas without electricity (peasants bought them, and some used them as wardrobes) when the Party guideline was to give priority to peasants to buy consumer durables. Countryside revolutionaries had a difficult choice: to improvise as best they could and not waste time waiting for help from Luanda, or pit themselves against the Luanda 'system'.

They were always sure of help at the Party. Senior Party officials often stepped in to order civil servants to carry out the country's demands. Lucio Lara as Organizing Secretary, defended the peasants' cause unremittingly. They had fought the Portuguese during the first liberation war; produced food for their sons and daughters in the MPLA guerrillas; been tortured and killed by PIDE. Now they must receive help, 'And they are not just asking, they are demanding'.

The root of the problem of building links between town and country lay in marketing the peasants' surplus. Government buyers wanted priority over private buyers, but many peasants were committed to the private market; because 1) government purchasing was disorganized and infrequent, centring on market towns but lacking transport to get the crop to the market place; 2) government tended to pay in scrip instead of cash; 3) government prices were lower, and finally the adverse effects of inflation and shortages on the money economy by mid 1978, resulted in many peasants bartering their crops for industrial goods, which private traders willingly provided.

Some provincial authorities half-heartedly tried to cut out private buyers, instead of improving their own buying organizations and providing more industrial goods to attract the producers. But the Party, and Neto himself, had guaranteed the private traders' future, and they were clearly necessary, given the inadequate state trading structures. Consequently private purchasing continued to grow, a proportion of which increasingly supplied the black market in Luanda, and further demoralized the state marketing boards.

Finally, in 1981, a special government marketing campaign was launched. Learning from the peasants and its cadres in the countryside, the government at last responded to the producers' needs. A series of purchasing and bartering markets were organized to coincide with the harvesting of specific crops in intensively farmed areas. A government 'caravan' moved into rural districts carrying industrial consumer goods, seeds, machinery, fertilizers and cash, to buy from or barter for the local harvest directly with the producers.

Life in the countryside was unquestionably hard, and in some areas affected by the war there had been famine, but usually food was more plentiful than in the cities – especially Luanda. By 1981 life in the capital was so inflation-ridden and food so scarce, and dominated by inexorably increasing black market prices, that a concerted and well executed government project offering jobs and housing in the countryside it seemed might well attract some of the city's workers.

This has been part of stated government policy since Independence, but not put into practice. The Central Committee reported to the 1980 Special Congress:

> The specific guideline issued by the Party, based on general guidelines of the First Congress, was that the surplus labour force in Luanda should be channelled to other regions and involved in production. But this was not done by the State organizations entrusted with the task. Nor was any analysis made of possible mistakes, and the matter was not taken up again. But the organization of labour, the security of our people and better living standards largely depend on the solution of this problem, even if partially.

Creating an Agricultural Work-Force

In the early years the reallocation of unemployed city dwellers to state owned farms – especially coffee plantations – had been discussed. But the primitive and insanitary infrastructures provided by the settlers for the contractual labourers who had worked the plantations had first to be abolished and replaced. If the government was to invite the unemployed to better their position by working on the plantations, decent conditions had to be provided.

The provision of cheap, rapidly built housing from local materials, electricity, by repairing the inevitable local generators and running water by harnessing the plentiful rivers was not impossible. But bureaucrats apparently lacked the imagination, creativity and above all the will to organize such schemes, which would have taken them out of the relative comfort of their Luanda offices and into rural Angola. Life in the countryside was unattractive and mysterious to the Luanda petty bourgeoisie. Furthermore, would the unemployed urban dwellers go, and if they did, would they stay?

The provision of adequate medical care and educational facilities when there were insufficient qualified teachers and nurses for existing structures was impossible. City dwellers might consider that driving a tractor to plough and harvest was an acceptable way of life, but what of such jobs as cane cutting, and coffee cleaning and picking?

With planning, adequate political and material support, efficient organization and co-operation between Ministries these problems probably could have been overcome.

Coffee: Mechanize or Collectivize?

In terms of production today, Angola is at the bottom of the African league. Colonial coffee production had peaked at around an annual 200,000 tonnes. By 1980/81 it had shrunk to a quarter of that, far below the planned output of 120,000 tonnes.

Six years after independence, most settler coffee plantations had been irrecoverably lost owing to neglect. The State Coffee Board was thoroughly overhauled in 1981, because the government considered it to be top heavy and inefficient. Twenty-six 'Territorial Enterprises' covering 185,000 hectares, were hived off with full autonomy for production, finance and investment decisions; but the labour problem remained unsolved.

State coffee farming cannot succeed without organization, planning and construction to create adequate conditions for a permanent all year round work-force on the state plantations. Until the 1982 crop, the government relied on wage labour from local peasants and the voluntary work of urban dwellers. Production figures have shown, however, that voluntary work could by no means compensate for the absence of around 120,000 contract labourers.

Mechanization is technically impossible at present. No machinery has so far been devised to clean, weed and select ripe from unripe beans for harvesting.

Probably coffee farming by small-holders must now provide the backbone of coffee exports. An official colonial inquiry showed that in 1970, 263,300 small-holders were growing 2-4 hectares of coffee, accounting for 36% of the total coffee producing area. Presumably most of this has been under continuous cultivation, unlike extensive parts of the former settler-owned 64% of coffee plantations which consequently have been lost. From 1976 to 1978 most of the Coffee Board's sales were derived from settler coffee that had never been taken off the plantations, plus a contribution from the small-holders.

Around Uije, where an MPLA veteran from the eastern region of the guerrilla war took charge after the Alves coup, peasants enthusiastically proposed forming coffee co-operatives, and by 1979 there were around a dozen projects receiving government support. This co-operative movement has continued to grow.

The Party's decision to favour small growers still receives insufficient practical support. The sharp decline in coffee prices (52% from 1979 to 1980) has affected financing of state aid. By 1982 the colonial peak production of 240,000 tonnes was still a distant target. The aim of 120,000 tonnes for 1980 had not been reached, and prospects for the 1982 harvest were so unreliable that the Central Committee appointed some of its members to take overall charge of the state's territorial coffee companies and direct the organization of the harvest.

Contributions towards the coffee sector by foreign technicians have included maintenance of coffee mills by Western companies responsible for their construction, and organizational and management assistance from Cuba. Coffee Board sales have been made overwhelmingly on the London market through the Angolan coffee company with offices there. Most of the crop is being used in the US, as it was before Independence, although small direct sales have been made to some socialist countries that provide assistance to Angola; particularly Cuba and GDR, and to Algeria. The Angolan government wished to present a gift of coffee to Cuba, but appreciating the importance of the crop's value to Angola, the Cubans insisted on paying the world market price.

Other Cash Crops

There were other areas where Cuban assistance was fundamental: the sugar industry had come to a standstill with the Portuguese exodus. Under Angolan directors, Cubans immediately took over technical jobs at the country's four sugar plantation and mill complexes, and began training Angolans in all aspects of production. Cane cutters were taught Cuban burning and cutting methods, which brought in an extra eight inches of cane. Cubans also assisted in mobilizing workers to join the union organization, and mechanization was increased. Again, finding a work force has impeded progress because, the sugar industry too, had depended on contract labourers.

Sugar production is a priority in the national plan, and with growing mechanization of the industry the way seems clear for expansion. In 1982 a major contract was signed with Tate and Lyle for technical assistance to Azucarias do Norte.

Sisal and cotton, both important foreign exchange earners before Independence, are also beginning to reach normal output levels. Here, too, mechanization has facilitated a rapid recovery of former output. Both crops are now under state production on former settler land.

Cotton is particularly important because it feeds the national textile industry, based almost 100% on pure cotton. Until 1982, national production of raw cotton was insufficient to satisfy the industry's demands, particularly after Africa Textil – a partnership between the state and French private industry – was established in Benguela.

Self-sufficiency in Food

Before Independence, Angola was almost self-sufficient in food. This statement must, however, be analysed: only 350,000 settlers were able to eat what they fancied, and only the urbanized 12% of Angolans were in daily contact with the Portuguese diet. Nutrition studies revealed severe protein deficiency in northern and tropical Angola, where meat and eggs were rare, and fish expensive. By contrast, the diet of semi-nomadic ranching tribes in the south was based on milk and meat. Market gardening was almost entirely limited to the Portuguese. Most Angolans derived their proteins from beans, groundnuts and certain leaves used in sauces; staple foods varied from north to south. Uije, Zaire, Luanda and Malanje are in the cassava belt, the central highlands and south rely on mealies from maize, and the deep south cultivates sorghum and millet. Potatoes and rice also formed part of the national diet. Meat was scarce except from hunting, or cattle raising near the Namibia border. Fish is the national dish – supplemented by local river fish, dried, salted sea fish was sold all over the country. A cold storage system also brought fresh sea fish to the main towns.

Colonial studies in the Luanda *musseques* showed that urban working class families survived on a mixture of traditional and Portuguese foods, according to their spending power. In general, meat or chicken was eaten once or twice a week, fish every day. These were the labour aristocrats, most Angolans ate less well.

Independence raised expectations, but there was the vast problem of setting up a national retail food system. All branches of food wholesaling and retailing had been run by the Portuguese.

Food shortages have become characteristic of Independence. Distribution problems, as we have seen, were partly responsible, but inadequate food production is the root cause of the shortages.

Meat, and Poultry Products

At Independence, pork products factories operated in Lubango, Huambo and Lobito. Traditional African farmers supplied the pigs, which were bought by Portuguese middlemen and sold to the factory. A few Portuguese farmers practised scientific pig farming, on a small scale with 30 or 40 pigs. Because the African farmers were grossly exploited; the Portuguese middleman worked a 12 hour day, and the market was limited, this system was successful. Now there are government pig farms in all provinces, although so far production is insignificant.

The Ministry of Agriculture has also sponsored state chicken farms on a mass scale across the country. Production from these has at times made an impact on local markets, but shortages of chicken feed, water and electricity cuts, problems with refrigeration of the carcases have militated against total success. Peasant poultry farming has slowly improved, but production is clearly insufficient to create a surplus to sell in urban areas.

To build up the national herds, decimated by the war, slaughtering of Angolan cattle was limited by government order after 1976. Pedigree herds had been imported by the Portuguese. Charolais, Aberdeen Angus and other well known European breeds have been crossed with local cattle, and the absence of tsetse fly in all but the extreme south-east, makes the southern uplands and border area ideal for ranching. But the South African war against southern Angola has practically demolished government efforts to reorganize ranching. Vaccination of the herds, by Comecon technicians went ahead in 1980 (practically under the barrels of South African guns). Most meat eaten by Angolans was being imported at huge cost, first from Argentina, then from Botswana, which, although it proved to be of better quality and much cheaper was still a drain on foreign exchange.

The Fishing Industry

Higher fish production would have reduced the need for meat imports. But at Independence the fishing industry was totally disrupted, again owing to the exodus of Portuguese.

Based on Portuguese trawlers and family businesses, the fishing industry had employed Angolan crews, scrubbers and cleaners. Now the country's six million people were dependent on traditional fishing fron dugout canoes. Major government contracts with the Soviet Union and Cuba provided for part of their catch to be landed in Angola for national consumption. Foreign factory ships swept unobserved and unchallenged down the Angolan coast harvesting their catches until around 1979 when, after a series of dramatic pursuits, the young Coastguard patrols steered Spanish and other vessels into custody. Despite the contracts with the Soviets and Cubans, fish landed for the national market was of poor quality and insufficient quantity. Quotas landed at the fishing ports largely fell in the hands of black marketeers and never reached the government controlled markets. Eventually, after repeated government enquiries into the fishing scandal President José Eduardo dos Santos declared that Angola would never have enough fish until it had its own fishing industry. This was being developed through co-operation agreements with Cuba and Sweden, and entailed building a national fishing fleet, training Angolans, and constructing a national cold storage system.

In spite of domestic shortages, the government honoured its promises to General Mobutu of Zaire, by exporting fish there in a determined effort to establish economic co-operation with its hostile neighbour.

Industrial Production

Concentrated around Luanda, Benguela-Lobito, Huambo and Lubango, pre-1975 industry was dominated by agribusiness, followed by light import-substitution. Heavy industry represented a small fraction of total production, built around cement, paper pulp, steel from scrap and ship repairs.

Since Independence light processing industry has taken the lead because of the decline in agricultural raw materials for the food industry (by 1980 agricultural production provided only 15% of industry's needs) and increased government investment in light industry. The industrial investment plan, approved by the 1980 Special Congress, divides 32% of public investment to the food industry, 31% to light processing industry and 37% to heavy industry. The Special Congress recommended that for the 1981 to 1985 period industry's main task should be to organize, strengthen and develop,

> removing all obstacles preventing levels of production and productivity

> from rising close to capacity; diversification of production through studies and investments in new projects to correct current sectorial and regional imbalance.

In the majority of cases industrial production has failed to regain its 1973 levels, and for at least some weeks every year many factories are virtually moribund. Frequent calls by the Party to prune spending, avoid factory floor wastage, and increase output – plus a tough incomes policy – have failed to transform loss into profit. The increased cost of raw materials, the government's austerity policy and consequent sharp cut-backs in imports of industrial raw materials, and especially management failings, delays in arrivals of technicians and maintenance spares from overseas, along with crippling water and electricity cuts are all factors militating against full and effective production.

In 1976 the government's efforts were concentrated on making a national inventory of industry, which occupied the next two years. The extent of plant, the state of equipment, the raw material stockpiles and the supply of parts were all unknown. Acquiring parts to restore output in sabotaged units, or those inadvertently damaged owing to lack of skills, was dependent upon Western companies to supply the parts and send technicians, and in 1976 they were rarely willing to do either. Many factories were maintained by improvisations by technicians from the socialist countries; a few young mechanics and electricians, members of Western solidarity organizations, also made their contribution. In general, not until 1977 and 1978 did large numbers of Western technicians return to sign service and supply contracts with the government, and only then could regular industrial training schemes for Angolan workers begin. At least another ten years was needed before there would be sufficient skilled Angolan mechanics and electricians to undertake the maintenance of industrial plant themselves.

In Malanje, where there was some agribusiness, there was no piped water for months. Lubango was constantly plagued by electricity power cuts as South African attacks and UNITA raids damaged the high tension cables that fed the city from the Matala dam, itself protected by heavy concentrations of FAPLA troops. Luanda suffered constant water and power cuts, due, not to sabotage, but to maintenance problems and overloading.

By 1981, a new Ministry of Energy was drawing up plans for heavy investment in electric power, mostly from hydro schemes, but also solar and wind energy; oil conservation was by now a priority. The Luanda industrial belt had been helped by the installation of extra turbines; power generation had also been boosted in Huambo, Cabinda and Moçamedes. The Luanda industry's water problems were reduced by construction of fresh pipelines, but generally water shortage continued in the capital until fresh reserves could be tapped.

These were the reasons for fluctuating production charts, and which made it almost impossible to fulfil production plans and run companies profitably. Often, planned levels of output were maintained for a few weeks and then plummeted to zero because of an extended power cut, or a faulty machine.

Western trading companies readily sold consumer goods to Angola for cash, but industrial firms resisted persuasion to commit their technicians and sign parts supply contracts. Western – especially British – banks, refused all credit once they knew it was for MPLA; some British firms lost valuable contracts because they were unable to finance their end of the bargain.

After 1979, when Western industrial and trading links with the People's Republic were fairly well established, industrial production was impeded by shipping and unloading delays at the docks, and the tardiness of bureaucratic import licence processing.

There was also some demobilization of the work-force. As we have seen, conditions in the big cities were difficult, salaries had failed to keep pace with inflation and workers were forced to join lengthy food queues. To pay rent and other bills often necessitated queuing during the office hours. Absenteeism became a problem.

The processing industry, however, did increase the volume of output, by 60% from 1977 to 1980. Particular progress was made in the production of maize meal, margarine, dried, semi-cured, and tinned fish, soft drinks, leather goods, textiles and clothing, bicycles, motorcycles, car and van assembly and the cutlasses used by peasants to clear bush and cut wood and cane.

The year 1979 to 1980 saw uneven progress; agricultural input was so low that the food industry's production actually fell. But output increased by 39% in light industry and 14% in heavy industry.

Planned output for industry overall in 1981 was to be raised 75% compared with 1980, particularly in heavy industry and the beverages sector. Overall 1981 output still stood at a planned 89% of the 1973 pre-Independence record level.

Most successful was the mining and mineral products record. By 1980 there had been a 400% increase in production of diamonds and crystalline quartz, and a substantial rise in output of decorative marble. Angola's crystalline quartz is of the finest optical quality. A small, private operation started by the Portuguese and Brazilians in 1974 discovered high quality quartz south of Luanda which they began exporting in 1975. After Independence the new Mining and Geology Department began to investigate the quartz market. It was discovered that there was a world shortage of fine quartz for the optics and electronics industry, and it was being stockpiled in the US. But the Portuguese and Brazilian firm were putting an astonishingly low value on their exports. A thorough enquiry revealed not only that Angolan quartz was of the highest quality, whereas on the official specification chart the company was declaring it to be only second or third class but that its value was at least five times more than the company was declaring. The owners were nationalized without compensation, and the state owned company has subsequently expanded strongly.

Future major industrial projects will centre on consumer essentials such as shoes and clothing, and on heavy industry. A phosphate crushing plant in Zaire province is to produce fertilizer for national needs, then for export; a compound fertilizer plant is to be built later. The possibility of chemical industry investments linked to the refinery expansion project is also being studied.

Regional industrial development is being promoted with the development by Sweden's Alfa-Laval of a large dairy farming and industrial plant in the centre of the country. Food processing industries are due to be built at Moçamedes where the Mediterranean climate is suitable for intensive horticulture. New mining projects are underway: phosphates in Zaire province, and iron ore in the north, where new deposits are being mined near Dalatando. The oil industry is generating more regional jobs, around the new concessions south of Luanda and on the Zaire river estuary.

Infrastructural Changes

All the 149 road bridges destroyed during the 1975-76 war had been rebuilt by 1980, mainly owing to technical assistance from the socialist countries. Angola's few qualified engineers took charge of a special bridge building unit and military engineers from FAPLA construction and logistics units also assisted. The construction workers from Cuba and the Soviet Union who helped in the building, simultaneously trained Angolans. They were often in the line of enemy fire, or subject to South African air attacks and sophisticated sabotage.

Owing to road and bridge rebuilding, road freight traffic has increased at a steady 20% annually. Following government investment in rebuilding the trucking fleet, skilled drivers are now scarcer than trucks. The bombing by South African and UNITA commandos of the rail bridges on both the Moçamedes and Benguela lines, has resulted in a continuing standstill in international rail freight on the Benguela line, and total tonnages are still below 1973 levels.

Government investments have built a national airline and merchant navy fleet. New aircraft were bought from the Soviet Union, Holland and the US. Intensive pilot training began in 1976 both for the military and TAAG, the civil airline; a civilian pilots training school operates out of Luena, few foreign pilots are now needed for civil flights. The merchant navy has four new long haul vessels, of 15,000 dwt tonnes, and three ships and two barges for coasting. Principle ports have been re-equipped with cranes and new loading and unloading equipment.

There were large-scale imports of earth moving equipment, transport equipment and tractors in the 1977 to 1980 period. The Central Committee later noted 'marked imbalance between the volume of investment in acquiring new equipment and volume of investment channelled towards improving technical assistance, as a result of which a high proportion of machines are not operational'.

Finance and Banking

MPLA's firm move to nationalize all banking business was simplified by the

1975 Bank nationalizations in Portugal which also affected the principal banks operating in Angola. At Independence it was a matter of transferring already state owned banks from Portugal to Angola. Negotiations soon became impossible owing to the war: Lisbon backed FNLA and UNITA after the November 1975 coup in Portugal. Because of Lisbon's series of reactionary governments diplomatic relations were not established until 1978. The question of compensation was by then no longer on the agenda.

Formal nationalization took place on 10 November 1976, when Saydi Mingas, Finance Minister, announced confiscation of the Bank of Angola and the Commercial Bank of Angola, which were renamed the National Bank of Angola and the People's Bank of Angola. Depositors' interests were not affected. Some foreign owned banks which had acted as merchant banks, closed their offices and left. The next step was to launch a national currency and leave the Portuguese colonial escudo zone. This was done in three days, from 8 January 1977, when escudos were exchanged for national currency. The new national currency, the Kwanza, named after a major river, is subdivided into 100 Lwei, named after a Kwanza tributary, and is non-convertible, and the Angolan central bank fixes international exchange rates every week. It rapidly acquired a firmer value than the Portuguese escudo.

The currency change mobilized tens of thousands of volunteers and was seen as an important step towards further independence from reactionary forces. Approximately a quarter of the Angolan escudos in circulation were held outside the country by settlers and Portuguese capitalists intent on using them to sabotage the revolution; their holdings were made worthless overnight. Hoarders, smugglers and petty bourgeoisie within Angola were now forced to declare their cash assets in order to exchange them for Kwanzas, and legislation decreed that any assets above Kwanzas 20,000 (about $700) must be banked, at least for the first few months. The currency exchange exercise unearthed some diamond smugglers with huge cash assets – hardly reflecting their 'unemployed' status!

Subsequent legislation has reinforced the state's monopoly over banking and financial institutions. Insurance and credit are state monopolies through state owned companies created since independence.

Production and Management Problems

In June 1979, disturbed by the performance of the economy, the Political Bureau issued an analysis of the economic and financial situation. No production statistics were included, but an increase in heavy industry output of 123% over the 1977 figure, and 10% increase over colonial production in the diamond industry was reported. Light industry had increased production by only 27% over the extremely low 1977 levels. The Political Bureau's view was that 'the fall in production is largely the result of the poor organizational capacity of our companies and the shortage of qualified cadres, especially in management, as well as a fall in discipline at work and shortages of raw materials and other inputs.'

Management of state owned concerns should be 'efficient and dynamic' and far greater effort should be made to avoid wastage. The issue of unsatisfactory management had arisen almost two years before, with the amendment of the original 1976 State Intervention Law's concept of collective industrial responsibility, in October 1977. From that time management had individual responsibility for plant and while obliged to fulfil production plans drawn up under the supervision of the central planning authorities, had some degree of initiative.

This greater flexibility however, had few positive results. In many cases, it was difficult to determine whether incompetence at managerial level was the result of sabotage or irresponsibility. The local, and more particularly, Luandan petty bourgeoisie still dominated the technical jobs, despite Neto's appointments of MPLA politicians or worker-cadres to leadership positions.

The petty bourgeois cadres were astonishingly complacent. Disinclined to learn from their foreign advisors, or become immersed in their revolution, they treated their functions as sinecures and adopted bureaucratic practices to conceal their ignorance and incompetence in decision making and administration.

The Political Bureau also recognized that owing to poor organization foreign technicians already in Angola were underemployed. Agricultural technicians sat in their hotel rooms waiting for transport to their farms; the Health Ministry was sluggish in allocating doctors to hospitals.

Significantly, the Political Bureau also called for foreign investment in mining and in manufacturing contracts for the national market: food, clothing and shoe production were the priorities.

The following month the Foreign Investment Law was passed. This law expressly prohibited foreign investments in defence, telecommunications, financial and credit institutions, insurance, foreign trade, public utilities and services (health, education, water and electricity supplies), as well as mass media and publishing. Otherwise, all foreign investment must correspond to priorities in the plan.

The law lays down foreign investors' duties: output must comply with Angola's guidelines, and companies' operations will be controlled by appropriate Angolan bodies which will oversee their accounts, their recruitment and training of Angolan nationals, and their cash reserves and social security funds. There is flexibility on the extent to which private ownership is acceptable. Private companies may be authorized, according to the law, 'in exceptional circumstances and where there is a clear national interest'. A significant reduction in imports might be considered as such an interest. But the general rule is for mixed enterprises between foreign and Angolan state companies, with Angola owning a minimum 51% controlling stake, to include plant, terrain, and equipment as well as cash spending. A single profits tax will be levied by contract on the foreign investor. The law offers guarantees of a period of operations from 10 to 15 years and mutually agreed compensation in the event of nationalization.

The Political Bureau again tackled the country's economic problems in a long statement, issued for May Day 1980. Its themes were similar to those of 1979, showing that in spite of a correct analysis production problems had persisted. Management was once more held responsible for most failures to implement the plan. Directors of state owned firms in particular were strongly criticized for their failure to implement the 1977 law on worker participation in management. This law was intended to lay the basis for workers to air their grievances, and for an education process whereby workers would become involved in factory-level management problems. In addition, the work-force would have a deeper understanding of its role in increasing output and building economic independence.

The trade union congress, UNTA, had already sharply criticized management for the same failing. But for the first time the Political Bureau now singled out corrupt workers as a growing problem. Cadres, it said, had at various times given way to 'workers unworthy of their class, saboteurs, absentees . . . and had exacerbated problems instead of solving them. Speculators and black marketeers were also warned. 'Unless we pay enough attention to organizing and developing our economy, we shall be endangering the major victories we have already gained, and threatening our main aims of people's democracy and socialism.'

This critical moment in the economic struggle coincided with a sharp decline in Angola's foreign exchange earnings for the first time since Independence. In spite of a decreased output in major exports (coffee, diamonds and oil) high prices on the world market, particularly the oil price boom that began in 1973, had increased state revenue from these exports to a level above colonial incomes. But with the drop of 50% in coffee prices, reduction in the oil price under the influence of the Saudi Arabia-US plan, and a sharp fall in diamond revenues the situation was reversed, and a foreign exchange crisis resulted.

Austerity

The government faced two choices: because its conservative finance policies and good foreign exchange position had earned the Western banking system's confidence (Angola had the lowest risk rating in Africa) it could have borrowed, fairly massively, from the Western banks. The other choice – which in fact was decided upon – was to implement a policy of extreme austerity, and maintain independence from Western creditors. This decision came from the top Party leadership, strongly supported by the leading economic managers, Lopo do Nascimento at Foreign Trade and Planning, Jorge de Morais at the Oil Ministry and Ishmael Martins at Finance.

The international situation provided a sharp warning: in the White House, Ronald Reagan was promising to undermine all Third World countries seeking independence from US imperialism, because, allegedly they were Soviet satellites. In Poland, there was tangible evidence of the problems created by massive Western credit to a country building socialism. In general, World Bank and IMF interference in the national economies of those Third World countries heavily in debt to the West had reached such a pitch that they had been told to leave by countries as different as Jamaica and Zaire. The worldwide economic depression showed every sign of deteriorating, and interest rates of being raised still further. All Third World countries were deeply in debt, and their people went hungry to pay off foreign creditors.

Austerity had been the key note for imports, from time to time, since Independence. Unlike other recently independent African countries, Angola had a state monopoly of import trade, and private companies were under strict import quotas and regulations. Imports of private cars had been totally banned since Independence, as – virtually – luxury consumer goods. Consumer durables, such as refrigerators, cookers and air conditioners, were imported under strict government control and rationed, and distributed on the basis of government issued ration cards, through private and state owned commercial firms. Clothing and shoes were increasingly manufactured inside Angola, although they sold at high prices.

Food was the main import, mainly flour, rice, sugar, powdered milk, cooking oil, margarine, baby foods, and canned goods. But food imports were broadly criticized by revolutionaries because they serviced urban tastes, not the needs of the country's overwhelmingly peasant population. There were insufficient imports of mealies, and tomato paste for sauces. Soap and milk was always scarce. Meat and chicken imports were insufficient. When the austerity programme reached a peak in early 1982, the shops were literally empty for almost three months. People survived by travelling to the countryside for local produce, or, for those unable to do this, by turning to the black market.

Whether or not the Party had foreseen the effect its austerity plan would have on the black market, by mid 1982 it had entered almost every urban home, and was consolidating its power. The combination of black market power and the austerity programme had not yet brought any marked increase in locally grown food, although the government had clearly intended that it should. Attempts to foster market gardening by improved irrigation in the Luanda green belt, began in late 1982. A reasonable rainfall also held out prospects of a better agricultural year in the country as a whole.

Meanwhile, in industry, the President was determined to reverse the drop in production by improving organization at management level, and firmer discipline of the work-force. But again, he was impeded by shortages of raw materials precipitated by his austerity programme. After the 1980 Political Bureau economic statement, President José Eduardo began a series of presidential spot checks, beginning in the crisis-ridden Luanda docks. This was structured into a 'General Offensive against Liberalism and Disorganization' launched by the Political Bureau on May Day 1981. It called for

> a generalized offensive against liberalism and disorganization, to detect irregular situations of sabotage in firms and public services in the private and mixed sectors of the economy, to strengthen discipline, to

re-establish the authority of the Party and government in all sectors and to increase the pace of the forward march of the revolution.

Leading revolutionaries were seconded to the General Offensive's board of enquiry which made unannounced spot checks on all branches of private and state owned industry and services. Massive disorganization was uncovered, from the airport's mishandling of freight and baggage, to wholesale diversion of goods in the fishing industry and chaos in the health service. Some senior cadres were dismissed, but others retained as the Party judged that there was no viable replacement, and that constant reshuffling of portfolios did not improve performance.

Future Prospects

The MPLA will continue to pursue a strategy of state growth and collective production, and diversification of technological dependence through contracts with companies from different countries. The socialist Comecon countries are already taking a growing share of Angolan exports (though this is still less than 10% of total foreign exchange revenues) and are likely to continue doing so. Input to the Angolan economy from the socialist world is increasing. From technical assistance contracts and supplies of basic capital equipment, some companies from Comecon countries are now winning construction and mining contracts; but they must compete with Western companies and are sometimes less competitive, particularly Yugoslavian and Rumanian, whose state firms' technology is often purchased from Western multinationals and who must, therefore, charge an extra profit margin on their tenders. It is cheaper for Angola to go to the source for their processing or mining technology, and this is often in the US.

The Angolan economy, in many interesting ways, illustrates the growing economic interdependence between capitalist and socialist technology. The government's official Lada cars are Soviet manufactured Fiats. In many industrial factories technicians from socialist and from capitalist countries work side by side. Shop floor mechanics may be Westerners and the management consultants socialists. Industrial training schemes for Angolans are being run by Western multinationals and by socialist, state owned firms. Angola's wealth and its strategic position makes it attractive as a partner and the government can afford to choose the best.

The first six years of rebuilding the Angolan economy has largely depended on technical assistance from the socialist countries, provided at a time when these countries themselves desperately needed skilled workers and investments to expand their national production for a rising home market. Buses, trucks and other vehicles were exported to Angola at the expense of supplying their own people. Without the teams of Soviet, Cuban, German, Polish, Czechoslovakian, and Yugoslavian engineers and workers, Angola would have collapsed under a Western boycott.

Western input into the Angolan economy is made on a clear technological basis, with government guarantees that the company will not lose, although the company is not free to do as it likes. Neto provided the framework for this contractual co-operation when he said

> we do not want to deceive foreign capitalist monopolies by concealing the fact that we intend to follow the road of socializing our means of production, finance, trade, services, everything that can be socialized, and that we intend doing this as quickly as possible.

Balance Sheet of Six Years Independence

The government's economic strategy to restructure ownership of the means of production yet maintain output has been based on gradual substitution of the existing capitalist economy through nationalization and collectivization. Outside dependence is, of course, seen as inevitable for many years ahead: but it must be as limited and diversified as possible. Portugal was too technologically backward, and too politically unpredictable to become a major influence in the economy. Because of Lisbon's intransigence, diplomatic relations were established only in 1978, long after all the EEC countries had recognized the People's Republic. MPLA therefore set about recruiting technical assistance from socialist allies where this was advantageous; and where it was not (oil and diamonds were prime examples, and the manufacturing industry in certain cases) to diversify dependence on different Western countries.

Because of Portugal's neglect of African education and training and the relatively sophisticated Western technology that dominated industrial and mining output, the gap between Angolan skills and the industrial and mining skills needed to run the economy was far greater than in many other African countries at Independence. MPLA could have elected to request massive technical assistance from foreign countries and place foreigners effectively at the helm of the economy. But they considered that to replace Portuguese by other foreign nationals would have been politically disastrous. Contrary to Western propaganda that depicted newly independent Angola as a Soviet and Cuban run enclave, foreigners were excluded from decision making positions, and (except in specific, isolated projects such as the Soviet contribution to the Humpata state farm) from executive responsibility too. Instead, poorly trained, inexperienced Angolans, often virtually ignorant of the field they had to command, were placed at the helm. Inevitably, economic growth has suffered, but has the price been too high?

Economic targets set out at the first Congress, in December 1977, were completely unrealistic. The thinking behind the economic strategy was basically sound – agriculture must come first, then recovery of former levels of industrial output, and last of all, fresh investments to satisfy national consumer needs and generate more export earnings for buying capital equipment

– but the difficulties involved were grossly underestimated; neither was the extent of South African aggression foreseen.

The 1980 Special Congress, which should have been devoted to detailed debate on a first five year economic plan, instead had to engage in correcting the first congress targets, describing the state of the economy and analysing its crisis points. Continuing poor organization, reflected in unreliable statistics, made detailed central planning still impossible to achieve. Hopes rested on the first population census since 1970, to be undertaken in 1983. Lack of reliable statistics has also hindered the publication of detailed macro and micro economic figures. So far neither an annual budget, nor detailed balance of payments statistics have been published. The government may be reluctant to disclose that approximately 50% of state spending is, necessarily at present, on defence.

Once a Namibia settlement is achieved and SWAPO comes to power, the end of the war, and the end of South African logistical and military support for UNITA, will make it possible for the government to reduce defence spending, and no longer need to spend millions of dollars on constantly rebuilding the infrastructure repeatedly destroyed by the South Africans across southern Angola.

The war reparations bill has reached over $7,200 million in blown bridges, roads and railways, bombed schools, hospitals, factories, oil depots, administration buildings and homes. Obviously it is almost impossible to believe that Angola will be paid even part of these reparations.

This devastation has been documented and laid before the United Nations. But the number of Angolan cadres who have had to turn from civilian to military tasks: engineers, architects, mathematicians, accountants, mechanics, electricians has not been recorded. The Angolan army has trained tens of thousands of young workers and peasants, to read and write, and then to learn further skills, all of which will be economic dynamite when they are released from national service.

9. The MPLA: from Movement to Party

The People's Movement

The People's Movement for the Liberation of Angola arose out of a number of African, coloured and white political organizations, including a small communist movement of intellectuals, and was founded on 10 December 1956. Its Manifesto declared: 'the Movement will be the sum of activities of thousands and thousands of organizations (of three, more than three, dozens or hundreds of members each) which will be created throughout Angola'. The MPLA, in contrast to the origins of both UPA and UNITA, was born out of common ideals, not common tribal roots. Its long history of cultural resistance to colonial rule waged by African and *mestiço* petty bourgeoisie and intellectuals, had served to radicalize Angolans in the small, privileged group of literate Africans. In 1956 these men and women understood that a broad mass movement must be built up, and the most oppressed and exploited should organize themselves against foreign rule.

Understandably, this reorganization came later than it had in some other Southern African countries. Angola was immeasurably more backward economically, and since the 1920s had been in the grip of Salazar's Catholic fascism. A comparison between the powerful Defiance Campaign mounted by the African National Congress and its allies and involving tens of thousands of South Africans, and the careful, written appeals to the authorities by the Angolans in the same period – the mid 1950s – highlights the extent to which Angolans lagged behind in effective organization owing to conditions in their country.

At that time, because industrialization was virtually absent in Angola there was no African urban proletariat. The huge force of migrant contract workers was overwhelmingly employed in the countryside; the few in the cities were relatively recent arrivals. Divide and rule was the order of the colonial day. Traditional African society was under close scrutiny for signs of 'restlessness', wage labour on the farms was pinned down by contracts and surrounded by Africans from other tribes whose hostility towards the migrants was encouraged. Until the Armed Forces Coup in April 1974, open, mass political or trade union organization in any form had been impossible. The official Catholic Church strongly disapproved of Protestant Native Church organization, and the messianic and millenarist cults, with their message of defiance and independence from white rule, were pursued and persecuted by the political police.

In the Luanda townships there was an opportunity for underground political discussion, as there was wherever large groups of Angolan workers were concentrated. In the countryside, the more privileged Angolans with some education were closer to the peasants than the majority of the Angolan élite in the towns were to the unskilled labour force. It was a society to a great extent without classic and clearly defined class boundaries. A huge gulf separated settler and settled, oppressor and oppressed, but within the ranks of the oppressed Angolans, no national bourgeoisie existed in the accepted sense of owning substantial means of production. In a nation 85% illiterate and subjected to settler fascism, the petty bourgeoisie was a cultural and wage group: comprised principally of office workers, with a few artisans and an insignificant minority of professional men. These people had no means of production, but as a cultural and wage earning élite, they developed petty bourgeois tendencies and aspirations. As the colonial economy boomed and more Africans and *mestiços* were edging into such skilled jobs as, for example, nurses, teachers and mechanics, they too joined the elité and came to constitute a petty bourgeoisie in sharp contrast to the mass of working people.

This petty bourgeois élite began increasingly to identify with the Independence movement. More and more Portuguese continued to arrive to deprive them of the chance of economic advancement. They imitated the Portuguese culture and frowned upon their African traditions, seeking to learn whatever they could from their colonial masters. Ultimately, however, they wanted an end to white rule, so they themselves could take the helm. Few members of this social group risked their lives for their people; those who did included *mestiços* and such black Angolans as Saydi Mingas, Belarmino Van Dunem.

Political prisons were soon set up in response to the MPLA's mobilizing strength. The first full-time PIDE agents were sent to Angola in 1957, (the year after the movement was founded) and they finally exceeded the number deployed in Portugal itself. Those imprisoned were men who spoke out against injustice, signed petitions, or were simply indiscreet in expressing their hope for the future. These were not mass organizers, powerful trade union leaders or trained guerrillas. When the MPLA-led Luanda opposition stormed the political prison to free their comrades on 4 February 1961, it was a hastily planned action to coincide with the presence of many foreign journalists in Luanda who had come to cover a different story. Armed only with cutlasses and stones, many of those who took part – could neither read nor write. The assault failed but the armed resistance had begun, and, as has already been noted, it unleashed a white terror against the black population. Men such as Manuel dos Santos, a peasant farmer from near Dalatando who, with others, had earlier led a deputation to protest against forced labour by their pregnant women, and many nurses and teachers were murdered.

From 1961 and the launching of the armed struggle, it became increasingly difficult to undertake any political or trade union work in the urban areas. This was particularly unfortunate at a time when the colonial government needed rapid industrialization, services for the sprawling colonial army, and when an urban African working class was about to develop.

The Armed Struggle

In October 1961 UPA forces murdered a column of MPLA guerrillas infiltrating northern Angola; more guerrillas went in to take their place. In December 1962 a First National Congress was held in Leopoldville. There were 70 delegates, and Agostinho Neto was elected to head the Steering Committee. The people's army was formed, EPLA, *Exercito Popular de Libertaçao de Angola.* Tension in the Leopoldville headquarters caused by the new Zaire President's opposition to MPLA beset the organization in 1963. There were also ideological problems; Viriato da Cruz, a radical leftist, led a group of three others in a bid for alternative leadership. They issued a document dismissing the Steering Committee and appointing themselves in its place. Only another Congress was empowered to do this, according to the Statutes. Viriato applied to UPA for membership and finally went to China, where he died years later.

In January 1964 MPLA opened its Cabinda military front, the Second Region. In response, the Portuguese set up the Flechas ('arrows') special counter-insurgency units, and began to foster puppet groups such as MOLICA and FLEC, purporting to be Cabinda Liberation Movements. In Zaire's Shaba province, MPLA militants were also active and eventually joined the eastern front, launched from Zambia in 1966. The peasants of Moxico, Lunda and Kuando Kubango gave consistent mass support to the MPLA's guerrillas. Their liberated areas were far from urban centres, consequently it was the peasants who waged the war of national liberation. The active, mass scale participation of urban workers in the struggle came only in the second war of liberation against Zaire and South Africa and their FNLA and UNITA allies, and after Independence in the battle for Angola's right to self-determination and socialism.

Viriato's dissension was not the only one that threatened to weaken the MPLA during the anti-colonial war. In 1970 Neto had observed:

> Today we are going through the stage of a movement for national liberation, a movement in which all tendencies and persons willing to take part in the struggle against Portuguese colonialism are accepted. We are bound together by the common will to fight against Portuguese colonialism . . . but while there is one organizational structure there is not one ideological position.

Early in 1973 a number of guerrillas from the eastern front near the

Zambia border broke away from MPLA, and under the leadership of Daniel Chipenda, formed what was known as the 'Eastern Revolt' group. Zambian backing for Chipenda exacerbated its effects. Chipenda was ebullient, hard-drinking and a womanizer, notorious at the front for his non military exploits. There was a sharp fall in armed activity in Chipenda's zone after the Eastern Revolt group's formation. Soon afterwards came the April 1974 Portuguese coup. A fresh split followed almost at once. In May 1974, a group of 19 intellectuals, led by Father Joaquim Pinto de Andrade, issued a statement in Brazzaville, (the location of MPLA's external headquarters) accusing Neto's leadership of 'presidentialism' and disregard for internal democratic procedures. This group of 19 intellectuals and professional men, including medical doctors and lawyers, called themselves the 'Active Revolt'. But their case was weakened by the fact that most of them had left the ranks of the MPLA some years before and returned to ordinary life, though still in exile. There had been criticism of the movement's leadership on the grounds that rank and file had not been consulted over the 1972 decision to move for reconciliation with FNLA (the aim was to persuade Mobutu to end his hostility to MPLA and thus reinforce the northern guerrilla front through bases in Zaire). The two revolts came at the worst possible time for MPLA – when the Armed Forces coup promised a real impetus for change.

To what extent they represented tensions deliberately fostered by infiltrated agents can be only a matter for speculation. It is interesting that during the 1974 preparations for the Alvor independence talks, a group of wealthy Portuguese businessmen from Angola publicly announced their support for the Active Revolt. To these businessmen, they represented the 'civilized' MPLA: men of culture and goodwill, an elité sharply differentiated from the mass of workers and peasants that the MPLA, with its 'people's power' banners represented.

Transition from Movement to Vanguard Party

During 1974 and 1975 MPLA Action Committees were formed all over the country, in urban centres and in villages. Many consisted of individuals who had never met MPLA guerrillas but who had listened to its *Angola Combatente* radio programme and identified with the call for self-determination and independence. The People's Neighbourhood Committees in Luanda had carried community organization to almost half a million Angolans. Workers in the industrial and clerical sectors heard for the first time about genuine trade union organization. MPLA spoke of an end to the exploitation of man by man. 'From Cabinda to Kunene – One People, One Nation' was the MPLA's call for national unity and fierce struggle against the tribalism propagated by the enemy. The anti-imperialist nature of the independence war was made plain by Western and racist support for the enemy forces. 'Neto: imperialism's poison' was a popular slogan daubed on township walls. Thousands of Angolans sang and chanted 'the MPLA is the People and the People are MPLA'.

The People's Movement's campaign against racism, conducted at the height of the South African invasion, was reinforced by the concrete situation: white Cubans fought alongside the FAPLA, against the enemy forces, and many Angolans had suffered at the hands of black soldiers from UPA-FNLA and UNITA. To combat black hostility towards the *mestiço* population, who still comprised a de facto educated élite, was more difficult. The MPLA emphasized class lines, pointing out that some blacks were also guilty of petty bourgeois behaviour. The Movement's leadership was convinced that by building people's power and a vanguard party, the oppressed and exploited could soon be raised to positions of dignity, skill and leadership. In the early period the petty bourgeoisie was essential, if Angola were to be independent and rely on its own manpower. Meanwhile, workers and peasants would join the ranks of the literate and skilled. Class struggle would grow.

From their experience in other African countries, the exiled MPLA leadership had a clear idea of the pitfalls a vanguard party could encounter. How could they be avoided? The People's Movement had a head start over parties in the Congo and Tanzania, for example, because it had experienced 13 years of armed struggle before Independence; but it was severely hampered by the weakness of working-class consciousness in Angola. Indeed, in 1975 there was the question of whether it existed as such at all. The lack of trade union activities or even community welfare and solidarity associations (except those run as charities by the white church) seriously impeded effectual organization. In the urban areas, political organizing was really starting from nothing. Even traditional bonds of association and authority were absent in the townships.

After the bitter and disruptive experience of the Alves faction and ensuing coup d'état, the Movement was under great pressure from rank and file militants to clarify its commitment to building socialism in Angola. By mid 1977, the men and women who were MPLA members now included thousands of urban production workers, office workers, teachers and civil servants, as well as the hard core of first war activists and the peasants in the countryside. Particularly disturbing was that the recent factionalism was widely thought to have been made easier to engineer by the lack of clear ideological definition on the part of what remained a broad liberation front. The Luanda petty bourgeoisie's attempt to dominate the government and civil service – contrary to the Movement's banner of power to the people – was also a matter for concern. Although the majority of Angolans still did not recognize it as such, class struggle had now begun.

The coup had revealed the need for ideological study groups, to satisfy Angolans' thirst for education and scientific thought. The faction's emphasis on theoretical discussion had attracted a number of well-meaning supporters, especially among the student left, because of the existence of a vacuum in the MPLA political education structures during the difficult transition period and the early months of Independence. Theory had been left behind in the daily round of attending to urgent, practical business.

It was also time to reaffirm the movement's commitment to workers' power. Among the factionalists Neto said had been some 'ambitious workers, thinking they already had the leadership of the country in their hands and that the unity of all classes was no longer possible. They thought they alone – and they personally above all – could lead the whole revolutionary process in Angola.' Neto had warned that the struggle for national unity must now be waged 'with extreme care'. Ndunduma, in an editorial in the *Jornal de Angola*, wrote: 'If all patriots are not united, then imperialism will penetrate. The class struggle must be integrated into the more general context of the anti-imperialist struggle. The unity of all patriotic forces against imperialism should not be destroyed.'

Was the Movement to be abolished and a Party formed instead? This would have more rigid criteria for selection if it were to be Marxist-Leninist, and the broad front would be 'committing suicide'. If no Party were created, the kind of confusion evoked by the parallel organization and factionalism practised by Alves could easily recur. Was the Party to be open to illiterates or should it be strictly an educated cadre party? The decisive moment came during the October 1976 plenary session of the Central Committee – its first plenary session after Independence – when it decided to launch the transition to socialism.

First Congress

A resolution was passed to make every effort to hold a Party Congress by the third quarter of 1977. In a resolution on the stage reached in the struggle the Central Committee listed the changes in social policies and declared:

> These social changes will necessarily lead to the formation of a Party (guided by the ideology of the working class, Marxism-Leninism), the leading force of the broad national anti-imperialist front, a historic imperative for the continuing of our revolution since, as Lenin says, socialism cannot be built without the leadership of the working class party.

1977 was declared 'Year of the Founding of the Party and of Production for Socialism'. Preparations for the Congress began at once. On 12 February 1977 the first National Party School was opened in Luanda, with a first course for militants from all over the country who would later set up province Party Schools. Angolans gave the courses on political economy, philosophy, MPLA and Angolan history; Cuban instructors gave classes on organization and method. Carlos Rocha (Dilolwa) who had delivered the inaugural address stressed that the aim was to transmit Marxist-Leninist ideology. In April, the first National Preparatory Meeting for the Congress was held in the School and was conducted by Lucio Lara as Organizing Secretary, and Manuel Pedro Pacavira. Lara, of course, had been with the guerrillas. Pacavira had been a member of the underground and become a political prisoner. The

FAPLA Political Commissariat was represented by Bakaloff and Dino Matross.

During the early months of 1977 considerable effort was made to explain the idea of forming a Party to the people. The Political Bureau, in a January statement, had noted that socialism required a people's democracy and that could be achieved only if the 'whole people were led by clear and scientific political guidance that will necessarily be Marxism-Leninism'. At a rally in Dalatando in February, Neto outlined the Marxist analysis of society moving from primitive communism through slavery, feudalism and capitalism to socialism, and of the proletariat as the only revolutionary class. He went on to outline the principles of democratic centralism in Lenin's terms.

In August, after the coup, the Central Committee plenary session selected 22 candidates for the 22 vacancies on the Central Committee that was to be elected at the Congress. It also strongly criticized 'the opportunist race by certain sectors of the petty bourgeoisie for official posts' which had become increasingly acute after the defeat of the Alves faction. In August, too, a National Seminar on Congress Organization was held in Malanje, and conducted by Lara, Dino Matross and Bernardo de Sousa. In October, Neto undertook a provincial tour to explain the Congress; special radio programmes broadcast Congress news; seminars and discussions were held in factories, offices and public halls in towns and cities, while action groups and the mass organizations arranged concerts, dances and sporting events, in order to raise funds.

The education and organization seminars provided workers and grass-roots militants with the tools for effective action at the Congress. Through the publicity, mass rallies and fund-raising events, the mass organizations and the people were drawn into participation at the birth of the new Party.

A party comprising only an educated civil service élite was out of the question. In the run up to Congress, the petty bourgeois assault on the power structures, in a bid for Party membership, concentrated upon proving they were the most militant of MPLA militants. In November, Lara warned of some civil servants who questioned the ability of illiterate workers and peasants to govern the country. Neto said, that in a society which had undergone centuries of colonialism, it was difficult for anyone to understand that 'a carpenter might direct a military unit'.

There were meetings all across the country to select delegates to the Congress. Provinces were given places on a principle of proportional representation. Luanda thus had the largest number of elected delegates (19). Militants' assemblies, first in villages, then at town level and finally at Province level, chose the Province team. Of around 300 Congress delegates, 187 were elected in this way, 95 by FAPLA around the country, 87 by the provinces and 5 by students. Other delegates were selected from the existing Central Committee, from MPLA permanent departments, from the mass organizations and from amongst individuals who had made outstanding personal contributions to the MPLA's struggle.

Congress work was conducted in commissions and sub-commissions, and by 9 December delegates had examined main documents (all of which had been published previously in the national newspaper for discussion and debate) and drawn up resolutions based on the draft proposals. Carlos Rocha, the Planning Minister, had chaired the commission on economic and social development, Lucio Lara chaired the political and ideological commission, and Iko Carreira the defence and security commission.

The five-hour Central Committee report to the Congress, read by Neto in the opening session, set the tone of the debate: 'Either there is capitalism or there is socialism – there is no other way.' Ten days before the Congress had convened, a seminar for MPLA militants in FAPLA had been addressed by the President, and his speech had been widely publicized:

> If in the past our fight was against Portuguese colonialism and for our independence, which we obtained, today our struggle is being waged on different ground. It is a class confrontation today. It is a class confrontation which we cannot avoid and which we must try to transform into a victory of the proletariat, of the peasant class, so that those classes most exploited under colonialism should take up the leadership of the country.

The proposed programme for a new Party laid down its role clearly: 'MPLA is the party of the working class, uniting workers, peasants, revolutionary intellectuals and other workers dedicated to the cause of the proletariat in a solid alliance.'

The Party's strength as a vanguard detachment of the working class would be based on 'the synthesis of Marxist-Leninist theory with its own revolutionary experience acquired throughout the national liberation struggle and with the revolutionary experience of all the peoples of the world.' Democratic centralism, criticism and self-criticism would reinforce and consolidate unity. Proletarian internationalism was explicitly stated. A 'revolutionary school' should be created throughout the country in towns and villages from which new militants would emerge, struggling for 'a scientific and revolutionary mentality in Angolan society'. The Angolan revolution was entering a phase of democratic revolutionary dictatorship under the leadership of the proposed new working-class party, in which national reconstruction would build the economic foundations for socialism.

> The workers, peasants and revolutionary intellectuals in close alliance will exert democratic revolutionary dictatorship against internal and external reaction, creating conditions for installing the dictatorship of the proletariat in the phase of building socialism. [During the transition there would be] tremendous class struggle.

The economic path was mapped out in considerable detail. The question of people's power was also before the Congress. The People's Power Law (1/76) passed so soon after independence, was strongly criticized in the opening report of the Movement Central Committee, on the grounds that it had provided almost a theoretical and practical framework for the Alves faction's construction of parallel organizations to the Liberation Movement and government. The Central Committee report recommended annulment of the law on the grounds that it was based on 'mistaken petty bourgeois concepts' that failed to take into account the basic Leninist principle that the ultimate organ of people's power is the Marxist-Leninist Party. Now that such a Party was to exist, it would take on the role of guaranteeing the workers' seizure of power and building of the apparatus of the revolutionary workers' state.

It was evident that this would not be MPLA's last word on the subject. There was a clear case for first concentrating on Workers' Party building, its aims and the form it should take, and later on the reorganization of non-Party politics. Congress decided that urgent consideration should be paid to the question and new proposals made. Congress also backed generalized people's resistance, and enlarging the militias so that 'every citizen should feel himself a soldier, defending the revolution'.

The lengthiest discussion, and substantial disagreement, centred on the elections to the new Central Committee. The MPLA had 'constituted itself into a vanguard party'. It had not transformed itself into a Party (which would have maintained the same membership as the broad movement and the same leadership), and it had not created a Party outside the MPLA, retaining the latter as a front; neither had it created a Party called MPLA. In practice, this complex articulation meant that some Movement leaders might be considered ineligible for Party leadership. There was a statute rule that laid down the requirement of eight years militancy in the movement for any candidate to the Central Committee. This effectively excluded working-class members, who had been unable to join official militant structures until after the April 1974 coup. It did, however, leave the way open for peasant supporters who had joined active underground cells before 1974, in recognized contact with the MPLA Steering Committees and underground structures in the liberated areas.

Congress had to elect 45 full and 10 alternate members of the new MPLA-Workers' Party Central Committee. A full complement was 60 full members plus 15 alternates, but it was decided to leave places open for the inclusion of working-class members at a subsequent Special Congress, to be held three years later, in 1980. The MPLA's official candidates list had exactly 22 names for the 22 vacancies; but FAPLA at a pre-Congress meeting, had elected its own list of candidates, comprising 45 names, almost entirely of those from the ranks of the first war guerrillas. Now, at the Congress, province delegates added their own suggestions from the floor. Of the 22 candidates proposed by the MPLA, 6 were rejected, 13 were elected full members and 3 alternates. All the existing Central Committee were re-elected. Three were elected on suggestions from the floor: Ruth Neto (full member) a women's leader and sister of the President, Kundi Paihama, a southern peasant, underground activist and, since the South African retreat, the exemplary Commissioner of

Kunene province, and Kota Neto, an older veteran from the underground Committees, chosen *in absentia* for his outstanding work at Lucala on the northern front.

Three women were now on the top Party body: Ruth Neto, Rodeth Gil and Maria Mambo Cafe. The strongest criticism at the Congress was levelled at a small regional lobby, called the 'Catete' group because they all came from that area near Luanda; many militants were shocked by the open sectional canvassing of this group. Manuel Pedro Pacavira and Agostinho Mendes de Carvalho were members of the Catete group and the aim of their lobbying was to gain more places on the Central Committee and then a guaranteed position on the top executive Political Bureau out of the ensuing Central Committee vote. Coming so soon after the Alves faction, the group provoked a good deal of hostility and its members' score in the voting was relatively low. None of them gained a position on the Political Bureau. The Catete group, however, did include prominent political prisoners whose reputation was unflawed by any association with the other political prisoners involved with Alves; they could not be ignored.

On 10 December 1977 the MPLA-Workers' Party was founded. Now the transition from anti-colonialist front to Marxist-Leninist Party would be carried out through a rectification process of members that lasted for years, and in continuing reappraisal of members' records. At the same time, the youth movement, JMPLA was transformed into a Party Youth organization. The mass organizations, the women's OMA, and the trade unions grouped under UNTA, as well as the Pioneers, remained non-party. On 14 December the new Party Central Committee held its first meeting and elected the Political Bureau of 11 members and 3 alternates. All had been former members of the Movement Central Committee, and 9 of the 11 were in the previous Political Bureau.

Rectification

The rectification campaign began on the anniversary of armed struggle, 4 February 1978. Liberation Movement members upon whose experience the Party would now draw, would, in principle, be eligible for membership. It was stressed, however, that 'this does not mean they will be party members since they will have to be confirmed through a fresh analysis'.

New Party members were to join through their places of work. The criterion would be especially 'the attitude of a militant to his professional duties' and this would have to be tested at his work place. Lucio Lara explained the process:

> We have a list of members in a certain factory, according to the census taken by the MPLA Liberation Movement. This list will be put to the workers of the factory. We have decided all workers will be asked for their opinion, not just militants. A workers' assembly will give its opinion on the comrades whom we consider to be militants of the party.

At the same time, the workers' assemblies

> will indicate to us which of the factory workers are really exemplary and have a worthy attitude towards production and who for one reason or another have not been linked to MPLA when the liberation movement set up its structures inside the factory.

These exemplary workers will, said Lara, then be contacted by the MPLA-Workers' Party to join up as militants or aspiring militants. The system of two categories of membership would provide an additional way of checking on members' conduct. Party regulations actually gave a preference to industrial workers, since under the new statutes, they remained on probation as aspiring members for only one year, whereas a two year probationary period was prescribed for other candidates.

Through numerous rectification meetings held initially in Luanda, and then in other large towns throughout the country, the first group of urban Party cells was built up. The new structure was based on cells of from 3 to 30 members, and aspiring members at the work place. The cells elected a Party Sector Committee which, in turn, elected a Party Area (or Party Village) Committee with other sector committees. The next level was that of an elected Party Rural District Committee or Urban District Committee, and finally, the Party Province Committee.

The first round of urban rectification provided some sharp lessons. In order to minimize intimidation by petty bourgeois or unscrupulous local bullies, the workers' assemblies were presided over by outside militants. Nevertheless, it was a new process for Angolans. Among office workers and civil servants, and in such areas as the media and higher education, where petty bourgeois skilled workers predominated, shopfloor criticism and independent rank and file views of candidates were rarely articulated. In sharp contrast factory workers and all ranks in the armed forces participated vigorously.

Opportunists and provocateurs, the Party warned, would come to light during the rectification process and so would 'those more revolutionary than the revolution itself'. There was a pressing need to 'fight tirelessly against petty bourgeois ideology and all its manifestations'. The Political Bureau stated, 'The class struggle being waged within the Party should lead inevitably towards victory for the proletarian line.'

Neto almost invariably took care to explain the class struggle in terms that caught the imagination of the people. Early in 1978 he had exclaimed:

> the internal enemy is like a clam. He only comes out of his shell with a dose of hot water or jemmying with a well placed knife. Because the internal enemy is convinced he alone knows the whole truth, drunk in from books lent to him by the imperialists. He is the two-faced man who talks one way in meetings and another way at work. He is the one who will resist socialism because he cannot conceive that all men are

> equal and that social distribution into different jobs does not drive us apart. On the contrary it brings us together.

He stressed that the armed struggle was launched,

> by workers and peasants who took up cold steel to assault the colonial bastions of power. They were workers with the tools of their trades. They were workers, who ripped down the shroud of slavery and obscurantism, already denounced by the intellectuals, and felt by every Angolan in his flesh and blood, in a world that demanded freedom.

The rectification process was to be,

> an act of unity by militants in which the working class takes up its leadership role and brings all those found to hold incorrect ideas towards correct positions. Starting from the unity of militants, a broad movement of loyal and open criticism must be developed in which we shall seek to overcome our mistakes and correct our working methods. Criticism must always take into account that our aim is not to destroy but to reinforce party ranks and make us more capable of facing the difficulties that arise in building socialism.

At the time of the First Congress there were 110,000 card carrying members of MPLA. From May to November 1978 three phases of rectification were carried out. By 18 November, the Party had just under 2,500 full ranking militants, with 1,560 aspiring members on probation. The youth had 1,163 full members and 795 sympathizers; around 5% of the Party members were women. Reports on the rectification process showed that intermediate ranking MPLA-movement members had come in for the greatest mass criticism. Many had not been rectified and remained as sympathizers outside the Party structure, active in the non-Party mass organizations.

The interpretation of Party statutes was sufficiently flexible to accommodate sincere and hardworking proletarians as aspiring members. The ban on those holding religious beliefs was interpreted to allow Catholics and Protestants also to become aspiring members, even though in principle religion was seen as contradictory to scientific socialism.

Strict monogamy was a ruling that affected the urban population less than the rural. An important militants' seminar held in the southern city of Lubango, decided to modify their ruling for peasant supporters. Rural rectification began in 1979, a year after the main campaign.

At the Lubango meeting, militants objected that a rule imposing rectification priority on co-operatives and peasant associations meant that wage labourers on the state farms were excluded from the process. Specific guidelines were laid down to facilitate their inclusion in priority rectification work. These guidelines also stated that rectification should apply to former members of the MPLA Liberation Movement structures, who had been registered before the First Congress, and could claim to have had two years of regular membership if agricultural workers and three if peasants. In the case of the old Action Committees of the MPLA militants operating in areas where there were no co-operatives or associations, and who had not only played an active role during the First Liberation war but continued to promote MPLA directives and government policy, the Lubango seminar decided that they could be rectified if they accepted the statutes.

Other problems existed in the countryside: polygamy among the middle-aged and older peasants was practised openly, in a traditional and organized way, in contrast to the clandestine and anarchical concubinage of city life. The modifications to the monogamy ruling permitted older men with several families to maintain their polygamous unions but young peasants were expected to adhere to the ruling on monogamy. Literacy could not be demanded of peasant members. Thousands of people had learned to read and write under the national campaign, but coverage of the scattered rural populations was less thorough than in the cities where, by 1979, it was reasonable to expect skilled and semi-skilled workers to be literate. In the countryside, by November 1980, MPLA activists had supervised 2,542 peasant associations and 304 co-operatives which had formed 423 and 61 cells respectively. This meant that the Party was now operating in 16.6% of registered peasants associations and in 20% of registered production co-operatives.

By the December 1980 Extraordinary Congress, rectification had covered the entire country; with a total of 31,098 members, 8.6% of whom were women, 15,294 were MPLA-Workers' Party militants and 15,804 aspiring members.

There were 2,765 Party cells, 65 Party Committees at workplaces and 4 Sector Committees – the elected pyramid was rising. A study of the social composition of half the membership produced the encouraging evidence that 51% were workers and peasants. If members of worker and peasant origin who had become full-time Party office holders, or government and civil service office holders, were included the percentage would be considerably higher.

Party Control of Government

During the rectification campaign, the petty bourgeoisie accelerated its bid for the commanding heights of the government and civil service. Neto made a series of political appointments that displeased the civil service élite but heightened workers' consciousness that the class struggle had to be waged seriously in defence of the revolution. The MPLA-Workers' Party and its leaders stimulated class struggle by means of theoretical speeches, practical measures, and a growing network of party schools and seminars.

At a three day Central Committee meeting in December 1978, petty bourgeois action was discussed, and it was concluded that petty bourgeois tendencies were alive and active both in the Party and the government. Party unity also had to be strengthened. Lopo do Nascimento was dismissed from the Political Bureau but retained on the Central Committee; the post of Premier that he held was abolished, and Neto himself took on the role of head of government. Carlos Rocha 'Dilolwa' resigned from both the Political Bureau and the Central Committee and returned to the ranks as a grass-roots militant. He had been Planning Minister and was, like Lopo, a leading member of the MPLA old guard. No public explaination was ever made of do Nascimento's dismissal from the Political Bureau. Speculation centred around both men's economic policies. Dilolwa was thought to favour strong state sector planning and perhaps he balked at the predominant Party view favouring collectivization and association in the countryside around peasant farmers; Neto's determination to support small scale private enterprise, (Angola's shortage of skilled manpower was crippling to a centralized state economy) may have been an additional factor.

Lopo do Nascimento's dismissal from the post of Premier to some extent reflected Neto's impatience with the way government was impeded by endless Portuguese bureaucratic red tape. The Prime Minister's office, with its several associated vice premiers created to facilitate efficient administration had instead contributed abundant paperwork but little action. Neto wanted to bring the administrative desk work related to critical government decisions under his own control. There were also subsequent suggestions that the Premier had been criticised by some Party members for being too close to his foreign technical assistants. Do Nascimento had for some time wanted to return to Party ranks and work full time there, but after a short period out of government, he was appointed as Minister of Foreign Trade, and later, under President José Eduardo dos Santos, Minister of Planning. For almost a year he held down both portfolios until a replacement was found for the Foreign Trade Ministry, in August 1982, leaving him free to concentrate on the Planning Ministry, the most senior appointment in the government at that time.

The eclipse of both do Nascimento and Dilolwa at the December 1978 Central Committee Meeting was followed by a vigorous speech from Neto about Party independence. Recalling MPLA's 22 years of experience in struggle, he said:

> We learned something. We learned first and foremost that it is necessary at all times to defend the independence of the Party so that this independent Party can also contribute to the true independence of the country. If the Party is not independent, the country will not be independent either. [During the struggle] various situations arose that weakened not only the movement itself, but also weakened the people's driving force, doubts were launched and scepticism about the fruits of our struggle. So we must take increasing care to make our orientation clear and to know exactly what we can do at each moment to preserve our independence. Independence before everything.

The Central Committee had:

> reaffirmed the need to preserve our Independence and it also reaffirmed one more thing: the need for us never to permit anyone to divide us, anyone to place themselves amongst us, the leadership, or between us, the MPLA and the people. Nobody has the right to do this. This is one of the conditions for guarding our independence.

At the same mass rally, Neto outlined the streamlining of government, and inclusion into the Cabinet of Province Commissioners, who were all Party members; a practical step to speed up government action in the provinces. He also addressed the question of private enterprise. The Central Committee had decided to encourage small business in retailing and housing construction: 'This will not be a political step backwards. It is simply a question of allowing some compatriots to use private initiative to solve some of our problems.' The state, he said, had 'made strenuous efforts to solve most problems but at this stage we must recognize the fact that the state cannot solve singlehanded the majority of problems facing the rural population.' He launched the slogan 'The most important thing is to solve the people's problems.'

People's power had also been discussed by the Central Committee. A new Party department for installing People's Power was to be set up 'we are lagging behind with institution of people's power. There was a good experience of people's power unfortunately used by factionalists for their own ends'. The time has come to start again so that 'everyone and each group can make their contribution to national policy'.

During 1979, Neto revealed his appreciation of the need to create checks and balances to control political life, and increase the government's accountability by means of elections for People's Power structures. In his 1979 New Year message he had said:

> the structuring of the Party should mean that in the very near future we can organize People's Power clearly and openly dominated by the working class and peasants, classes that were far away from the influence of the colonial bourgeoisie and that can exercise their task of leading society.

Launching 1979 as the 'year of cadre training', Neto stressed the opportunities that were now open to workers and peasants to increase their skills. The petty bourgeois élite had already begun to experience the effects of this and, in what was clearly a test of their strength against the workers, the Benguela petty bourgeoisie went on the offensive.

The Class Struggle

Benguela the 'red city' had always been strongly MPLA. In colonial days, it had gathered progressive whites, away from the PIDE concentrated in Luanda, and it was one of the first cities to be industrialized. It lies on the Benguela railway line, 30 kilometres south of the railhead Atlantic port of Lobito. By Independence, 27% of the country's industrial work-force was employed in Benguela province, either in Benguela city, or in Lobito. Benguela's post-Independence problems began when Alves faction members gained control of the Province administration, and specifically of Party structures. After they were removed, the petty bourgeoisie – which in Benguela included agricultural small scale entrepreneurs, owners of small fishing companies and the bureaucratic élite – saw their chance to move in and take their places. Although the Party had publicly warned this could occur, it proved to be unable to prevent its occurrence in Benguela.

To understand why this happened it is necessary to examine the problem in practical terms. The manpower shortage still meant that few people were available with the minimum skills needed for running government offices. The continuing call for national unity and patriotic participation in reconstruction meant that the Party was still extending a welcoming hand to those petty bourgeois sectors which it felt could be won over to alliance with the workers.

By that time there had been enough public political education through the mass media to enable anyone reasonably intelligent and literate to appear revolutionary enough to satisfy the average Party militant. Additionally, the numerous difficulties facing administrators and executives could easily serve to excuse failures to carry out policy, or short-comings at work. These two different but related cover-ups would be used to increasingly telling effect by the petty bourgeoisie as a whole, throughout the country in the ensuing years. And it became difficult to assess where to draw the line between deliberate sabotage of Party guidelines and government policy, and *laissez-aller* or *laissez-faire* attitudes to work.

Inevitably, the Party continued to be short of experienced revolutionary cadres, and could not create them instantly. Crash courses of ideology and politics were no substitute for years of work in mass organizations and resistance. The Alves coup was a double-edged sword. If it had heightened awareness that the MPLA could be undermined from within, it also counselled caution in criticizing leaders.

In any case, the Party was a different structure from the old Movement, and until militants settled into Party life and cell activities, there was even some uncertainty as to how the new structure functioned. Although many militants had by now been rectified, bringing party cells to life was to prove a slow process. If this appears to be a fundamental contradiction, it is again necessary to recall the conditions in which the MPLA-Workers' Party was founded: after a period of only three years of legal political activity, on top of 50 years of fascism that had both crushed traditional community organization and lines of communication and prevented the development of modern industrial association and resistance.

In its report to the 1980 Extraordinary Congress, the Party Central Committee revealed that, 'there was insufficient effort put into setting up cells –

even provisional ones – during the rectification, as soon as there were sufficient members to justify doing so. This delayed the participation of rectified members in Party life.'

Neto spoke of 'breathing life' into the Party. It was, therefore, relatively simple for the Benguela petty bourgeoisie to operate against Party directives (which is what they did), without immediately facing disciplinary action.

From early 1978 onwards – even before rectification had really begun – the Party headquarters in Luanda was receiving complaints from Benguela individuals, both Party members and ordinary workers, that something was going seriously wrong. A series of surprise visits by the leadership to the Province began.

In April 1979 Neto and a team of top Party and government officials descended on the city. A communiqué noted that after the Alves faction had been dismissed a rightist group had moved in.

> This enabled infiltration into certain government sectors and even into local Party structures of élitist, colonial, anti-people ideas, against the working class, aimed at preventing it from wielding power . . . . A certain Benguela petty bourgeoisie still wants to impose its class supremacy on the basis of its scientific and technical knowledge and of its positions in the bureaucratic apparatus. It is essential to dismantle these petty bourgeois groups who are opposing the rise of the working and peasant classes in Benguela and sabotaging economic and social development, thus acting against the improvement of the people's standard of living.

Both the Benguela Province Commissioner and the Province Party committee co-ordinator (who had been appointed, as elections had not been held at the time) were dismissed and Colonel Dino Matross, FAPLA National Commissar, was appointed to head the Province, a measure of how deeply the Party was concerned at events.

Apparently, the most right-wing, privileged and élitist elements of the colonial bureaucracy had been called upon, and their appointment to senior positions justified on the grounds of their expertise and former experience. Working-class recruitment to cadre positions had been actively discouraged. This had contributed to an open climate of arrogance and superiority against workers, discernible even at street level. Workers' literacy classes had been suspended and other forms of worker education discouraged. Racism was implicitly fostered, in so far as many of the petty bourgeoisie involved in the power struggle were *mestiços*, and the workers against whom they struggled were black.

The situation in Benguela was corrected; but it was a sharp reminder that the country had entered upon a new phase in the class struggle. It was no longer a theoretical concept, neither was it 'decreed from above', as it had seemed to some West European Communist delegates attending the MPLA-Workers' Party founding Congress. Class struggle in Angola was now being consciously waged on a mass level.

The 1979 Political Bureau May Day statement focused sharply on this intensifying class struggle.

> The constant deepening of the popular and revolutionary content of our options has inevitably resulted in the increasingly clear delimitation of the various social groups – on one side, the working class, leading force of our revolution, with its scientific ideology, allied to the peasant class and other workers dedicated to the proletarian cause: and on the other side the petty bourgeoisie which, in its growing eagerness to take the place of the colonial bourgeoisie at various levels, is adopting various means to prevent the rise of the working class and of its ideology, to leadership of the country. [The petty bourgeoisie] is assuming the ideological and moral values of capitalism – disdain for the working class, failure to solve the concrete problems of the masses, love of luxury and the easy life, the spirit of ostentatiousness, negligence, political and economic corruption, opportunism, spreading of obscurantist and superstitious ideas – in a word, all the retrograde moral values of the enemy.

This was all quite accurate and perceptible during 1979. At the top, the growing relations with capitalist multinationals – the oil industry was the most obvious example, but other big conglomerates were also signing contracts – meant the government had to some extent given its approval to the infiltration of Western technology, and reactionaries were quick to take advantage of this and deride the achievements of the socialist countries. Since most Angolans had never travelled outside Angola, it was difficult to engage in helpful or enlightening debate on the issue. Party militants were convinced that the Volvos belonging to the Western technicians and diplomats were better than the Soviet embassy's official cars; all Westerners were kind and friendly, and anxious to distribute perquisites.

The new managers of Angolan-controlled factories were not chosen for their Party membership, many were petty bourgeois caught in the wages squeeze and rising inflation and had begun black marketeering with factory output. By this time, workers had achieved a measure of control over the factory, there were worker cadres on inventory work, and militias on the gate searching vehicles and demanding documents, consequently the black marketeers had increasingly to corrupt and involve workers if they were to succeed.

Reorganization of internal trade had taken place after the coup sabotage, and fresh contracts for food imports, fuelled by plentiful foreign exchange, had been signed. Better food then became available in shops in the cities than ever before since Independence, but there were still acute shortages of consumer durables and industrial goods. The petty bourgeoisie wanted more cash, it was beginning to feel the effects of Party policy to keep salary scales within narrow limits. Wages per month were around Kwanzas 3,500 for an unskilled worker to Kwanzas 20,000 for a top ranking government Minister (Party workers were paid low wages, with heads of department earning around Kwanzas 14,000 per month). On the MPLA's instructions the government had also removed the colonial civil service allowances (which had benefited only the petty bourgeoisie), and substituted universal family allowances, which were of particular benefit to working class families.

Petty bourgeois housewives were carrying out a lucrative trade from their backrooms, in black market goods secured by them or their husbands, or in articles they made themselves from black market materials. Petty bourgeois black marketeering spread gradually into the working class .

In condemning the reactionaries the Party was careful to add:

> There are sectors of the petty bourgeoisie who, although they have not rejected their class origin or position, are still today acting in a progressive way and contributing to the defence of the interests of the working class, placing their political, technical and scientific expertise at the service of national reconstruction, of organization and functioning of the state and of state firms, thus working for the creation of the material foundations of socialism.

Some working class and peasant members of society, it said, are 'no less guilty than the petty bourgeoisie of adopting petty bourgeois behaviour'.

The Black Market and the Party

The black market was in many ways the most intractable problem the Party faced. There was a clear understanding that until production could be increased and shortages eliminated, some form of black market would continue to exist. Perhaps this understanding led to an over-tolerant attitude by the leaders, or perhaps to attempt repression would have been futile until increased production could encourage a campaign against the black marketeers. In 1979 the situation was out of control, and in 1981, when imports of basic goods were sharply cut back owing to the decline in foreign exchange earnings (the decrease of oil price was largely responsible), the black market's hold over lives of the city people was further reinforced.

The Party, especially through the mass organizations, repeatedly attempted to engage the mass of working people in an anti-black market campaign. Government-fixed prices would perhaps have been more effective in the market, on fish, fruit and vegetables, if the government's inspectors had been backed by angry housewives. Faced by a consumer boycott, the market women might have brought down their prices. This did not happen. Instead, there were periodic campaigns by inspectors, police and the people's militias, that resulted in a temporary observance of the official prices, while a token number of petty traders were gaoled. But since there was often no alternative way to obtain many goods, the black marketeers never lost their customers, although on occasion they priced themselves out of the market.

The Party instituted controlled rationing, in favour of workers, of the few consumer durables and industrial goods available, through ration cards issued at places of work. It also improved workers' incentives by instituting Campaigns of Socialist Emulation, in charge of UNTA, in which factories and offices participated in a production campaign, with specific output targets. At the end of the Campaign, factories were graded for their record, and particularly outstanding workers were singled out for awards including material prizes such as refrigerators and other domestic appliances. If their production work was matched by correct attitudes and personal behaviour towards their colleagues, these workers were also approached by the Party for membership. By a variety of measures, the Party ensured that workers obtained a good share of the few luxuries that were available. In turn, the petty bourgeoisie intensified its manoeuvres and black market operations to steer these goods away from the state's outlets, and prevent them falling in to the hands of the workers. For example, at a trial held in a Luanda court in 1982 one Angolan was convicted of having appropriated millions of Kwanzas worth of television sets, which he had sold, at personal profit, to friends.

The Party as Privileged Élite

From the Party's commitment to building its ranks with workers who would lead the country, it was clear that these men and women were the new élite; inevitably, opportunists rushed to enter the organization. What improved conditions could they expect from Party membership?

There were two types of Party membership: members who were full-time Party workers, and those who held ordinary jobs. The latter had no special material privileges: they were paid the same wages as other workers, they shopped at the same shops, and the burden of Party work actually meant they had less free time, since party cell meetings took place outside normal working hours.

Party membership did hold out the promise of reaching higher positions in your profession, but this was not guaranteed. In 1982, many top administrative and technical jobs were still held by non-Party cadres, and there were very few posts which required Party membership. Cabinet ministers were members, but not their top civil servants who earned virtually the same salaries and shopped in the same 'leaders shops', a series of food and industrial goods stores reserved for senior civil servants and state appointed posts.* Participation in official delegations, on sought after visits overseas, was not

*These shops were justified on the grounds that they provided material incentives for skilled cadres and officials to stay on in Angola, at a time when conditions were difficult and people not seriously committed to building socialism might have left the country.

limited to Party members. In 1981, the Oil Ministry, which constantly sent delegations overseas, had only two Party members and thus not even a cell (a minimum of three Party members was required for forming a party cell).

Full-time Party workers were in a slightly different position. Those working at Party headquarters in Luanda had a separate food shop, which though similar to People's Shops occasionally stocked extra goods. This privilege became an easy target for criticism disproportionate to the service it rendered. Full-time Party workers could expect to be paid the lowest salaries at whatever civil service scale they were classified, to work longer hours and unpaid overtime. It was hoped in this way to discourage opportunists and to set an example.

By 1982 Party patronage, though not Party membership, was necessary in order to be appointed to a senior post. At lower levels, the importance of patronage from the Party depended on how strongly it was functioning in an individual's place of work. For example, in factories, cells operated that, along with the mass organizations (UNTA in particular), could vet workers' promotions. But in offices, especially in the civil service, the Party's influence over promotions at low and medium grades was fairly weak.

There was a distinct shift in the Party's choice of cadres in the 1980s. A spate of political appointments by Neto had been criticized on the grounds that people had been given jobs for which they were technically incompetent. This had not only created problems in national reconstruction, but had led to some ridicule of the Party and its stand on working class advancement. President José Eduardo dos Santos and the Political Bureau consequently took a rather different approach, placing non-Party technicians in more senior positions, and relying on improved control by the Party over implementation of its guidelines and the increased accountability demanded from all top executives.

The Party and Security

It was difficult to tackle the problem of security in a country that was still fighting external aggression and destabilization, (which involved some Angolans), and at the same time heal the wounds of the country's brief, tribal Balkanization as well as those inflicted by the war. The MPLA was committed to a people's security service, and to mobilizing the working people to defend the revolution. Ultimately, the security of the revolution would depend on the FAPLA, as far as conventional defence went, and on the hundreds of thousands of armed militias. If either force became dissidents and turned their guns on the Party, the Party would be crushed.

But a conventional security service also had to be built up. It was subject to the same political education as applied to the FAPLA, and its members were drawn from all classes. It was partially infiltrated by the Alves faction and used by them to arrest those who got in their way.

Neto, however, received so many reports of abuses by the DISA that he dismantled it, and instead created two new Ministries: in July 1979 he appointed Central Committee member Kundi Paihama as Minister of a new Ministry of State Security, and placed Major Alexandre Rodrigues at the head of a new Ministry of the Interior which was responsible for the police force and internal law and order. A number of specific measures were taken to limit the powers of the security services, including a ban on house searches between dusk and dawn, and the right of citizens to demand to be shown a search warrant. Neto also set up a special Office of Public Prosecutions to act as Ombudsman and respond to individual complaints against state or government.

While Neto, as head of state and of government, announced these innovations, they had been decided collectively at Political Bureau or Central Committee level, by the Party leadership.

The Party and the Mass Media

Before Independence, Angola's mass media had included a national radio station, regional commercial radio programmes, and privately owned national and local newspapers and magazines. There was also a Church radio '*Radio Eclesia*' run by the Catholic Church. Until 25 April 1974, the mass media had been under rigid official censorship by members of the fascist government who were specifically appointed to the task. Black journalists were unheard of, white journalists either muzzled themselves or were convinced fascists. The papers reflected an apartheid society, white faces on the beaches, in the nightclubs, in theatre advertisements and at social functions. Few exiled Angolans entered journalism or studied mass media development. Anibal de Melo, the Movement's representative in Zambia in the late 1960s, had written for journals, but most MPLA writers were poets and novelists rather than pamphleteers.

During the transition period, the mass media opened their columns to readers' letters, and these soon provided the most radical material. Until the last days of the transition government and the massive August-September 1975 exodus of whites from Angola, journalists remained much the same individuals who had accommodated their writing to fascist diktat. The MPLA's fight to have its views expressed, several times led to the arrest or even torture of its media personnel.

As the settlers fled, so too did the newspaper proprietors and backers of the commercial radio stations. After Independence, the commercial stations were incorporated as regional stations of the national broadcasting network, *Radio Nacional de Angola*, which operated from around 5 am to midnight on two channels, mainly in Portuguese but in all principal Angolan languages too. The new state reserved a broadcasting monopoly, though it allowed the Catholic Radio station to continue until 25 January 1978 when it was closed down in response to a vicious attack on the government by the Catholic hierarchy.

A handful of media technicians was able to maintain radio broadcasting, and in a nation of mainly illiterate people this was the most important medium. A shortage of receivers restricted the influence of radio, as later did continual problems of acquiring batteries for transistor sets. Nevertheless, news still travelled faster and more widely by radio than it did by the written word. Copies of the national newspaper were distributed by the national airline's freight service to province capitals, but they rarely circulated beyond. Television, in a pilot stage before Independence, was launched in Luanda and extended to Benguela and Lobito. Cinema was not nationalized and a Board was set up, similar to the British Board of Film Censors, to preview all films brought in by the Portuguese distributing companies. Pornography, racism and extreme violence were banned from the screen.

The Party's influence on the daily newspaper was stronger in theory than in practice. Young, inexperienced journalists were unable to provide efficient news coverage and for the first few years the quality of national reporting was low, owing to technical reasons. The young journalists were hampered by a low cultural, general knowledge, as well as by their petty bourgeois city lifestyles which had not fitted them to understand national issues or to put much effort into improving that understanding. Political activists had constantly to insist that the news relating to rural Angolans should be adequately covered and their viewpoint represented, while in the cities, workers' problems and culture, not the concerns and aspirations of the petty bourgeoisie, were of prime relevance. A programme of recruiting voluntary, part-time correspondents in the countryside to contribute to fuller reporting of national events was successful.

Not until 1982, did the Party finally hold a seminar on information to debate the shortcomings of the mass media and the propaganda work of the Party itself. The seminar was frankly critical of past performance and singled out lack of co-operation by the authorities to improve reporting standards, as well as the generally low level of journalists' expertise, as fundamental impediments that had to be rectified. The newspaper's opinion columns all too frequently provided the sharpest and most constructive criticism of society, and the best written prose. This was encouraging, since clearly, people felt free to express stronger views than the newspaper staff seemed inclined to write; it also reflected the lack of lively and vigorous performance by the national press' staff. A national magazine *Novembro* and many other journals were also being published by the trades unions, by the armed forces, by literacy centres and different economic sectors – oil, agriculture, social affairs – with the aim of educating and informing their workers.

The Party was strongly critical of these shortcomings. Wherever strong and creative Party influence was felt, there was good media work. One example was the National Cinema which had produced a series of documentaries and was discussing the production of its first two feature films, to be based on novels by two Angolan writers. Both works were wide-ranging examinations of the problems of post-Independence Angolan society, the role of the Party, the quality of its members, and the material difficulties that accompanied Independence.

The Party and the New Society

While it was leading the way towards the new society, the Party and its members still reflected the divergent cultural and political trends and values in post-Independence society. In no sense was it a homogenous, or monolithic group of men and women. Party members diverged sharply on details in relation to the kind of new society it was desirable to build in Angola, even though everyone agreed on the broad lines of improved health and education, better housing and equal job opportunities for all.

The question of the women's role was largely controversial and the Party succeeded in supporting the women's movement through specific government action on work-related issues, rather than in launching ideological or political confrontation. Traditional customs were another source of potential conflict within the Party. It was easy to announce that good, positive customs should continue and bad, retrograde ones wither away. But to go to battle over the bride price, or the loss of working hours caused by traditional attendance at three day funeral wakes was less easy, and the Party made no attempt to do so.

Instead of trying to enforce desirable attitudes by decree or repressing activities that were ideologically in conflict with its principles, the Party relied on literacy, education and the direct experience of organization for the advancement of the workers and peasants' cause to gradually evoke changed attitudes. Contact with the outside world, as well as with foreigners in the country, also broadened the vision of the Angolan people.

The Party and the Church

Angola's Methodist Bishop, a strong supporter of the MPLA Movement, and an active member of the World Council of Churches, likes to draw attention to those leading members of the new state who are practising Christians, and the number of the MPLA-Workers' Party leaders who were educated in religious institutions. He travels a great deal on international church conferences, and battled almost single-handed in the early years of Independence to prove to anxious Christians outside Angola that the promise in the MPLA's Constitution, that freedom of conscience and freedom to worship would be observed, was a reality.

The Protestant Church early on rose to the challenge launched by the MPLA for 'frank ideological struggle'. It accepted the fact that Jesus Christ was not born in Africa any more than Marx or Lenin, but that they each had a universal message to propound.

The Catholic Church's attitude was quite different. Under colonial rule it had been sharply divided. The Catholic hierarchy was closely bound to the fascist state. Luanda's Archiepiscopal seat was an integral part of the Governor's Palace and the link was more than symbolic. Leading churchmen were almost all white Portuguese, and most of the Church's effort was expended on the settler community. But within the official Church, and more especially in the separate Catholic Missions, many men and women were angry and ashamed at the hierarchy's fascist politics and its disregard for the African masses. As the colonial war sharpened contradictions in the society, so it did in the ranks of the Catholic Church. The most notable battle against the hierarchy was fought by the Basque Fathers of Malanje, with the firm support of their superiors in Spain. They drew up critical documents proposing new and different uses of their Mission funds in the diocese and discussions within the Church regarding what its role should be towards the most impoverished and oppressed section of the community. They met inflexible opposition from their local Bishop, who, interestingly, was promoted Archbishop of Angola after Independence, as the country's only black Bishop. Rather than welcome Independence and the MPLA's vision of a new society, the Catholic hierarchy under his leadership first proceeded to wreak revenge on their internal opponents.

The Basque Fathers were a main target. Like many other priests and missionaries they had recognized the MPLA's principled rule and enthusiastically set to work to help in national reconstruction.* The Archbishop denied them the right to administer Holy Communion, without which a Mission cannot function; it was tantamount to an order from the Church for the Basques to be expelled. The Fathers went to the MPLA and set out their case: they had unanimously agreed that their place was in Angola, and that they should remain and continue with their work even without the right to dispense Mass. They appealed to the Movement to allow them to stay on; after consideration the Political Bureau agreed to do so.

The Catholic hierarchy now drafted a Pastoral Letter at a meeting in Lubango in December 1977. It was read in Catholic churches around the country on 8 January 1978, and taken up overseas. On 21 January Vatican Radio reported:

> The Bishops in Angola have protested about the frequent and lamentable violations of religious freedom in the People's Republic of Angola . . . . The Angolan Bishops say that Catholics – half the population – suffered discrimination for their beliefs and often lost the custody of their children.

Lucio Lara stated that the first information the MPLA received of the Bishops' complaints was a report in a right-wing Portuguese newspaper. The Pastoral Letter, which one Western diplomat described as 'fuller of vitriol than of holy water' had complained that church property was being systematically damaged and altars profaned, that children were being taken away

*They had assisted the peasants co-operative movement and provided expertise to operate tractors previously the property of local settler landlords.

from their parents without parental authority to study abroad at the risk of their faith, that Marxism and materialist philosophy would bring dire consequences.

These slanders brought a strong response from Lucio Lara. At a public rally in Beguela, he rejected the Pastoral Letter as 'an insult to the dignity of our people, our government and the MPLA-Workers' Party'. Isolated incidents of disrespect for Church property were neither condoned nor authorized, and such incidents had arisen from situations of war. He pointed out that scholarships offered to hundreds of Angolan school children overseas, notably in Cuba, had been accepted by the government because of the shortages of schools and teachers at home. As for the Bishops' claim that Angolan vernacular languages were not being encouraged, the MPLA had been encouraging them in literacy programmes in the liberated areas. Marxism-Leninism's values were no more foreign or alien to Angola than Christianity, 'Does the Bible say that Christ was born here?'

The Bishops' attitude prompted government closure of the Catholic radio station, established under the concordat between the fascist state and the Catholic Church. It had been allowed to continue for over two years after Independence.

The hierarchy's attitude became more subdued as it was forced to admit that religious freedom was a fact of life under the Party. Although religious teaching was now undertaken outside normal school hours, as in such other countries as France, where church and state are separate, Sunday Schools continued to be full, as did the churches, and although the Church had lost the prestige it acquired from the fascist state, this by no means weakened it spiritually.

Priests and missionaries, who were on good terms with the MPLA authorities, frankly rejoiced that Angola was now turned towards helping the masses of its people. Many spoke movingly of their silent anger under fascism, and their sympathy for church people working against apartheid in South Africa.

In 1982 the Angolan Council of Churches organized prayer meetings to commemorate the 1976 Soweto uprisings and 26 June, South Africa's Freedom Day, in conjunction with members of the African National Congress. The Catholic hierarchy was conspicuously absent.

Neto's Death

In August 1979 Neto went on a tour of the provinces; he was clearly tired and apparently ill. In speeches in Malanje and Uije on 21 and 22 August, he apologized for the hoarseness and weakness of his voice. He seemed to be outlining what he saw as the most important issues for the country and returned repeatedly to the theme of People's Power: 'We lack People's Assemblies, in order to have a People's National Assembly in which the workers and peasants will be properly represented. Until this happens, we will not have sufficient control over the state institutions' he told a mass rally of peasants in Malanje. He also spoke of his view of socialism, and of the urgent need to recruit more working-class members for the Party 'the execution of what we call the daily tasks of the militant can by no means be guaranteed solely by revolutionary intellectuals. There must be a majority of workers and peasants in the Party apparatus to ensure we carry out our watchwords'. Neto also stressed his earlier theme 'the most important thing is to solve the people's problems', and spoke frankly of the material shortages that afflicted the young republic.

At one point, he seemed almost to be bidding his people farewell: 'The revolution is continuing. The revolution will triumph. Some of us may go. Some of us will be liquidated at the next corner. But the revolution will continue.'

In early September Neto and his wife, Maria Eugenia, left for Moscow on what was officially described as a private, friendly visit. He went, in fact, for medical treatment. Emergency surgery was performed on 8 September. Agostinho Neto died on 10 September.

The medical report on Neto's death, signed by eight leading Soviet physicians and his personal physician from Angola, Dr Eduardo Macedo dos Santos, stated that the surgical operation confirmed serious lesions of the liver and a tumour of the pancreas. As a trained medical doctor himself, Neto had no doubt evaluated his own condition and may have understood that his death was near when he chose to embark on what was his last visit to provincial Angola.

The Central Committee was unaware of the seriousness of Neto's condition. News of his death stunned the country and was followed by an outpouring of grief. Men, women and children wept in the street, and when Neto's body was brought back thousands flocked to greet the coffin and the state funeral ceremony, dignified and solemn though it was, expressed national anguish.

Forty-five days of national mourning was decreed by the Central Committee's Political Bureau, and planning began for a mausoleum to Angola's first President and political leader. The succession was conducted in accordance with Party statutes. On 21 September 1979 José Eduardo dos Santos, whom Neto had designated to take charge of the Angolan government in his absence, was elected as President of the MPLA-Workers' Party by the Central Committee, 'unanimously and by strong acclamation'. Under the terms of the Constitution he thereby became President of the People's Republic of Angola.

At his investiture as Head of State he swore 'to struggle for strengthened national unity, for the fulfilment of the worker-peasant alliance and for the building of people's power'.

The new Party leader was a young man of 37, the son of a bricklayer from Luanda, who had joined the MPLA in his teens and left for military training in the ranks of the guerrillas. Later, he studied in the Soviet Union and graduated in petroleum engineering at Baku in 1969. After a military telecommunications course he joined the Cabinda guerrilla front telecommunications unit and had been elected to the Central Committee and Political Bureau at the September 1974 Inter-Regional Conference of Militants.

Building People's Power

The new President appointed Pedro Maria Tonha 'Pedalé' as Central Committee Secretary for Provincial Control, moving Roberto de Almeida to the post of Secretary for Economic Development and Planning, and later Minister of Planning. In November, he announced a partial reshuffle of government portfolios, bringing Lopo do Nascimento back as Foreign Trade Minister. In December, Defence Minister Iko Carreira left Angola to study in the Soviet Union (he returned in mid-1982), resigning his seat on the Political Bureau executive, which was taken by Dino Matross.

From 1979 until the 1980 Party Congress, the Party's main task was to build people's power institutions. Rectification was still proceeding, but the first recruitment of members for the new Party was complete, and the leadership lost no time in moving on to create the structures of control and mass participation envisaged under People's Power.

1980 was designated 'Year of the First Extraordinary Congress and of the Creation of the People's Assembly'. The new institutions would eventually rise from grass-roots local assemblies at village and urban district council level, to Provincial Assemblies, and finally the 'People's Assembly' or national house of parliament.

In August 1980, the Constitution was amended to replace the Council of the Revolution by the People's Assembly. A commission, chaired by Bernardo de Sousa, Secretary of the Central Committee for the Department of Institution of People's Power, proposed that the Assembly should have 206 deputies and Provincial Assemblies from 55-85 deputies, with proportional representation in the People's Assembly.

Article 34 of the revised Constitution now states: 'The deputies are representatives of all the people without any distinction based on race, social class or religious, ideological or political status.' Article 37 states: 'The People's Assembly shall promote the execution of the objectives of the People's Republic of Angola as defined by the MPLA-Workers' Party.' The Assembly has power 'to authorize the President of the Republic to declare war and to make peace'.

The People's Assembly is composed of ordinary working people who hold other jobs and for whom the task of being a deputy is not a full-time occupation. Consequently it meets only twice a year in ordinary session, but it can be called into extraordinary session by the President, the Central Committee or its own permanent commission, or at the request of one third of its own deputies. Sessions are held in public except in extraordinary circumstances; they have been televised and broadcast live since the Assembly began work. The quorum for an assembly debate is over half of its members, and decision is by simple majority of those present, with the exception of constitutional changes, which require a two thirds majority of all deputies. Between sessions, Assembly work is carried on by a permanent commission of the President of the Republic, deputies who are members of the Political Bureau and 11 deputies elected by the Assembly on the recommendation of the Central Committee.

When the Political Bureau launched the election process in February 1980 it tried to clarify how the People's Power institutions would be related to the supremacy of the Marxist-Leninist Party. After all the Alves faction experience was still very much present in most people's minds. The Political Bureau declared that the Party leads the building of a democratic state 'where the working class have a direct and organized role in the exercise of power from the grass-roots to the commanding heights'. It cautioned:

> In order for the content and aims of the process of building people's power not to be warped, the Party must be sufficiently well organized and coherent at all levels and throughout the country so as to be able to lead the process, that demands a continuing work of clarifying, mobilizing and organizing the broad masses.

The Central Committee in criticizing the first People's Power Law for 'petty bourgeois tendencies' had reported to the First Party Congress that:

> the term people's power expresses a new concept of the essence and role of power, of the new relations of the masses of the people to power, and contributes to the mobilizing of the masses to transform society . . . . As Lenin said, the question of state power cannot be evaded or set aside since it is the basic question which decides everything in the development of the revolution . . . . The State apparatus is the principle instrument in the hands of the working class under the leadership of the party, to achieve its political domination and the exercise of people's power. The State apparatus represents the power of the people which means that the organs of people power cannot exist outside it, separate from the state apparatus. The organs of the state apparatus are themselves the organs of people's power.

Reflecting on the mistakes made during the 1976 elections for people's power, the Central Committee said:

> the third plenary of the Central Committee analyzed past mistakes and decided that elections should be held only where the structures of the movement are sufficiently strong and stable organizationally and where they are mature politically and ideologically. This is because the process of establishing people's power where socialism is being built, is a function of the revolutionary vanguard and not just of the state.

The former people's power law had been guilty of presenting people's power 'as a mass struggle which could also be used against the Party'.

What was the essential meaning of all this? Lucio Lara explained: the People's Assembly would not be under direct instructions from the Party. Party members elected to the Assembly would 'seek to influence debate'. There would be no organic link between Assembly and Party 'nor should there be'. Candidates for the top assembly were proposed by the Party, by the Party Youth JMPLA, and by the mass organizations, OMA for the women and UNTA for the trade unions.

During the campaign, Bernardo de Sousa warned that opportunists would again be active trying to be nominated as candidates.

> We are working to set up people's power so the people will have confidence in the Party and so that our people can become part of the structures and help the government to work towards serving mass interests better [but] we must be vigilant against those wanting to infiltrate the people's power organizations and become the most talked about deputies.

Why was the Party starting with the top of the people's power pyramid, instead of the grass-roots assemblies? One reason given was the absence of any reliable population statistics until after the 1983 Census* which made electoral rolls impossible to draw up. Equally there were delays in rectification of Party members in rural areas, which meant that some areas would be unable to fulfil the Party's basic stipulation of minimum Party organization and function before the elections were launched.

In the Central Committee's view, the establishment of people's power required, 'qualitative changes in the political ideological and organizational spheres, required the creation of a Marxist-Leninist party and its consolidation and development on a national scale, as well as the structuring of the mass organizations.'

The first elections were for the People's Assembly (national) and these were followed by elections for the Provincial Assemblies. There was not direct suffrage but the mass of electors voted for an electoral college; the college then voted for the list of candidates. However, candidates did have to be approved by workers and peasants assemblies, where they were presented and their lives and records discussed by all Angolans who wished to attend.

The electoral colleges were elected in places of work, by state economic units and co-operatives, military units and other institutions chosen by the Provincial Party committees and Provincial Commissions (generally places of work where unionization was strong). While, in practice, this meant that not every Angolan over the age of 18 actually cast a vote, it did ensure

*The last census was taken in 1970.

that the majority of assemblies deputies were workers and peasants. The social breakdown of the province assemblies was reported to be 40% workers, 30% peasants with 10% each for three other groups – combatants and security workers, workers in the state machinery, and intellectuals. The National Assembly is a rather different body: one third (31%) of its 203 deputies are political and administrative leaders (in a sense, the former Council of the Revolution); 29% are workers, 24% peasants, 10% defence and security workers, 3% intellectuals and 3% workers from the state machinery.

Before his death, Neto stressed that the fundamental role of the People's Power assemblies would be to demand accountability from the government and the state machinery.

This was long overdue, and the Party had frequently called for greater individual responsibility and accountability from government leaders and workers. The question asked by deputies during the first sessions of both province and people's assemblies were closely related to urgent material problems afflicting workers and peasants. Many Party cadres felt that the Assembly, with its access to publicity and opportunity in public to attack inefficient leaders, would provide the pressure necessary to invoke change that the Party itself was not always able to apply successfully. In its report to the 1980 Special Congress, the Party Central Committee stated the problem it faced in trying to lead and control the government and state:

> On the one hand there are sometimes shortcomings in the leadership activity of higher Party organs, which stem from the fact that the present structure of the Secretariat does not allow for day to day control of implementation of the Party's general policy because of accumulation of tasks by its members and the poor ideological technical and professional level of some cadres in the Secretariat's supporting structures. On the other hand, State bodies sometimes ignore the guiding and supervisory role of the Party, which leads to people losing sight of the priority tasks laid down, and prevents the timely introduction of necessary corrections in government activity.

The Assemblies did not serve simply as a rubber stamp: draft legislation was hotly debated and amended; Province assemblies took their role of control over economic and government action seriously. But President José Eduardo dos Santos, as head of the national People's Assembly was clearly of the opinion that more could be done. In 1982, after the assemblies had been functioning for a year, he rebuked deputies, and suggested that if they concern themselves more closely with people's problems, the standard of debate might be elevated further.

Continuing Rectification and the 1980 Special Congress

Convened under the banner of the struggle for economic independence, the 1980 Special Congress, held in December, had two main tasks: to rectify the economic targets set by the First Congress – now revealed to be unrealistically high – and set guidelines for economic development over the next five years; and politically, to elect more working-class membership to the Central Committee. The 1977 Congress' decision to postpone the ballot for the full complement of members, had been specifically in order to give working-class members a chance of election. The rule of eight years militancy as a condition of candidacy was amended to five years for working-class members. Those who had joined the Movement in 1975 were now eligible to stand for election to the top Party body.

The Congress itself had 463 delegates, compared with 300 in 1977. With 160 elected by provincial militants conferences, 89 others by Provincial Party committees, over half the delegates now came from provincial structures, by election rather than nomination. The FAPLA elected 52 delegates, a smaller share than in the first Congress, while the trade unions were given a larger share of the delegates: six from the Trade Union Congress General Secretariat and ten more from trade unions themselves. The Women's Organization had six delegates, plus 40 women elected as ordinary delegates along with the men. The Congress Mandates Commission reported that 57% of the Congress delegates were members of the MPLA from the period 1974-77. Only 17% had joined between 1956-61 and 25% were recruits from the period after the armed struggle was launched and until the 1974 Armed Forces coup.

The strong representation of new members made for lively criticism and debate. The youth in particular, many incorporated in the FAPLA representation, strongly attacked those older leaders whose life style they considered did not contribute to the fulfilment of their revolutionary tasks. Rectification of members had resumed in May 1980, when, as Co-ordinator of the National Preparatory Commission for the forthcoming Congress, Lucio Lara had spoken of the need to purify the party ranks.

> Some people who were approved during Rectification do not deserve to be Party members. Worse still, some were cleverly and energetically able to get themselves elected as grass-roots organizers, but have proven to be poor militants. There must be much greater vigilance and political courage shown by other grass-roots militants to stop these individuals from continuing to monopolize responsible positions or to continue as delegates of various different levels of assemblies.

Meetings were begun at cell level, and later at provincial level, to examine the practical work undertaken by the Party cells and to review membership.

The Special Congress and continuing rectification after it, enshrined the principle of a permanent review of the Party's membership. It also elected more working-class members to the Central Committee, though the majority of the successful new candidates were of rural, peasant stock.

The Transition to Socialism

By 1982, a lively class struggle was underway everywhere in Angola where people met to work together: in offices and factories, in the countryside and in the towns, in schools and university. The new society was being forged as growing numbers of workers and peasants joined the ranks of the literate and organized. Was this the transition to socialism promised by the MPLA?

The crucial question for the theoreticians examining Angola was whether such a backward and economically underdeveloped society could in one bound leap from colonial capitalism to building socialism, thus bypassing what Marx had propounded as an inevitable period of building capitalism. For the Angolans themselves, certainly in the Party leadership, the question was how it was possible to achieve the transition to socialism without undergoing a phase of capitalism – a phase that the masses of people could not afford. The MPLA calculated that it would result in the kind of anarchy and corruption typical of Zaire, Ivory Coast or Zambia, where international monopoly capitalism creamed off the important profits, and the rest was manipulated into the pockets of small scale national operatives, with possibly the addition of a section of expatriates, exploiting African labour as they had done before independence.

The MPLA set out to enter the transition to socialism by creating a Marxist-Leninist vanguard Party of the working class, establishing the foundations of a People's Democracy with elections for the workers and peasants assemblies, and ensuring that all practical measures taken by the government and state 'in the political, organizational, ideological, economic and social fields are directed towards achieving the tasks of the People's Democratic Revolution'.

The socialist sector of the economy had been continuously expanded, the social policies of the government were in marked contrast to previous colonial discrimination, and had increased ordinary people's access to education and health care, although inevitably much remained to be done.

By 1982 the revolution was being defended by a million workers and peasants, armed with weapons ranging from MiGs to Mausers, in the FAPLA and in the militias. The commanding heights of state power were in their hands.

10. Counter-Revolution: UNITA

Today, the creation and support of counter-revolutionary Third World forces has become well established. The roots lie in the 1950s and the cold war policies of John Foster Dulles. Returning from a South Asian tour in 1953 he remarked 'the Western powers can gain rather than lose from an orderly development of self-government. I emphasize, however, the word orderly. Let none forget that the Kremlin uses extreme nationalism to bait the trap by which it seeks to capture the dependent peoples.' For 30 years this was to be the key to all US thinking on national liberation. There is still no sign of any change.

In the 1950s a vigorous black renaissance had developed. The national liberation movement that flowered after the Second World War brought together militants and intellectuals from America the Caribbean, and Africa.

The US Central Intelligence Agency (CIA) became active on many different fronts to undermine the mounting black radical movement. By 1955 it was involved in the promotion of black culture as a means whereby to penetrate and undermine black consciousness. When the Society for African Culture held its first congress, in December 1956 at the Sorbonne in Paris, it was attended by Mercer Cooke and his American Society for African Culture (AMSAC). *Ramparts* magazine later wrote:

> The great question during the heyday of AMSAC and other similar CIA organizations was what formal African independence would actually mean once it became a reality. And at some point the CIA decided that the development of a safe cultural nationalism was critically important to US interests in Africa. It was essential not only as a way of keeping cultural energies in line but primarily (though the two are intertwined) to channel the explosive force of nationalism itself in directions suitable to the US.

The black, cultural movement became increasingly radical. In Paris, African, US and Caribbean writers, artists and political and social scientists gathered round the journal *Présence Africaine*; in Rome, radicals organized the 1958 Congress of Negro Writers. In the United States, black Americans had begun the search for their roots, simultaneously the black civil rights movement was campaigning fiercely against institutionalized discrimination. In South Africa, open defiance of racism was on the agenda: mass protest action reached a peak as the African National Congress organized the campaigns of the 1950s when tens of thousands took to the streets regardless of danger. There were the radical movements in Ghana, Egypt, Guinea and Mali. Even Houphouet Boigny was voting with France's Communists in the French National Assembly. This prompted CIA intervention in the growing black trade union movement. Although the key CIA-backed African American Labor Center was not founded until 1964, the AFL-CIO was active in black trade unionism several years earlier, to such an extent that a 1959 British Cabinet Paper 'On Policy in Africa' added in annexe:

> The Americans are not interested in the creation in Africa of genuine trade unions. America has no labour party. Her trade union movement has been built from above by highly paid trade union bosses. As a result the American trade union leaders such as Meany can afford directly and openly to execute government and particularly CIA policy. [The aim was to] take advantage of the difficult situation in which the UK and other European powers find themselves and to replace their influence and interest by direct US machinery of the ICFTU and American contacts.

It was against this background of American black cultural and trade union penetration that Nelson Mandela wrote his 1958 article in *Liberation*. He warned that:

> American imperialism is all the more dangerous because it comes to Africa elaborately disguised. It has discarded most of the weapons of old type imperialism. The American brand of imperialism is imperialism all the same in spite of the modern clothing in which it is dressed and in spite of the sweet language spoken by its advocates and agents.

And he pointed to soaring US business investment in Africa: from £150 million in 1945 to over £660 million a decade later.

In 1960, massive, direct, armed US intervention snatched the Belgian colony from Lumumba's revolutionary forces. It was 'the opening salvo of more general US involvement in Southern Africa'. Immanuel Wallerstein considered that

> US involvement in Zaire was the launching pad of a new US attitude towards Southern Africa; Zaire was the first to flirt with the idea of drastic political realignments . . . it is rather clear that a Lumumba government securely in power would have given extensive support to an Angolan national liberation movement. The potential of such support to Angola is analogous to what Tanzania later gave FRELIMO with two differences: it would have come much earlier on and from a

> country with far more resources to throw into the fray. It could have made a considerable difference to the whole history of liberation movements in Southern Africa . . . . The US wanted what it eventually got: a politically stable, economically conservative regime in Zaire whose only true interest in Angola is to help establish there a regime of exactly the same variety. Translated into the terms of the Angolan liberation movements, this has meant obstruction of the MPLA.

When MPLA launched its 1961 armed struggle, first in Luanda, then in the north, Adlai Stevenson told the United Nations 'the United States would be remiss in its duties as a friend of Portugal if it failed to express honestly its conviction that step by step planning within Portuguese territories and its acceleration toward full self-determination is now imperative.' Angola, he said, could become another Congo if step by step planning were neglected.

Because of the backwardness of Angola's economy and class structure, and the repression practised by the fascist regime, it was not necessary to set up elaborate trade union penetration, or black entrepreneurial organizations to undermine the nationalists. Trade unions were forbidden to blacks and black entrepreneurs were extremely rare. Attention therefore centred on creating a counterweight to the People's Movement for the Liberation of Angola, founded in 1956.

UNITA: Portugal's Counter-insurgency Force

The National Union for the Total Independence of Angola – UNITA – was proclaimed on 13 March 1966 in Muangai, eastern Angola. Its founding members were a small breakaway faction from Holden Roberto's UPA-FNLA. Jonas Savimbi, its President was former UPA Secretary General and Foreign Minister of Holden's government-in-exile GRAE (*Governo Revolucionario de Angola no Exilio*).

The UPA had been formed in 1958 as *Uniao das Populacoes do Norte de Angola* (Union of the Peoples of Northern Angola – UPNA) an openly tribalist organization aiming at independence for the north and re-establishment of the old Bakongo Kingdom. When Holden attended the All-African Peoples Conference, in Accra, in December 1958, he had changed the organization's name to UPA, eliminating the northern restriction in the face of strong African criticism of tribalist politics. From 1962 he was on the CIA payroll.

Savimbi and his faction of southerners resigned from UPA in 1964. At the Cairo OAU Summit, in July 1964 Savimbi called a press conference and charged that UPA was 'in collusion with American imperialism', and was tribalist, racist and corrupt. He supported the MPLA's accusation that during the 1961 uprisings Holden had ordered the murder of Angolan contract workers from the south, who were working on northern coffee plantations.

He did not explain why, as UPA Secretary General, he had not taken action or denounced the murders at the time. He called for OAU member states to reconsider their support for UPA, and urged that instead, they should support him and his call for a Congress of Angolan Patriots.

Jonas Savimbi was highly ambitious. In August 1963 he was already building up a personal base of support in the UPA-FNLA. He told John Marcum, author of *The Angolan Revolution* that he had plans 'to build an organization loyal to himself among Ovimbundu, Chokwe and other Angolans residing in Katanga'. In the same month he sent his right hand man, Jorge Valentim, to Katanga to find recruits and take them back to UPA's Kinkuzu training camp.

Why did he not join MPLA when he left the UPA? The MPLA was already based in Brazzaville, across the river from Kinshasa, and had provided assistance to the Savimbi group, helping them to organize their escape, and providing financial support in Brazzaville. Savimbi had talks with the MPLA leadership. The MPLA was happy to welcome him as a rank and file militant, but Savimbi insisted upon an immediate position on the top MPLA policy-making body, the National Steering Committee. When this was denied him he apparently lost interest.

Perhaps this was understandable. Only three years earlier he had achieved speedy promotion to the post of Secretary General within one year of joining UPA; the mechanism of this unprecedented advance is not recorded. Savimbi had grown up in the central highlands, he was educated at the Protestant mission schools and in 1959 left Angola for Lisbon's Passos Manuel High School on an American scholarship. In 1960, with US Protestant funds, he was sent to Switzerland to study medicine at Fribourg. He joined UPA whilst at Fribourg (according to one source, on the recommendation of Tom Mboya whom he had met at a student conference). In 1961, still in Switzerland, he had been made UPA Secretary General. There is no record of Savimbi engaging in any political activities inside Angola before he left for Lisbon and Switzerland. Neither his friendly biographers, nor John Marcum, who has carried out diligent research on the subject, make mention of any political work by Savimbi in Portugal where student activists of MPLA and Portugal's own Young Communists were risking imprisonment and torture to organize student opposition to the fascist regime. Some African students allege that Savimbi was a police informer in Lisbon.

Marcum records 'As a student in Switzerland, Savimbi had always lived well,' and built up a reputation, 'as something of a playboy', a life style later pursued in Zambia at a time he was claiming to be deep inside the Angolan bush.

Other future UNITA leaders were also studying on scholarships, largely funded by US missions. Jorge Valentim was at Temple University, Jorge Sangumba at Manhattan College and later London University, Luciano Kassoma went to Michigan State University. The Swiss group included José Ndele, Toni Fernandes, Fernando Wilson, João Vahekeni and Jeronimo Wanga. Viewpoints in their student environment will have differed sharply from those in Portugal, where most MPLA supporters were studying at the same time. By the early 1960s there was a strong anti-fascist student underground in both Porto and Coimbra where most 'overseas Portuguese' went. It was not necessary to be a communist to understand the relationship between Britain, the US and Lisbon, bolstering fascist colonial rule and exploiting Portugal's national and overseas labour and resources, or to assess NATO's role in supplying arms to the fascist regime. The opening of mail, tailing, and approaches to become a PIDE informer that black students routinely underwent in Portugal were rather different to the problems facing overseas students in Fribourg, Lausanne or Michigan, living on scholarships from the American Church.

Savimbi's earliest contacts with US officials was most probably in Kinshasa, as a UPA-FNLA leader. According to Marcum's sources he was apparently on fairly intimate terms with the US Embassy there by 1963-64. Savimbi became concerned with an approach to UPA by Viriato da Cruz, an MPLA leader who had renounced the People's Movement on leftist grounds and applied for UPA membership. Marcum's sources state that Savimbi went to the US Embassy to warn them of Viriato's radicalism and suggest that they take steps to keep him out of UPA.

Following the 1964 split from UPA, after his short stay in Brazzaville Savimbi moved back to Switzerland. A few months later, in 1965 we are told he 'graduated' in Political and Social Science at the Lausanne Law Faculty (from where he derives his title of Doctor). But that summer he was in Dar-es-Salaam – the hub of liberation affairs.

The Tanzanian capital was the headquarters of the recently established OAU Liberation Committee, under Oscar Kambona, who at this time was very much engaged in the affairs of the Pan African Congress of South Africa. In 1967, Kambona fled the country to London; he reappeared in Caetano's Portugal, and in Mozambique shortly before the Armed Forces coup in 1974. Savimbi claims that he and 10 others, including Samuel Chiwale, UNITA's C-in-C spent 9 months in China in 1965 on 'intensive military training'. At what stage UNITA became an instrument of imperialist counter-revolution is a matter for speculation, but the process took place some time between 1966, when it was formed, and 1972 when Portugal's PIDE files contain letters between Savimbi and the Portuguese high command, detailing UNITA's anti-MPLA actions and joint UNITA-Portuguese plans for the future. The letters were first published by *Afrique-Asie* in 1974, and were dismissed as forgeries by UNITA. Their authenticity has since been proved by on-the-spot enquiries in Angola, in the area where UNITA operated with the Portuguese, and finally, in August 1982, correspondents in Lisbon were shown the PIDE files by the Portuguese government. They were incomplete 'in order to protect persons still living who would be implicated'. But the Savimbi correspondence was there.

Savimbi claimed to have been living in the bush from 1966 to 1974, as a guerrilla and political activist mobilizing the people and organizing communities of resistance to Portuguese rule, carrying out literacy programmes, health care programmes and collectivization of agriculture.

The Portuguese military do not mention UNITA as a military opponent in their reports. In September 1966, General Gomes de Araujo, the Defence Minister, toured Angola and reported back on MPLA's Eastern Front. He made no mention of UNITA, although the organization claimed in its first Bulletin (like all UNITA early publicity published in London) that in March it had attacked the Benguela railway, set fire to petrol pumps and destroyed many small bridges in the east.

On Christmas Day 1966 UNITA did attack the railway line and in February 1967 Savimbi was in Lusaka for talks with the Zambians, who were in a difficult position. Dependent on the railway line, Kaunda had supported the opening of an MPLA delegation under Anibal de Melo, in Lusaka in 1965, a few months after Zambia's Independence. Talks on opening MPLA's military front in the east had hinged on the MPLA agreeing not to attack the railway. Now Savimbi seemed to be involved in an attempt to gain Zambia's support in exchange for stopping attacks on the railway. Kaunda continued to support MPLA.

In February 1967 UNITA again attacked the Benguela line and in June Savimbi again arrived in Lusaka: not from the bush but from a long tour outside Angola. This time he was arrested and spent six days in prison, and was then promptly expelled. There are several accounts explaining Savimbi's unpopularity with Zambia at this time. Basil Davidson states that Kaunda was suspicious of Savimbi because he had close contacts with Simon Kapwewe, then Vice-President, but suspected of plotting to sabotage the liberation struggle. Kapwewe's subsequent career as centre-piece for destabilizing Kaunda's government, and linkman with Pretoria, leaves no doubts as to the influence he would have had on Savimbi. Savimbi's letters to the Portuguese in 1972 explicitly link UNITA with anti-government action inside Zambia designed to force a change in the Zambian government.*

John Marcum's sources criticise Savimbi's life style. An on-the-spot African observer told Marcum:

> Savimbi collected sacks of money from people inside Angola around 1967, and left with it saying he was going to buy arms. When I got to Zambia in 1968, I met a number of South African ladies with nice, big radios and other things and the name Savimbi was on every one of their lips – the presents he lavished about, what a good dancer and entertainer he was and finally he had taken off with one of them (who was married) to Cairo.

*Much later, in 1978, Agostinho Neto said Portugal had been giving military training to a group of Zambians for an eventual military coup. The Zambians were being instructed in techniques of sabotage and guerrilla warfare, and Savimbi was connected to this opposition movement.

According to Marcum it was SWAPO people who helped Savimbi 'slip back through Zambia into Angola' in June 1968. From then on, his permanent presence in the bush is even more open to doubt. Several sources say he was actually living in Zambia, furthering his ties with his Zambian friends and slipped in and out of Angola with foreign press reporters. Zambian newspapers carried a number of articles which were the only news about UNITA.*

The main written source on the UNITA thinking is Savimbi's letters to the Church. John Marcum includes a number of them in his book. In 1965 Savimbi wrote to the United Church Board for World Ministries, New York: 'this struggle is not ideological because it cannot exclude anybody. It has to unite all. Political and economic theories which are supported in atheistic attitudes do not fall in line with the feelings of Africans' beliefs.' In October 1969, and again in October 1970 he wrote to the New York missions from 'Central Base, Freeland of Angola' (an address that seemed to appeal to him since he still uses it today). Marcum relates that the letters emphasized political and not military action, there were quotations from Mao. Savimbi said 'scientific socialism' was UNITA's 'base'. UNITA was 'nationalist and anti-imperialist including anti-Soviet social-imperialist'.

From 1967-70 the UNITA claimed to be immensely successful. In 1967 Savimbi said he had 2,900 party branches and 66 military detachments in Angola, and in 1970 he said he had 'control' over one million Angolans. (This seems to be the first time Savimbi used the word 'control' vis-à-vis his compatriots.) Marcum describes Savimbi's 'exaggerated claims' and quotes a US State Department 1970 paper entitled, 'Angola: an assessment of the insurgency', in which UNITA is estimated to have 200 armed men and 'perhaps some 2,000 sympathizers' west and south of Luso.

In 1972, UNITA claimed it had 4,000 men under arms and that it was operating militarily in Bié and Huila provinces, and south to the Namibia border. The evidence is different. By this time, UNITA owed its existence solely to Portuguese support. The South Africans already knew of its agreement with Portugal, and it is therefore reasonable to assume that so did Washington and London.

The South Africans joined the Angola war in 1966. South African helicopter squadrons began cross-border patrols in that year. In 1968 an agreement gave Pretoria an air base at Kuito Kuanavale in the south-east, from which Alouette III helicopters and Cessna 185s were flown 'inside the south-east operational sector assigned to South Africa'. Quoting a State Department source, Marcum says the South Africans were 'carrying out visual and photo reconnaissance and even transported assault troops in actions both against Angolan nationalists and Namibian guerrillas'. MPLA was gaining ground in northern Kuando Kubango. Luso was surrounded by MPLA guerrillas and to

*John Stockwell later detailed how the Zambian press became a tool of the CIA propaganda war against MPLA and for UNITA in 1975 and 1976.

the south-west they were reaching Huila. Operation 'Attila' was launched against the MPLA in 1972, napalm and defoliants were used, but there was no defoliation west and south of Luso, where UNITA was.

A biography of Savimbi by his supporters: *Jonas Savimbi: um desafio à ditadura comunista em Angola* (*Jonas Savimbi: a challenge to communist dictatorship in Angola*), states that 1968 was UNITA's 'worst year'. They cite the MPLA's strength in the east, describe many desertions from UNITA and refer to a certain Castro Bango who 'tried to betray Savimbi's camp' in 1969. The result, they say, was a Portuguese offensive; PIDE rounded up 300 Luso supporters of Savimbi. Then

> more or less at this period Savimbi received a letter from Dr Sao José Lopes, then head of PIDE in Angola, proposing a meeting in a place to be selected in the eastern bushland . . . . The UNITA leader ignored the content of such a strange proposition. He never replied.

The biographers next refer to Savimbi's combat plans which, we are told, 'were intercepted by PIDE agents while on their way by messenger from him to the operational units'.

A Spanish missionary priest, who had been in Angola since the early 1960s, worked at Ringoma, near the Cuanza river, and served another parish further east at Umpulo. This was the area in which UNITA collaborated with the Portuguese to bar the westwards advance of MPLA's guerrillas. The priest reported 'there is no doubt whatsoever that the Portuguese had an agreement with UNITA to act as a buffer'. He recalled that:

> MPLA found it difficult to move in westwards, they only had a fairly weak presence in Bié province, and were under constant attack by the Portuguese forces who clearly dominated Bié, and by UNITA. On the other hand, UNITA were left alone by the Portuguese. In conversations with Portuguese officials and district officers from 1968 onwards, they clearly let it be understood they had an arrangement with UNITA. They told me Portuguese troops were under orders not to attack UNITA bases, not to cross such and such a river as this was a UNITA area. The dividing line between the MPLA and the Portuguese was the UNITA and roughly the last defensive line UNITA was supposed to hold was the Cuanza river.

In a Memorandum addressed to General Luz Cunha and dated 26 September 1972, Savimbi writes:

> however far off the final solution may be, we are sure the authorities are already in a victorious position thanks to the enormous means at their disposal . . . thanks to the policy of renewal within continuity practised by the government . . . . As far as we are concerned we want the decisive eradication of war in this eastern sector. We have done

> everything we could to weaken the forces of the common enemy . . . . Our analysis leads us to conclude MPLA is the main obstacle to peace not only in the east but right across Angola.

Later, after considerations of OAU politics and some information about UNITA action in Zambia, he continues:

> Whatever the government's intentions, we shall never make the mistake of taking up arms against the authorities. We shall use them to the full so that the MPLA will be forced, one day, to abandon the east. Peace in the east in our view should take the following into account:
> a) Weakening until liquidation of MPLA forces inside Angola. This task can be carried out by the joint efforts of the military forces, the militarized forces and the UNITA forces.
> b) Liquidation of MPLA camps in frontier regions in Zambia. This could more easily be carried out by UNITA as we have no political status which would allow for proceedings against us in the international courts. Our plans have already passed the drawing board stage . . . .
> c) Launching discredit against MPLA . . . . Here we are targeting the OAU itself. Once the MPLA is weakened or destroyed in the east, the way will be open towards broader horizons for us.
>
> Thank you for the official note from the Portuguese Government dated 4 July 1972. UNITA will try to reach an agreement with the Moxico authorities to facilitate transit of these persons between the UNITA regions and the district offices without the people running undue risks.

Savimbi then goes on to give a glimpse into the future:

> I maintain my philosophy until today, that is that the mass surrender of our population and their leaders can only be a partial aspect of the solution to the problems that are seriously affecting peace in Angola. For me, it is the existence of a force that can combat those who cause us all these various horrors at all levels without limits imposed by international conventions, that can in the long term be a most useful factor for the nation's government. There is nothing better to fight a subtle enemy like the MPLA, supported by a whole range of influence, than to know the enemy and its sources of strength at their very source. Nobody will be better placed than ourselves to know with 80% certainty what is going on at the OAU, in Zambia, in Tanzania, within MPLA, once all our UNITA people will have taken up their posts.

Savimbi then details some anti-MPLA operations and MPLA positions. He also mentions the Portuguese timber merchants:

> We are going to station an armed group on the other side of the

> Mucanda river towards Cangumbe to prevent UPA from hitting at the forces stationed at Cangumbe or the timber merchants which would place our correspondence in danger. [But he adds] I do not think UPA constitute a serious enemy at present.

The Portuguese timber merchants were linkmen between the UNITA and the Lisbon officials in Luso. They also channelled supplies to the UNITA forces and in the same letter Savimbi writes:

> I request again from your excellencies to supply me with at least 1,500 bullets of 7.62 calibre as our actions against the MPLA and UPA always take place with guns of this calibre.
>
> Please take particular care with this request as we shall no longer use these calibres against nationals. My request for hand grenades is cancelled since we have enough to be going on with.
>
> As for camouflage we shall ask the timber merchants for another cloth, that you should recommend, but I request that you send me if possible at least two uniforms in real good camouflage, one for me and one for Puna.

A second letter, published by *Afrique-Asie*, written by Savimbi in October 1972, was to Lieutenant-Colonel Ramires de Oliveira, at Military Headquarters, Luso. Again he details operations against the MPLA and explains why his men had to move outside their normal permitted zone of operations, in hot pursuit of the MPLA guerrillas. He requests permission to move into a fresh area in pursuit, 'for one month maximum or until the operation is completed. Our forces will withdraw immediately afterwards'. Savimbi claimed to have an OAU document

> which covers arms supplies to MPLA and to other movements operating in the Portuguese territories: quality, quantity, financing, means of transport etc. I think it is useful as it reflects the spirit of the last summit meeting in Rabat last June. As soon as I have finished studying it I shall forward it by the usual route.

Savimbi also mentions plans for installing a radio transmitter. On 4 November 1972 de Oliveira replied to Savimbi, also outlining his view of long term co-operation:

> The national authorities agree that the best thing as far as the UNITA is concerned is to maintain the region of Upper Lungue-Bungo out of the war and to strengthen secretly the co-operation with our army. So in this phase we cannot conceive of any mass surrender of the population and the guerrillas . . . . What we want is for the population to remain of its own free will in the region it is occupying. We have always suggested, in this sense, a programme of promotion, with our assistance.

> As for the movement, the UNITA, there is no talk of surrender but of 'integration', although the concept must be better defined in meetings in which you shall take part. So what we want now is to maintain a peace zone which will gradually be enlarged at the cost of promotion campaigns with the population and co-operation against the guerrillas of MPLA and UPA. Small pilot integration projects could be started, as far as the conditions in eastern Angola permit.

UNITA and the Future

In August 1973, the UNITA held its Third Congress in 'Freeland of Angola'. The Final Communiqué states:

> 221 delegates representing the members of the Political Bureau, Central Committee, Armed Forces for the Liberation of Angola (FALA), delegates of the People's Assemblies and of the Branch Committees attended. Nine foreign observers also attended, five were journalists and there was a film crew. All UNITA's overseas official representatives were present at this historic congress; they took part in the meetings and debates and especially contributed to the study of UNITA's relations with the African continent and the rest of the world. It was comrade Jonas Savimbi, President of the UNITA, who pronounced the opening address. In a speech of remarkable clarity, our president stressed the following points:
> 1) The UNITA must pursue the struggle against all intrigues fomented by colonialism and international imperialism.
> 2) Self-reliance must be our principle. Of course we should welcome foreign assistance; but the development of the Angolan struggle should never depend on problematic support from overseas.
> 3) So that the leadership of the struggle is not taken out of the hands of the Angolan proletariat, so that the Angolan proletariat firmly grasps it, the cadres and the people must pay particular attention to the class aspects of the Angolan liberation struggle.
> 4) At this stage of the national and democratic revolution, the unity of all the Angolan liberation movements is essential.

Among declarations of support for UNITA, the document states, were messages from the PAC of South Africa and ZANU. Three black Americans were also present from the African Liberation Support Committee. The UNITA thanked the People's Republic of China for 'its faithful support to our national liberation struggle'. An account of the Congress by one of the black Americans, Malik Chaka appeared in the Zambia *Daily Mail*. He reported the ALSC donated 5,120 Kwachas to the UNITA. He also reported

> the Afro Americans will transmit to UNITA the results of their research

> on foreign investments in Angola, will publish pamphlets on the UNITA and will publish accounts of all political activities favourable to the liberation movements. Charles Simmons ended his address by presenting to the delegates photographs taken in Detroit where 5,000 Afro Americans celebrated African Liberation Day. In one of the pictures the UNITA representative in the US was speaking to the crowd.

Chaka related the appearance of Savimbi: 'It was announced that Savimbi had been unanimously re-elected President. The news was greeted with songs and cheers. A few minutes later, Savimbi reappeared, dressed as usual in a military uniform captured from the enemy, revolver and grenades at his belt.'

The whole elaborate show had been held by courtesy of the Portuguese Army Eastern Region High Command.

On one occasion, ordinary working people in Bié were summoned to a public meeting at the Bié city basket-ball building. Portuguese troops presented UNITA leaders, who addressed the crowd. This was before 25 April 1974 and the people in the Gymno-Desportiva building were puzzled. 'It was as though the Portuguese wanted us to know about UNITA' said one. 'They, the Portuguese, were the first to tell us about UNITA, at the Gymno-Desportiva meeting' said another. Unfortunately, no one could date the meeting precisely. Other Angolans stated that occasional small, UNITA news items were published in the local Bié newspaper, but not in the national press.

What is clear is that when in June 1974 UNITA signed a 'ceasefire' with its Portuguese allies, it was now merely a question of reinforcing the partnership. This was the task of the leader of the Portuguese military delegation, Lieutenant-Colonel Fernando Passos Ramos.

Passos Ramos was operating during most of 1974 and 1975 out of the Lisbon Presidency Decolonization Office and the Ministry of Foreign Affairs. He was assiduous in his publicity for UNITA. Before 25 April 1974 he had been part of the Angolan Eastern Region command, under General Bettencourt Rodriguez, who, according to Premier Marcello Caetano in his memoirs *Depoimento*, had been responsible for the UNITA alliance. Caetano wrote that Bettencourt had 'managed to pacify that region including an understanding with the UNITA people'.

Immediately the April coup was over, Portuguese army platoons began touring the central highlands with UNITA 'guerrillas'. They entered villages, held public meetings, and informed the astonished Angolans that UNITA was the movement they should support, and that nobody should harm the white settlers.

Most Angolans had never before heard of the UNITA. Everybody knew about MPLA and many people listened to the *Angola Combatente* MPLA radio broadcasts from Brazzaville. Now, suddenly, Savimbi and the UNITA were being talked about. A Portuguese journalist working for Radio Clube in Lobito decided to go and see for himself. Fernando Martins set off by rail, for Luso in May.

On arrival, he went straight to the High Command and was received by Colonel Ferreira Macedo. A strained and cautious atmosphere prevailed at this interview, and Martins was told to leave his tape recorder outside the room. 'Off the record' Macedo claimed that he did not know how to contact Savimbi, but went on to talk openly about the operating agreement between the Army and UNITA: to leave each other alone and concentrate on hitting the MPLA. The interview ended inconclusively.

In Luso, Martins was told of a UNITA 'representative', Jorge Dotel, a white Town Council employee. He was also told to contact Father Oliveira, a Roman Catholic priest. The priest told him to write a letter to Savimbi requesting an interview, he should expect a reply in about a week. By the time he set off for the camp, two West German and one Spanish journalists accompanied him. Organized by Dotel the party set off on the Benguela railway from Luso with Dotel as UNITA representative and the Benguela Railway Company's local Chief of Security, a Major Baptista. At Cangumbe, they were met by the District Officer who sent for a timber merchant to provide a truck, which left with the group at 3 am. They were asked to take their own food, and the timber merchant sent some chickens for Savimbi. At dawn they were ordered to proceed on foot, and reached the camp about two hours later.

> It was all part of the mystique to make out this was a jungle base but look how we had got there! The links in the chain made the whole thing clear. The camp was a very recent affair, though I don't know if the European journalists recognized the signs. It may have been a week old.

Only Savimbi and Nzau Puna spoke to the journalists, though Vakulukuta and Sabino were also present. Unfortunately, Martins' tapes were lost in the South African occupation of Lobito; but he has not forgotten that when they arrived at the camp, Father Oliveira was waiting to greet them.

Shortly afterwards, and under Passos Ramos' expert guidance, a ceasefire was signed between the UNITA and the Portuguese.

On 18 June page one of the morning paper *Provincia de Angola*, carried a banner headline "SUSPENSION OF HOSTILITIES WITH UNITA. MEETING IN EASTERN ANGOLA". The article stated:

> We have received the following communiqué from the High Command of the Armed Forces in Angola:
>
> SUSPENSION OF HOSTILITIES WITH UNITA
>
> 1. A meeting has taken place somewhere in eastern Angola on 14 June. Present for the UNITA aside from the President Dr Jonas Malheiro Savimbi, were the following leaders of the movement: Major C. Tchata, Captain Eduardo Andre, Captain Samuel Epalanga and Lieutenant Verissimo Sabino. The delegation from High Command was composed of the following officers: Lieutenant-Colonel Fernando Passos Ramos, Major Pedro Pezzarat Correia, Captain Manuel Moreira Dias and Captain Benjamin Almeida.

> 2. After a long and fruitful exchange of views the two delegations agreed to suspend hostilities under conditions laid down in the communiqué below.
>
> As a natural follow-up to contacts made between the High Command of the Armed Forces in Angola and the President of UNITA, through the good offices of a Catholic missionary as has already been reported in the Press, a meeting was arranged between representatives of the High Command including elements from the Office of the Armed Forces Movement, with elements of the UNITA Central Committee headed by its President Dr Jonas Savimbi, on June 14th 1974 in the interior of Angola in an area where UNITA had been carrying out its activities, which took place with great cordiality and mutual respect and during which, after having discussed the various points of view on the current political situation in Angola, arising out of the April 25th Movement, it was decided to suspend all armed actions of hostility as soon as possible in order to create an atmosphere favourable to development of political dialogue leading to the restoration of peace in Angola.

The paper published a facsimile of the handwritten communiqué plus signatures. But the High Command added in its own point three

> Aside from the obvious satisfaction with which we view this decisive step towards re-establishing of peace for Angola, in accordance with the principles laid down in the programme of the MFA, this High Command wishes publicly to make known the atmosphere of friendliness and sympathy in which the talks took place, in which the political maturity, loyalty and true love for the Angolan people on the part of Dr Jonas Savimbi were made plain, and to which, therefore, we pay due tribute. As is evident, the suspension of hostilities will be followed at a higher level by political talks, so that within a few days, officers of the High Command will go to Lisbon to report back to the Provisional Government and Junta of National Salvation on the details of the conversations that have taken place.

Savimbi's image of a 'pragmatic nationalist' now had to include the self-reliant Maoist-influenced guerrilla emerging from years of hardship and deprivation in the bush. He made few public appearances between April and September, but from then onwards, he began to campaign at mass meetings. Heavily bearded, clad often in military fatigues, decked with African bangles, swagger stick and necklaces, he clearly intended to convey an image combining traditional chiefly qualities and daring bush warrior.

UNITA had a headstart in its campaigning. The MPLA remained underground until it signed a ceasefire in November. UPA-FNLA began infiltrating troops into the north after the September Sal agreement, but its campaigning took the form of intimidation and bribery.

UNITA's Ideology

Savimbi had told the Church that the UNITA was 'nationalist, and anti-imperialist, including anti-Soviet Social-Imperialism'. He had also said:

> the African believes in a higher Being whatever his name may be, or whatever the place he is worshipped. There is an ancestral force which transcends man. All alienation from this feeling which is profoundly popular will tend to divide the forces which could openly show themselves against colonial domination.

In 1963, when Savimbi barred Viriato da Cruz from UPA he was against Mao but by 1969-70 this opposition no longer applied. At some stage, the UNITA claim, Savimbi and 10 others underwent a nine month military training course in China. It is unlikely that this took place in 1965, as Savimbi said, because in that year he was engaged in his crash doctorate course and visited Dar-es-Salaam.

Certainly, from 1970, Maoist sentiments appear in the UNITA documents. Self-reliance, no outside assistance, people's war – all are liberally used to convey genuine struggle. Maoist-style pamphlets were also distributed inside Angola by the UNITA in the destabilization campaign against the People's Republic (the South African Defence Force also took to leaving behind Maoist literature after their raids).

But the main impact of the UNITA's message was simple: to gather the Ovimbundu together, promise the resurgence of the tribe into its former wealth and power, hearken back to the 'days of the rubber', and integrated with the tribal theme was the idea of an 'ancestral force which transcends man'.

Markedly absent from the UNITA campaign were the mobilizing ideals of the MPLA. Instead, the UNITA encouraged and increasingly relied upon the most retrograde and backward notions, on fear and mysticism, to mobilize mass faith when reason and logic argued that the organization fell short of expectations. The UNITA's campaign against contract labour, and its links with the Protestant missions in the central highlands, were instrumental in procuring its rapid rise to popularity in the early days.

The African Church

The Roman Catholic Church came to Angola with the earliest seafarers and built its churches in the north and around Luanda, and gradually spread into the interior. The Protestants are relative newcomers. US and Swiss missions entered the central highlands from around 1911 during the construction of the Benguela railway line. They not only spread Protestantism amongst the Ovimbundu, but also undertook studies of the local people. Three major studies of Ovimbundu life are linked to the Dondi Evangelical mission, and were written between the 1930s and 1960s, by G.M. Childs of the mission itself, W.D. Hambly and Adrian Edwards. No other area of Angola attracted so much Anglo-Saxon attention.

Edwards, an anthropologist, visited the highlands in 1955. He was particularly interested in the Church's influence in the area and in his book *The Ovimbundu under Two Sovereignties*, he describes the differences between Roman Catholic and Protestant Church.

The Catholic church worked closely with the state; it made little or no effort to educate Africans, or provide welfare services. On the other hand it employed black labour at the usual exploitative rates. On the Protestant work in the central highlands Edwards reports:

> most of the Protestant Missionary work among the Ovimbundu has been achieved by joint effort of the American Board of Commissioners for Foreign Missions (Congregationalists) and the United Church of Canada, though the Swiss Mission and the Plymouth Brethren should also be mentioned. The headquarters of the American-Canadian mission at Dondi includes a seminary for pastors, a boys' secondary school, a girls' boarding school, the printing press, a hospital and leper settlement.

The American-Canadian mission had been confined to the Ovimbundu and 'the Native Church it has founded is the only all-Umbundu social grouping that exists'.

When Edwards was in the area, he noted that there were only 32 African Catholic priests, but more than 70 black Protestant pastors. In the Catholic Church 'the most significant distinction is between priest and layman, among the Protestants the significant distinction is between the American and Canadian missionaries and the Ovimbundu members of their Native Church, including the pastors.' Edwards further notes:

> with the Protestants there is a division of functions, the missionaries providing supervisory and specialized services such as agricultural advice, education and medical work, and the Native Church being responsible for village work . . . . The missionary salaries [are] being paid by the mission boards and those of the pastors and the village schoolteachers by the Ovimbundu Protestants. Socially there is less contact between missionaries and pastors than between (Catholic) black and white priests. The African Catholic priests then have approximate equality and identity of status with their white confreres within the hierarchic framework of the diocese of Nova Lisboa [Huambo today]: the Ovimbundu pastors lack this . . . but instead possess greater independence and opportunities for leadership within the Umbundu Native Church, which functions as a partly autonomous body. The difference in functions of the priests and pastors is related to the ultimate aims of missionary action: for the Catholic missions the establishment of a

local clergy is part of the complete incorporation of the Ovimbundu into the Universal Church; for the Protestants the establishment of a local clergy is part of the building up of a totally independent local Church.

Edwards' comments are of relevance because of the part the Native Church was to play in building the UNITA following in 1975.

Under fascism, religion had to be closely controlled. The Protestant missions were viewed with hostility and suspicion, and their presence was sternly limited under Salazar. The control exerted by the Portuguese over animist, and other Christian sects, was even more rigorous. These religions, none the less, also had their influence in the central highlands.

Periodically, exponents of messianic liberation cults travelled into central Angola by way of the Benguela railway line communicating directly with the Katanga and Zambian copper belts, and further south with South Africa. Many of the cults were manifestations of the Watch Tower sect of Jehovah's Witnesses that first appeared among the Witwatersrand miners in 1897.

In 1952-53 Ngola Chiluanji preached anti-colonialism and black dignity, along the railway line east of Bié. He spoke of a new generation; peasants killed off their livestock as a means to hasten its coming. Chiluanji was finally arrested in Lumege.

In 1963, after the launching of armed struggle, there were several prophetic movements working underground. Documents recorded by PIDE were found in Huambo, Bié and Alto Catumbela, further west. In 1967 the PIDE accused the US of directing a fresh Watch Tower campaign at Benguela. They were preaching that the son of God was born white, but the whites killed him and he would return one day as a black; to ensure that the whites did not kill him again it was necessary to exterminate them all, or at least the bad ones.

Johann Maranke's African Apostolic Church, founded in Lusaka in 1932, also earned a sizeable following among the Chokwe, and like *Kitawala* (Watch Tower), spread along the railway line. In 1955, at Bela Vista (also on the railway) a prophetic movement of both men and women, who were regarded as saints risen from the dead, arose. According to Edwards, the Bela Vista saints' movement was spread through the Protestant mission catechists. In 1960 another Bela Vista sect grew up around David Jorge 'the Evangelical Flood of the Church of God'. In November 1964 an administrator in Bailundo was asked by another millenarist for permission to set up a church. He too foretold the second coming of Christ as a prelude to 1,000 years of peace. Promising miracles, the prophets also demanded sacrifices: killing of all livestock. Later, a priest described the UNITA meetings around Ringoma in 1974: 'It was empty promises. After independence you will have everything you ever wanted. Angolans won't need to work and even the oxen will be able to rest as everyone will have machines.' Miraculously no work was needed.

Savimbi promised the old men false teeth free of charge; the young men cars and a university education without bothering about secondary school. To the women, he promised agricultural machines, refrigerators, cookers. All this while everyone rested. On the spiritual side, the UNITA promised 'mystery, the marvellous, endless wonderful promises, tribalism and nepotism and the retrograde in customs'. Savimbi could do anything, and his troops were made to believe that they were immortal.

Savimbi's portrait stood upon the altar, and hymns to him were composed and sung in Protestant village mission churches. The slogan 'God in Heaven and Savimbi on earth' was scrawled on the walls. Elsewhere in Angola, the Protestant Church was firmly in favour of MPLA. The black Angolan Methodist Bishop Emilio de Carvalho had always supported the People's Movement and had seen successive generations of young Methodists go off to join the MPLA underground and the guerrillas.

Christians from both the Catholic and Protestant Church hierarchies gave full and active support to the MPLA during the war, risking their lives in underground work against the FNLA-UNITA-South African coalition. The pro-Savimbi Protestant missions were a continuation of the Native Church 'independence' Edwards noted. Any appeal to the Ovimbundu as a people must closely involve that Native Church. And Savimbi's most persistent and powerful appeal was: 'Ovimbundu of the world unite, you have nothing to lose'.

Later, at mass meetings, the UNITA would address the crowd in two languages, Portuguese and Umbundu; the content would be quite different. Scandals erupted and were reported in the *Provincia de Angola*. At Cuma, Savimbi had told an audience in Umbundu that after Independence there would be no white people in the secondary schools and university; but some settlers in the crowd understood Umbundu and this pronouncement was widely and quickly circulated. In Huambo, the UNITA information department issued a denial; Savimbi had meant that the directors of these institutions would now be Angolans. UNITA speeches in Portuguese told the whites they could stay on, their property would be left intact.

The violence soon began, initially against fetishists. 'It was enough for your private enemy to denounce you as a fetishist and you were dragged off and killed horribly: cut into pieces, burned or buried alive.' One Bié worker who had lived through the terror felt this was a cultural reaction, linked not to the Church but to liberation. Sensing freedom, you turn against the former evil power, the fetishist, and prove that you can kill it. But more often than not the victims were innocent men and women. The killings created a new climate of violence and fear.

The MPLA had turned its attention to the question of fetishists, but separated the genuine herb doctor or '*curandeiro*' from the fetishist engaged in vengeance and trials by ordeal. They called on the people to analyze the contribution of the two groups in traditional society and report cases of fetish action to the local police or authorities.

In the UNITA's Angola, alleged or imaginary fetishists were dealt summary justice: there were knifings at public meetings. Later *mestiços* were dealt with in the same way and racism gave way to hatred of educated blacks. Finally, by 1977 Ovimbundu peasants, sickened by the UNITA horror and anxious to return to People's Angola from their bush imprisonment, were victims of the same brutalities.

By the end of 1974, the UNITA was preparing its people for war. Word went out that young Ovimbundu must return to the Ovimbundu heartlands, and there, make their way to the 'bases' for military training. They rode on the Benguela railway, walked, hitched rides along the roads, in answer to the tribal call.

UNITA and Western Imperialism

While there were two UNITAS speaking to the people inside Angola, one in Portuguese, another in Umbundu, a third UNITA spoke to the West. The June 'ceasefire' organized by the Portuguese, gave UNITA a head start to spread its message in the central highlands, it also gave the UNITA a head-start with its international publicity. It contained hardly any radical content, in marked contradiction to the image of Maoist guerrillas propagating people's war.

On Monday 3 June 1974, the *Provincia de Angola* had reported:

> Savimbi, polled by a Catholic missionary with a view to opening negotiations for the laying down of arms, has shown his concern over an early independence of Angola, alleging the people are not prepared.

In July, the Paris daily *Le Monde*, quoted Savimbi direct, 'the people of Angola are not ready for independence. Don't let us ask for the impossible.'

In July, too, the South African *Star Weekly* reported:

> Significantly, Dr Savimbi has been having talks with white businessmen which suggests UNITA might be about to enter an electoral agreement with the giant southern-based MOPUA party which has apparently unlimited white financial backing. MOPUA is led by a multi-racial élite of professional men. An agreement between UNITA and MOPUA would virtually clinch the southern and central regions where well over two thirds of the population are found.

The battle for 'control' over the Angolan people seemed to have begun.

The *Daily Telegraph*'s Rhodesia correspondent went to Luanda in August 1974; he knew where to find information.

> Dr Jonas Savimbi, founder of UNITA the smallest of the three guerrilla movements in Angola, is now being hailed as a future president by many of the territory's 450,000 whites and there are indications that Dr Savimbi and his movement have the tacit backing of Angola's ruling junta and several large commercial concerns, and the tall, articulate bush fighter has recently been entertaining leading businessmen at his camp.

At the same time, the UNITA's Paris offshoot was distributing press communiqués. One 'war communiqué' dated May 1974 and signed 'the FALA High Command, Freeland of Angola', claimed five engagements with Portuguese forces that month including 29 Portuguese army troops killed and large quantities of weapons captured. It ended, 'the struggle will continue until the total independence of our country'. On 24 June, ten days after the joyful announcement of the ceasefire, the UNITA political bureau, denied that it had ever taken place 'UNITA has never laid down its arms because this would mean surrendering to the enemy'. The statement was distributed in the form of an official communiqué.

By November, South Africa's *Star Weekly* was able to add:

> If the UNITA party gets power in an independent Angola they will not help any liberation movements in attempts to seize power in South West Africa. The pledge was given by Dr Fernando Wilson, UNITA's top man in Luanda and head of a delegation which will negotiate independence with the Portuguese.

In May 1975, it returned to the same theme

> Dr Jonas Savimbi has hailed the Prime Minister Mr John Vorster as a responsible leader. Armed liberation struggle would not solve the problems of South West Africa and Rhodesia said Dr Savimbi. He favoured dialogue and a policy of détente he said. South Africa had shown its sincerity by refusing to grant Rhodesia military backing he said. This is a period of readjustment in Southern Africa said Dr Savimbi.

Savimbi spoke in May 1975 to the South African *Financial Mail*:

> I hope the future leaders of Angola will co-operate with South Africa. We have that dam at Kunene. We have other investments with South Africa. What are we going to do? Are we going to ostracize them? I think not. I hope that any leader here will be realistic and accept political and economic co-operation with any country, despite differences in political systems . . . . Chiwale and I were trained by the Chinese in 1965 . . . . We have gone past the stage when we were expecting aid from the Chinese and it did not come . . . . I have gone through several stages in my thinking. Now, I am thinking in a different way altogether after my own experience of fighting for six and a half years in the bush.

In July 1975 Savimbi gave an interview to *African Development*. With his usual aplomb he denied that there was any idea of an alliance with FNLA 'We will never make such a coalition'. He returned again to the subject of Southern African liberation.

> Whilst there is a possibility of talking and getting peaceful settlement

> we shall never support an armed struggle. Let us take the case of Namibia. Any government here which supports armed struggle in Namibia must know that South Africa assistance to individuals or groups of will fight back. When this happens the population in the southern part of Angola will suffer.

South Africa's military were in Angola with the UNITA by August 1975; the armoured columns rolled in through the south in October. On 25 September 1975, the *New York Times* had published the story of CIA support for FNLA and UNITA. MPLA reported South Africa's invasion, and all the Western governments ridiculed the notion: possibly a few mercenaries were involved. In November 1975 the *International Herald Tribune* reported from Lusaka 'the UNITA office here tonight issued a statement denying reports that white South African soldiers were fighting for UNITA.' The denials continued. In December, Radio Zambia reported, 'Dr Savimbi said South Africa was not giving aid to UNITA in the current war. He told *Newsweek*'s Andrew Jaffe, 'I have never gone to the South African or Rhodesian governments for help.' After the South African withdrawal in March 1976 the UNITA's campaign of lies was, if anything, stepped up. John Stockwell has given extensive details of how the CIA ran the UNITA press operation.

A white South African soldier involved in the Angola campaign later told Granada Television's 'World in Action' of his experience.

> I think the original intention was to go and fight as an equal force with UNITA; it became very clear fairly early on in the operations though that the UNITA troops weren't up to standard and we had to do all the fighting ourselves. For instance on the eastern front there was a big battle that our battalion (Sixth South African Infantry) was involved in at Luso which involved UNITA troops. The South Africans had to do all the fighting themselves.

Asked how he found UNITA troops, he replied, 'From all I saw of them they were a very motley bunch .... I don't think there was any battle that I ever heard of where UNITA actually played a major role.'

After the retreat into Namibia, the ex-SADF soldier said,

> we were operating in Northern Namibia and it was quite clear from small bands passing through our base that immediately after the South African withdrawal, small bands for operations were set up. For instance there were a number of Permanent Force members of the Parachute Battalion who were crossing the border into Angola regularly at night to blow up shops, mine roads, basically to make life difficult for the MPLA. Also we had passing through our camp a small group from the Reconnaissance Commando. They are the South African élite troops, they always operate in small bands, these people didn't wear South African uniforms, they didn't carry South African weapons, they

> carried AK47s. As far as I could understand they were hitting inside Angola at any sort of solid structures I think it was an operation really starting to try and destabilize the area.

UNITA in Namibia and in the Angolan bush

SWAPO's guerrillas fought UNITA immediately after their retreat into northern Namibia where they were sheltered by the South African army. By July 1976 the war communiqués of the People's Liberation Army of Namibia gave details of attacks against UNITA camps in Namibia. In SWAPO's *Namibia Today* number 2, 1977, SWAPO states:

> South Africa's military strategy in Namibia now includes the use of UNITA troops which it equips and trains against SWAPO. UNITA units in Namibia are divided into two sections. One group is stationed in the north and has been used as South Africa's first line of defence against PLAN cadres crossing the border from Angola. Posing as SWAPO units, UNITA men burn down people's houses, steal their cattle and terrorize the local population. The blame is laid on SWAPO.

The SWAPO journal continues,

> The other UNITA section is stationed in central Namibia and in Windhoek. They are used to create disturbances by beating up people, especially SWAPO members and supporters. In Katatura, the black township outside Windhoek, and at Rossing and other mine compounds, UNITA has been responsible for stealing money, clothing, and food, and for destroying people's belongings. UNITA itself has declared war on SWAPO. Their leader, Jonas Savimbi, has vowed to continue to fight SWAPO and to disrupt any elections to try to prevent SWAPO coming to power. He has also said that he will get Angolan 'refugees' in Namibia to vote for the Turnhalle puppets. These so-called refugees are Angolans who were recruited by force by UNITA and made to cross the border at gunpoint into Namibia earlier this year. South Africa immediately made propaganda out of them, saying they were fleeing from the MPLA government.

UNITA led the bulk of its men into Namibia, but small groups who knew Bié well from the times of collaboration with the Portuguese stayed behind to organize South African supply bases. There was a lot of cash available to buy friends. A Catholic Father testified, 'In March 1976 they [the South Africans] gave the soldiers a lot of money, 10,000 escudos each, I know because several asked me to keep their money for them.' The groups organized weapons and then began rounding up villagers and forcing the people to abandon their homes and take to the bush. The propaganda used to achieve this varied: sometimes that Savimbi was returning with heavy airpower to bomb all towns and villages and he had instructed the people to live in the bush, or that the MPLA and Cubans were going to kill all southerners. Sometimes they simply pointed their guns at the people and ordered them out. The villages were then looted and often burned and abandoned.

MPLA supporters' lives were again in danger, so, too, were the lives of educated Africans, as they had been during the occupation. In 1977, however, this attitude changed: educated Africans were kidnapped. The UNITA apparently wanted nurses and teachers to take into the bush where the thousands of peasants taken there by the UNITA were starving and complaining of the chaos and horrors. The nurses and teachers could not perform miracles, the people wanted increasingly to leave the bush and return to their homes. The UNITA then began a two pronged strategy to prevent losing their 'control' over these unfortunate peasants.

Mysticism and fear were the key: spies were posted everywhere. Anyone suspected of wanting to leave was killed: chopped up into pieces, or burned alive; or had limbs amputated. The UNITA's other alternative was to mobilize these starving and desperate people to tear down their villages, destroy their churches, and their shops. Whole areas became ruins: visiting these eerie villages it seemed the millenarists had returned to the highlands with their orders to destroy everything and hasten the second coming of Christ. The destruction included the murder of those priests accused of helping the MPLA, of shopkeepers, of peasants and of children.

Over the next six years, regardless of the UNITA's well established record for issuing blatant falsehoods, the Western press faithfully relayed its claims to have 'control' over vast areas of Angola, to have killed hundreds of Cuban and Soviet soldiers, and taken cities of over 10,000 inhabitants.*

A series of reporters entered Angola to visit 'UNITA controlled zones'. One, Richard Harwood of the *Washington Post*, was more guillible than most. His report was published in July 1981 in the middle of South Africa's largest ever anti-Angolan invasion, 'Operation Protea', which the SADF described as the biggest South African combined operation since World War Two. Harwood reported,

> the demoralized band of 3,000 to 4,000 guerrillas who fled into the bush five years ago has been transformed into an effective fighting force. Savimbi claims 15,000 guerrillas now, operating in fighting groups of 50 to 150 men in every province up to the 10th parallel. [That would be about 80 miles south of the capital.] Here in the

*On one occasion the BBC broadcast that the UNITA had taken the major towns of Ngunza, Huambo, Bié and Luena along the Benguela railway line. They checked the story with their correspondent in Luanda only after the broadcast. The programme editor should have known it was false; in fact, he could have telephoned Huambo direct.

> south he has raised, trained, equipped and put into the field ten conventional combat battalions. He promises to have 15 in action by Christmas.

Harwood quoted Savimbi

> Our battalions have modern weapons – SAM7 ground to air missiles, 81mm and 82mm mortars, recoilless cannon, anti-aircraft guns, Stalin Organs. Most of these are Soviet weapons we have captured. We have shot down Russian planes and many helicopters. You will see them. We have Russian prisoners. You will meet them. We have liberated most of this province (Kuando Kubango), most of Moxico province and half of Kunene province. We will show you. We control territory containing 2.5 million people and we continue to move to the populous areas in the north and west.

In Mavinga in Kuando Kubango, UNITA said it had killed 800 MPLA troops to take the town, this was faithfully recorded by Harwood.

After hearing the stirring tales of the great Mavinga victory Harwood concluded

> Before coming out here, I had heard from UNITA critics and from British journalists that any military success UNITA might have was the work of South Africans. It was a racist argument, based on the prejudice that Africans are not capable of fighting, particularly with modern weapons. That argument is untrue. These lads knew what they were doing. Puna is pleased with the regiment . . . .

By his sixth episode, Harwood is still 'wondering where do the South Africans fit in?' Savimbi soon set his mind at rest,

> Beginning in 1978 he said South African and UNITA people began to co-operate on certain matters. Specifically, the South Africans agreed to allow UNITA people to bring badly wounded troops across the Namibian border for treatment. They agreed to sell UNITA medicines, trucks, gasoline, food and miscellaneous items. They also agreed to buy ivory and diamonds from UNITA. But, said Savimbi, South Africa provides no weapons and engages in no joint military operations with UNITA.

By 1982 Savimbi's once charismatic image was virtually destroyed. A Windhoek newspaperman taken by South African military 'five minutes into Angola' from Namibia, to meet him, commented on Savimbi's large paunch and spotless appearance, as he looked around for the showers and changing-rooms in the tick-ridden bushland. He singled out the death's head insignia on Savimbi's uniform and cap and commented on his lengthy posing for the photographers. As for his expertise in handling the press, the Windhoek pressman compared him with Dirk Mudge, the unhappy white politician leading the Turnhalle alliance.

Years earlier, Agostinho Neto, revealing Savimbi's antics with the South African helicopter squadrons that lifted him in and out of Angola had said, 'Poor old Savimbi. Today he is nothing more than the servant of the South African racists. Our enemy is not poor old Savimbi. It is South Africa.'

11. Destabilization

The Undeclared War

> The imperialists can come with their warplanes, tanks, cannon and gunboats. They will not stop our heroic people from our duty to the people of Namibia, Zimbabwe and South Africa to whom we again pledge militant solidarity. Let them come! The racists and their allies will meet the impenetrable barrier of our people's determination. We stand ready to defend our freedom, our country and socialism.

Neto's words were not empty slogans. Namibians and South Africans defended Angola's revolution. Neto and the MPLA leadership openly supported the liberation movements fighting racism. Close ties had been built during the struggle against the Portuguese with the African National Congress of South Africa (ANC), and later with the Zimbabwe Patriotic Front and SWAPO of Namibia.

A socialist Angola in southern Africa therefore threatened imperialist interests, not only because of its Marxist-Leninist, national policies but also because of the material support it would give to the liberation fighters. After South Africa's defeat the West tried to put pressure on the frontline states – Tanzania and Zambia in particular – not to invite Angola to join the group. Foreign Office and State Department officials briefed the media that Angola was not in the frontline – overlooking its 1,200 miles of border with South African occupied Namibia. Angola had to be isolated. Zaire was still hostile, in spite of Neto's plea for normal relations as early as 4 February 1976. Zambia was ambiguous. Western intelligence sources filled the media with accounts of 'fierce fighting in southern Angola', implying that the UNITA was a force to be reckoned with, when it was in full retreat or sheltering in South African army camps in Namibia. But the majority of African states were now clear about the issues in Angola.

The OAU Liberation Committee met in Luanda in June 1976, a few days before the Soweto uprisings began. Neto firmly restated MPLA's solidarity for the Patriotic Front, SWAPO and ANC (SA). He briskly called for strong OAU material support for the struggle – 'boots and kitbags'.

Neto wanted to sweep away the cobwebs at the OAU and stated the issue starkly. Words were not enough: there must be action. While he would not compromise on the liberation of Africa, Neto constantly tried to reassure the West that Angola had not closed its doors to it or joined the Warsaw Pact. MPLA's foreign policy was based on non-alignment and a desire for relations of mutual interest with all countries of the world. Socialist countries were singled out as allies, because of their political commitment, but there would be no foreign bases on Angolan soil, and this applied to the Warsaw Pact countries. South African and CIA intervention had forced Angola to request the Cuban troops to come and help to protect the country from outside aggression. Neither the OAU nor the Non-Aligned Movement ever questioned Angola's non-aligned status, and by 1980 even senior officials in the British Foreign Office had to admit that the Cubans were not fighting in Angola but were grouped in camps for possible deployment in the event of a major South African invasion.

In a statement on 4 February 1982, Angola and Cuba pointed out that every attempt they had made to reduce the numbers of Cuban forces in Angola since 1976 had been halted because of escalation in acts of aggression by South Africa. Cuban troops, they said, would leave only when there was no longer any threat of a South African attack.

In the early days after Independence, MPLA set out to practise non-alignment with those Western capitalist countries who were not hostile to it. Italy, Sweden and the Netherlands fell into this category and soon had Embassies in Luanda; so did Brazil. Their presence also brought industrialists and traders so that some supplies of Western goods were always available. Western investors were also welcomed.

France was the first major power to realize the economic possibilities in Angola. President Giscard d'Estaing was deeply implicated in anti-MPLA intrigues involving mercenairies and fake liberation movements, organized through French connections in Zaire. But France was the first EEC country to open an Embassy in Angola (having deliberately announced recognition of Angola 24 hours ahead of the time agreed with other EEC countries). By 1982 there were 650 French residents in the People's Republic, representing by far the largest Western business community.

But US hostility continued; the Americans claimed that this was due to the Cuban presence. This hostility, plus British and French manoeuvring, encouraged some African countries to maintain support for UNITA and FNLA. Once the South Africans retreated, covert operations against the new state had once again to take the lead. Zaire, Morocco, Senegal, the Ivory Coast, and Gabon provided African diplomatic assistance or channelled CIA and South African aid to the traitors.

Zaire and Angola

Obviously, Zaire would have to remain the CIA's logistical African base for these operations; Mobutu agreed. He had been informed of efforts by the

Zaire opposition to gain MPLA's support in December 1975, when his forces were invading northern Angola. Neto asked the Brazzaville government to help in negotiations to end Zaire's hostility, and went to Brazzaville for a summit meeting with Mobutu in late February 1976. The joint agreement that resulted was followed by ministerial talks on specific economic questions, such as reopening the Benguela Railway to imports and exports for Zaire. But Mobutu did not formally recognize the People's Republic until more than a year later, in February 1977. No reasons were given for this long delay.

In the meantime, Mobutu had announced closure of FNLA, Cabinda separatists' and UNITA camps in Zaire (February 1976) and had pocketed more than $1 million that the CIA had sent to him to pay their Angolan underlings. These anti-MPLA groups continued to use strings of camps along the Angola-Zaire border to launch raids into the north of Angola, with civilians as their target. Mobutu had also signed a secret contract with OTRAG, a West German ballistics company, leasing them 100,000^2 kilometres of countryside, part of which ran along the Angolan border. The contract gave the company exclusive administration of the area and barred inspection even to the Zaire state authorities. Since the recent discovery of the involvement of some other West German firms in nuclear deals with South Africa, the Angolan government felt entitled to ask Mobutu for reassurances and to request to visit the area; this request was not granted, but Mobutu did later cancel the agreement with OTRAG.

Information of plans for a military operation to be launched against Angola from Zaire and Namibia in September 1977 was leaked to the MPLA, by a source in Zaire, and was made public by Neto several weeks later, on 24 February 1977. The main target of this 'Operation Cobra' was Cabinda and its oilfields. US army personnel were heavily involved, along with the South African Defence Force.

The US officers and marines were already in Zaire when the plans were revealed to the MPLA. Units due to take part included 1,800 FNLA under US and Zairean officers and the Ditrala Zaire army battalion, with air support by F 104 amphibious fighter bombers which had been on standby at the US Army Kitona base in Zaire since the CIA ordered them up in May 1975. US sea cover was to include warships detached from the Sixth Fleet, frigates with long range missiles and two troop ships. Kamina base, also in Zaire, would continue with Cyrano radar monitoring of Zambian and Tanzanian airspace to intercept any friendly relief flights entering Angola during the operation. US high altitude reconnaissance covered Angola itself. Simultaneously, the South African army units were to go into action along the Kunene border, and a third prong of the attack would aim at the Benguela railway on the eastern Angolan border with Zaire.

The 'Independent Government of Cabinda' was meanwhile waiting in Kinshasa. It comprised the usual traitors and renegades who had been living off oil company and CIA funds after their former paymasters, Portugal's PIDE political police, had been ousted by the 1974 coup. There was Nzita

Tiago, Ranque Franque, Bahn Alexandre, Fernando Lubota and others.

Two days after Neto denounced 'Operation Cobra', Zaire retaliated. The village of Pangala lies south of the Zaire border, and consists of a cluster of eight hamlets, their population swollen by the arrival of Angolans returning home from Zaire. Pangala had organized MPLA action groups; it had a People's Shop, a school and adult literacy classes. At 4.30 am on 26 February 1977 Pangala was assaulted by a force of 200 Zaireans and Angolans under the command of three white mercenaries. For two and a half hours, until dawn, the hamlets were under intense gunfire. With the first light, the murderers moved in on the houses. They found mainly women, children and old men as the young and strong had fled. Forty-three people were killed and many were wounded. They were sliced up with cutlasses, skulls were battered in with staves, some women were disembowelled; others were burned alive as the invaders set fire to the village. Among the bodies buried in a mass grave were those of dismembered children. As they assaulted Pangala, the murderers had screamed 'You like FAPLA – now you will pay with your lives'.

'Operation Cobra' never took place. But attempts to seize Cabinda and to attack national reconstruction targets in the north of Angola continued. The MPLA veteran Commander Bolingo, a Cabindan and one of the Mayombe forest guerrillas there, said that the Cabinda 'separatist' movement was started by the Portuguese in 1964, in response to MPLA's opening of its guerrilla front in Cabinda. Such people as Alexandre Taty joined Portugal's Special Forces (*Tropas Especiais*), counter insurgency units formed to fight MPLA. Taty had been a member of FNLA but left it at the same time as Savimbi to found the UNITA. From there he moved to FLEC (Front for the Liberation of Cabinda). A series of such organizations were set up from 1964 onwards: MOLICA (Movement for the Liberation of Cabinda), and UPC (Union of Cabindan People) as well as FLEC. The oil companies were heavily involved, French interests in particular as they wanted Gulf Oil out of its monopoly oil concession.

The most serious threat to Cabinda was on 2 November 1974, when a large force led by French mercenary Jean Kay attacked from Zaire. There were four days of heavy fighting during which enemy troops got to within 20 kilometres of the capital.

In Kampala, at the time of the 1975 OAU summit, Ranque Franque declared Cabinda's Independence during a press conference he held in the conference centre's press room. Another splinter group made a similar announcement in a Paris hotel. For years news agencies in Paris relayed FLEC communiqués, dreamt up by a French businessman, Marcel Bory, styled 'FLEC representative in Paris and member of the provisional government of the Republic of Cabinda in charge of Foreign Relations'. These communiqués spoke of 'sweeping military operations' and called on the press to visit 'the liberated areas of Cabinda, two thirds of the province'. Bory also sent Gulf Oil a telegram demanding 'immediate evacuation from Cabinda'.

FLEC remained the most well organized of these splinter groups. By November 1977, when the Angolan Defence Ministry detailed 19 bases inside

Zaire, connected with Cabinda destabilization, FLEC had a military headquarters at Tombo Vanga in Zaire, and a training base at Tishela in Zaire. A FLEC prisoner, Pascoal Manuel Gomes, captured after a FLEC attack on 14 March 1977, described how there were hundreds of French and US mercenaries at the Tishela base. All FLEC attacks in which he had taken part had been launched from Zaire. Other prisoners said FLEC troops were under the command of Zairean, Belgian and French officers.

March 1977 marked the first attempt by Mobutu's opponents to launch armed rebellion against his regime. On 8 March units of the FLNC (Congo National Liberation Front) went into action in Shaba province. They won the support of the people, and Mobutu had to call in help from Morocco, Egypt, France and the United States to protect his regime.

There had been Zairean exiles in Angola since the Katangese secession, and some had worked with the Portuguese army against the MPLA. After 1974, the Portuguese suggested that they should go to South Africa. Instead they chose to remain in Angola where they contacted the MPLA and turned down an approach by Savimbi to join UNITA. Attracted by an independent Angola, and faced with poverty and hunger in western Zaire, thousands more Zaireans flocked into Angola between 1974 to 1977.

After the March 1977 Shaba uprising, the numbers of Zairean refugees in Angola increased dramatically. Young recruits to the FLNC overseas began trying to draw together the opposition splinter groups in Brussels, Paris and East Africa. The result was a second armed uprising, launched a year later, in May 1978, and involving Zairean exiles in Zambia. This time, the US moved in with accusations that Cuban forces based in Angola, and Angolans too, were involved. This was strongly denied by Angola, and no evidence was ever produced to support the US claim. The Angolan government moved all Zairean exiles further away from the border and encouraged the FLNC leadership to leave Angola. Zaireans were to return home if they wished, under a previously agreed but not implemented plan involving the United Nations High Commission for Refugees.

By the end of 1977, the activities of the externally based opposition – FNLA, FLEC and UNITA – centred on terrorism against the civilian population. In August 1977 more than 30 Cabindan villagers were slain in a night attack on Cuma. In September a series of massacres took place in Huambo and Bié, in central Angola.

At Galanga, 35 civilians were slaughtered on 7 September; on 12 September, 5 died and 25 were wounded in Chitumbi, Bié; on the 21 September, at Lupatechi in Huambo province, 15 civilians and 10 militia men were killed; on the same night in Bié, at Kachingue, 93 civilians were murdered. In October, Zairean troops crossed the border into Moxico three times and pounded Angolan territory with heavy artillery. Neto cabled OAU Secretary General William Eteki, detailing UNITA, FNLA and FLEC bases in Zaire and recalling the OAU Mauritius summit resolution inviting:

> all OAU member states who have not yet done so, to end all aid and

> assistance to individuals or group sof individuals whose activities are directed against the peace and internal and external security of the People's Republic of Angola and who by this fact are working against the struggle for the liberation of Southern Africa.

After the second Shaba uprising in May and June 1978, Zaire finally agreed to talks with Angola. Neto went to Kinshasa on a first formal state visit in August 1978 and signed a mutual peace treaty ending support for the opponents of each regime. In October 1978, Mobutu came to Luanda and was received by hundreds of thousands of cheering Luandans, there was bunting in the streets, cavalcades of hooting cars, and joy as ordinary people believed that finally Mobutu had ended support for their enemies and there would be peace. But as long as Zaire remained the CIA headquarters for central Africa peace was impossible. By 1981 there were fresh signs that the CIA was preparing a new, major military campaign against MPLA. With Reagan now in the White House, there seemed reason to believe that this operation had received support at the highest level. A new opposition front was at the centre of the plan.

COMIRA (*Comite Militar de Resistencia de Angola*) had been put together from FNLA (without Holden Roberto, who was now considered a liability), FLEC and mercenaries in Zaire. A former Biafra mercenary, Frenchman Armand Agnarelli, was a key figure. Moved to Kinshasa in 1975 as a SDECE (French intelligence) operative, Agnarelli was now involved with the CIA, the Zaireans and the South Africans. Between 2 and 5 June 1981 he was in Paris for talks with Colonel Pretorius, the South African military attaché. Colonel Pretorius had promised military aid to COMIRA and a first shipment of ten tons, which was to include 60mm mortars, RPG-7 anti-tank rockets, grenades and 800 kilogrammes of plastic explosive, plus communications equipment and 100 individual combat kits. These were later taken by a C-130 South African Air Force transport plane to Franceville, Gabon.* The plane then changed course for Zaire and finally parachuted its cargo into Angola, near Mount Quibokolo.

Agnarelli now reported to Mobutu's personal advisor that COMIRA had 4,200 men under arms on three fronts: 1,500 in southern Zaire province, north of Luanda, 1,200 in the north-east near the Cuango river and 1,500 in central Malanje province. The advisor reported to Mobutu, 'on the diplomatic front Zaire would not of course be able to support COMIRA and would even have to declare that COMIRA activities on our territory could not be tolerated'.

*Franceville, President Bongo's home town deep in the Gabon jungle, has an international airport built with South African aid. It has been used for Rhodesian sanctions breaking, mercenary airlifts and illegal arms running ever since the early 1970s when it was completed.

In July 1981 a meeting, involving Angolan exiles, the US, South African military and intelligence staff and a Gabon official, was organized at the Kitona air base. The report received by Mobutu, and leaked to the press, stated that the meeting was a follow-up to a visit to the US by Zairean officials. The Americans had asked Zaire to encourage all Angolan opposition forces to join together and draw up a military plan. At the meeting were three UNITA members, four COMIRA representatives, two South Africans, three Zairean officials, one Gabonese and two American government representatives, one of whom was described as a member of the CIA's staff in Kinshasa. Three main points were on the agenda: change of regime in Angola, independence for Cabinda, and political and military organization of the four Angolan opposition movements in a special intervention force.

Tempo magazine of Mozambique quoted the Zairean documents, 'The Americans spoke first and outlined their plan to place Jonas Savimbi as the head of state of Angola'. A separate Zairean document gave an account of a meeting between the US envoy and Savimbi:

> Although the meeting was secret the American position was clear: the US is negotiating secretly with a number of other countries to find a global solution and end the Cuban and Soviet presence in Angola. China is one of those countries. But first there must be a change in the country's current rulers. For this, there will have to be a special military intervention force which will intervene early on, directly in the Angolan capital. This has been guaranteed by the US representative who took part in the Kitona meeting. Mr Jonas Savimbi, future president of the Republic of Angola, confirmed this in an exchange between the two leaders in the presence of your special counsellor. The US envoy requested your special counsellor to facilitate the transit of all leaders of UNITA, COMIRA and FLEC as well as of Mr Armand Iannarrelli.

A further document drawn up for Mobutu by the special counsellor stated:

> As for the Special Military Intervention Force, South Africa is responsible for putting it together and is to present military plans in Geneva, but unfortunately we will not have access to these documents so we shall have to raise our antennae in the US. According to our sources, it seems the Americans and South Africans have already infiltrated themselves directly and indirectly into Angola. They have their double agents highly placed among the MPLA.

The Ben-Guerir military base in Morocco was also to be involved, as well as Gabon's airfields.

In December 1981 Portugal's *Diario de Lisboa* gained access to documents in Rabat, Morocco and Brussels. It reported a string of 15 COMIRA camps along the Zaire/Angola border and air-lifting of mercenaries from Egypt,

Morocco, Israel and F.R.G. (Federal Republic of Germany) through Gabon to Zaire.

From September 1981 through to mid 1982 armed gangs conducted a campaign of terror against civilians in Luanda. Their targets were both whites and blacks, foreigners and Angolans. Foreign technicians from both capitalist and socialist countries were assaulted and murdered in their homes; Angolan white doctors were attacked. There were also cases of violent sexual assault. In the Luanda *musseques* the armed gangs singled out school teachers and students going home from night school. This upsurge of violence coincided with the reported increase in CIA covert operations.

Terror from the South

Although their regular forces had been defeated in the 1976 Angola campaign, the South African generals knew that the survival of the white laager hinged on undermining SWAPO and the ANC, both of which needed MPLA in Angola. An undeclared war would now have to be waged against the People's Republic.

Vorster's resignation put Pieter Botha (who had been Defence Minister since 1972) into power, and he immediately set about militarizing the power structures in Pretoria.

There had been joint military and intelligence operations between the Portuguese and South Africans from 1970, but 1972 marked a qualitative change in Pretoria's policies to defend racism in Southern Africa. That year a serious start was made to create black counter-revolutionary forces for Namibia and South Africa, and black insurgency against independent African states, of which Zambia was then the main target.

According to trial evidence in Lusaka in 1976 Zambians had received training from the SADF in 1972. Unconfirmed reports allege that Zambians were also trained with UNITA by the Portuguese inside colonial Angola. Certainly Savimbi refers to UNITA's support for anti-Kaunda elements in 1972. According to the *Windhoek Advertiser*, in 1975, Adamson Mushala, one of the leaders of the Mushala gang operating against economic and military targets in north-western Zambia, spent months with the SADF in Namibia. They skirmished with Zambian forces, blew a bridge, and like UNITA, kept the SADF informed of SWAPO's movements.

In Namibia, groups of South African blacks were being trained for operations there and in Smith's Rhodesia. By 1974-75 the SADF journal *Paratus* reported that 988 black South Africans were receiving basic training in handling firearms while a group of 246 were being schooled in 'anti-terrorist activities'.

By the time of the March 1976 retreat, the SADF had several secret training camps for blacks. More were now set up for those Angolans fleeing into Namibia who were convinced that they would be murdered by the MPLA and the Cubans, just as they had murdered members of the MPLA. North of the border, the Angolans were disarmed and escorted into Namibia by the South African troops. Some were taken to South Africa for advanced training, others were placed in bush camps in northern Namibia. Male refugees were taken from their families and forced to join the military structure. During the next six years, kidnapped Angolan civilians were also thrust into this force.

In 1974 Africans were receiving combat training at the South African Army Bantu Training Centre (now renamed 21 Battalion), at Lenz, 30 kilometres from Johannesburg. By 1976 special training was being given to blacks at Dukunduku, near Durban, at Maleoskop counter-insurgency base, and at the Reconnaissance Commandos base, all in South Africa. Rank and file troops from Angola were concentrated at Picapau and Bagani, Namibia.

Commanding the black forces amassed to destabilize Angola were white officers, SADF regulars and foreign mercenaries. By 1982 foreign mercenary units were deployed inside Kunene province to occupy large areas of Angola.

Escalation in South Africa's Undeclared War Against Angola

Colonel Iko Carreira dates the FAPLA's effective occupation of the Kunene border with Namibia to 1 and 2 April, 1976. The Angolan Defence Ministry records consequently date South Africa's aggression against the People's Republic following its withdrawal into Namibia from 3 April. On that day, two SAAF planes flew into Angola at Ruacana. By 18 April three other acts of provocation were recorded in Kunene, and SADF soldiers had positioned artillery and opened fire on Angolan frontier units, wounding a FAPLA soldier.

In an interview in May, Carreira said,

> Nobody is talking about the war but the fact is the war is still going on. Our combatants are still dying in the struggle against the remains of the puppet forces. They are receiving South Africa's support; and the position of some neighbouring countries is still not very clear. We have got to understand that our opting for socialism has brought us into confrontation with imperialism, and imperialism is going to use every possible means of fighting us, from sabotage to the supplying of small armed groups to try to create instability amongst our people.

That month, Operation Ferro ('Iron') was launched by the FAPLA into the Lungue-Bongo valley, where UNITA had co-operated with the Portuguese to form a barrier against the westwards movement of MPLA guerrillas in their anti-colonial war.

During the second part of the sweep, the FAPLA intercepted a major UNITA supply column moving northwards from SADF bases in Namibia to UNITA soldiers hiding out in the highlands. With the weapons supplied by the SADF they were to have begun major guerrilla action in the centre of the country. Documents captured with the supply column enabled the FAPLA to move on and neutralize UNITA bases at Tempué, Sandona and Cangumbe, all in the 'traditional' UNITA-Portuguese army area of operations. The column's first base inside Angola had been at Savate, Kuando Kubango.

In subsequent operations by the FAPLA during June and July, more than 3,500 UNITA were sent back to their homes and 18 bases were dismantled. In Kunene province, a lightning two day operation (code-named Vakulukuta for the UNITA politician from the province) destroyed two UNITA camps. During the FAPLA attack on the UNITA base, the South Africans launched a diversionary movement with a company of SADF infantry and Panhard armoured vehicles.

In August 1976, 'Operation Kwenha', launched by joint FAPLA-FAR forces, swept South African troops, the UNITA, the FNLA and the ELP out of Kuando Kubango province where they had been since March. These groups moved 50 kilometres south of the Angola-Namibia border to Pica-Pau near Cuangar. SADF troops had been training groups of Angolans inside Kuando Kubango province and ferrying men, weapons and supplies via Unimog truck from SADF bases in Namibia to the Kuando Kubango bush camps, around Mavinga, Luengue, Cunjamba, Gunga and Baixa Longe. Minefields had been laid to protect the SADF occupied area.

Prisoners taken by the FAPLA-FAR during 'Operation Kwenha' reported that Pica-Pau came under the direct command of the SADF colonel commanding the giant SADF base at Runtu. They said there were more than 200 field housing units at Pica-Pau for SADF officers; and that two majors, seven captains and more than 30 lieutenants, and a number of NCOs (mostly Angolans) were there. The prisoners also stated that the SADF's operations inside Kuando Kubango had been stepped up from July 1976. Freshly trained groups of 150 counter-revolutionaries under the command of white South African officers had entered Angola by Unimog truck from Pica-Pau, and set up base camp at Luengue.

As the FAPLA advanced south, Angolan government forces had intercepted radio communications from Runtu command ordering the immediate retreat of the SADF-led counter-revolutionary groups to the Pica-Pau base. Two enemy groups were captured in the FAPLA ambushes, along with arms, including 48 plastic incendiary bombs, 15 crates of detonators, 22 timing devices, more than 80 anti-personnel mines, 128 c-75mm projectiles and dozens of grenades and magazines for FAL and G3 (NATO) rifles.

During 'Operation Kwenha', the SADF made repeated and unsuccessful attempts to divert the FAPLA into Kunene by advancing into the province and burning and sacking villages.

The operation was completed when the FAPLA occupied Mucusso on 29 August and captured a SADF soldier driving his Unimog truck, looking for stragglers.

By 1977 there were regular cross-border strikes in Kunene by South African ground forces, UNITA and unidentified black South African or Namibian troops. Chiede is a small village about five miles north of the border at a cross-roads of dirt tracks. On 20 February 1977 at 4.30 am a mixed force of black counter-revolutionaries attacked the village from Namibia. Fernando Penehafo was on guard in the MPLA village committee building; he threw a grenade at the attacking forces, and was taken prisoner after being stripped of his clothes. He later escaped and said that there seemed to be two components to the attacking force. Some were in civilian clothing, hungry looking and barefooted, as though they had been in the bush for some time. Others wore good uniforms and SADF brown military boots, and spoke Afrikaans to each other.

The cross-border strikes were aimed at clearing the extreme south of Kunene and creating a no-man's-land.

UNITA troops had specific orders to attack the civilian population. One old woman from the village of Kayolua near Chiede reported, 'They come from house to house forcing us to give them food. If we refuse or haven't anything to give they kill us with their guns'. She counted off the names of nine neighbours killed in this way, eight men and a woman.

The Ovamboland Bantustan Radio Oshakati bombarded Angola with propaganda. 'They tell us everything in Angola is destroyed by FAPLA and the Cubans.' Sitilifa Tamukwaya, an Angolan mine-worker, in Namibia at this time: 'We heard very little news about what was really going on in Angola there. Anyone caught listening to Angolan national radio is punished and persecuted.' Vaya Komueno from the Tsumeb copper mines, another Angolan continued, 'We know they are telling us lies to keep us away from home and make us work forever in their wretched mines. They tell us the Cubans and the MPLA are wrecking everything, don't go home.'

Inocencio Parente Vieira was captured by the FAPLA on 26 September 1977 in Savate, Kuando Kubango. He had been recruited by UNITA on 15 April 1975 in Bié. He received a summary military training at UNITA's Macive base, 30 kilometres from Cangumbe on the Benguela railway, and after his 45-day course was promoted to sergeant and sent to Luso. Later he was transferred to Lobito and from there retreated on 7 February 1976 to Lubango, Menongue and Namibia. After crossing the border at Calai he was taken to the SADF Runtu base. Contact with Angolan civilian refugees was forbidden, and six days later, under the escort of SADF armoured cars, Vieira and other Angolans were returned to their country to engage in counter-revolutionary military operations.

Among the Angolans trouble broke out almost at once. A Zairean lieutenant in the party abandoned the group, along with three others. The remainder moved up along the Kubango river valley. Shortly afterwards the captain in command was murdered by a fellow UNITA officer, in a bid for leadership of the small force. From September 1976 until January 1977 it remained in the Quatire-Luatuta area and then moved back into Namibia for weapons. These included Bulgarian and Chinese AK 47s, 60mm mortars, mines and explosives and new green uniforms. Once they had ferried the weapons into Kuando Kubango, their group was taken by helicopter to a nearby SADF base. It was now the end of May 1977. Vieira and others were despatched to a 106mm fieldgun training course. Firing an average of ten shells a day, they were also trained in the use of land to air missiles, 60mm mortars and ground orientation. The eight week course ended in July and the group was then dropped back into Angola to the same spot where the helicopter had picked them up. Unfortunately for their SADF command, they had been in the area barely 36 hours when the FAPLA mopping-up operations forced them to move. Stores were abandoned on the left bank of the Cuvango river in an area where Vieira knew 120 UNITA men were operating. The company was linked to the SADF Command post by field radio.

According to Vieira, there was a string of small UNITA-SADF bases along the Cueio river, from September 1976 – after 'Operation Kwenha' – until January 1977 and the next FAPLA mopping-up operation. Weapons were being moved north from Namibia via these bases to the central highlands once or more a month. Vieira had been told that 'foreign forces would be placed at strategic points'. South Africans would not be used inside Angola, but French and Canadians instead. 'French technicians were to train us to use the armoured personnel carriers, tanks and long-range fieldguns, and a powerful radio transmitter would announce the proclamation of a republic, and French air power would be used.' He testified that French, US and Chinese weapons were being supplied to UNITA. Vieira did not enlarge upon the groups' on-the-ground activities.

In Kuando Kubango province the UNITA had no tribal support. Consequently, the first task was to evoke this from the local people. At Catota in mid-1976, the hearts-and-minds campaign took the form of a massacre of more than 100 peasants and their families. According to survivors, a black Angolan commando force was air-lifted to the village by SADF helicopters. Catota had refused to co-operate with the UNITA and was wiped out in revenge.

Between 3 April and 30 July 1976 more than 17 SADF raids were launched into Kuando Kubango and prisoners were taken back to Namibia to join the counter-revolutionary forces. Survivors tell how they were kept on starvation rations in SADF camps until they promised to fight against the Angolan revolution.

South Africa's Tool: UNITA Terrorism

Terrorism against supporters of the MPLA, a feature of UNITA action from the start, was now the order of the day. Any village could be the target if it had an MPLA cell, and salt or other food supplies, a functioning school or medical post, and was selling its produce to the government. On 7 October 1976, an attack was launched at Canhala, near Vila Flor in western Huambo, where potato farmers were bringing in a record crop. Supporters of the MPLA from 1975, the people of Canhala had contributed recruits to a whole company of the FAPLA. During the 100 days of UNITA-South African occupation, the villagers had fled into the bush. Overnight 287 men, women and children were murdered in their beds; many were hacked to pieces. Armed UNITA troops were involved in the mass killings but so also were villagers from neighbouring areas who were unable to explain how they had come to participate in such an orgy of bloodshed. Later, evidence was uncovered of drugs smuggled in from Namibia and administered to peasants before the UNITA carried out this and similar terrorist attacks.

While UNITA stepped up its terrorism in the central highlands, South African weapons and explosives were used increasingly against the Benguela railway. Zambia and Zaire were patching up relations with Angola and the railway threatened Pretoria's strategy based on drawing Zaire and Zambia, as well as Rhodesia and Mozambique, into a transport network relying upon South African railways and ports. Economic ties would culminate in an African common market dominated by Pretoria.

The Benguela railway, efficiently organized, could take most of Zairean and Zambian import-export traffic, thus the southern 'white' route they had been forced to use since 1975 could be by-passed. To use this route had cost them millions of dollars in foreign exchange, as well as loss of prestige: no black African state wanted it known that they were relying on Pretoria for foreign trade. To sabotage the 1,000 kilometre Benguela line was easy, but to hit targets that would immobilize the trains for any length of time was difficult. Over the years, the explosives planted along the track became progressively more sophisticated. Pretoria's war against the railway cost Angola millions of dollars to rebuild bridges and replace wrecked locomotives and rolling stock. But the railway continued to function as best it could internally, and backed by international finance a major rebuilding plan went ahead with Zambia and Zaire to increase its capacity.

SADF Combined Operations

Meanwhile, Kunene, on the Namibia border, was increasingly the target for SADF operations. National reconstruction was progressing as the Luanda government made Kunene a national priority area. The Defence Ministry report on 'violations and provocations by South African forces stationed illegally in Namibia' for January-September 1977 states: 'the South Africans have considerably increased their actions during the period under review. These include provocations with conventional and flare mortars, machine guns and artillery, armed incursions of troops and violations of Angolan airspace.' By March, the SAAF tested Angola's air defences with the incursion of jet planes – previously only helicopters and light planes had been used. Angolan frontier posts and villages were direct targets for South African ground attacks; SADF ground units also carried out supply runs for UNITA. On 13 July 1977 four FAPLA and one Cuban soldier were killed at Calueque frontier post by artillery fire from the SADF. Angola made an official protest at the United Nations. Columns of Boer troops were held at the ready for a new offensive against Kuando Kubango, which began on 29 July 1977 when they crossed into Angola, 80 kilometres from Calai, in a major campaign which took them to Cuangar and Dirico.

The plan was to reach Mavinga, Menongue and Kuito Kuanavale and then install Jonas Savimbi and his High Command in the area, and declare Savimbi's Black African and Socialist Republic of Angola, (*Republica Negra Africana Socialista*).

The 1977 Kuando Kubango offensive resulted in South Africa and the UNITA groups under their control occupying Cuangar, Dirico, Mucusso and almost reaching Mavinga. Greater quantities of heavy weapons were used than ever before.

From now on, small FAPLA garrisons had to be stationed all along the border and supplied by air: road transport in the rainy season, when much of the province is a marsh, is impossible. In the dry season, the dirt roads are passable but extremely slow. These outposts of the People's Republic face the might of the SADF, hundreds of miles from help.

In May 1977, Makaio Temba, member of the MPLA action committee in Mavinga was taken prisoner inside Namibia. 'I had gone to Namibia to get diesel fuel. A SWAPO comrade gave me a drum of it and I was able to bring it back to Angola. Then it was all gone so I went again and brought back three. When that was finished I went back again: but that time South Africans caught me and took me prisoner.' He was tortured by being made to squat, balanced on the balls of his feet until nightfall.

> The next day they took me to one of their prisons where they only keep SWAPO and MPLA. They left me there for a month. Then they brought seven FAPLA comrades they had taken prisoner from Cuangar. They told me: 'We are going to take you to UNITA, to Savimbi. You must work with them for a year and you'll get well paid.' But I replied 'You had better just kill me here and now instead of taking me to UNITA.' But they said 'We don't kill black people, we take them to UNITA, because UNITA is your friend, they are black like you and so they won't hurt you.'

He refused to go to UNITA and was left in gaol for another month. Later he was transferred to another prison. 'We were all put in a place so cramped we could only eat and sleep sitting up. We couldn't stand because the walls and ceiling were covered with sticking out nails and you got hurt unless you sat.' Eventually he was put to carpentry work and finally called again and told to 'go back to Angola and see where the FAPLA commanders' houses were and then return to give the information.'

Temba recalls:

> When I got to Calai, I told the FAPLA commanders that the South Africans were planning to take the war there. Then I went north to Kuito. Seven FAPLA comrades are still there, in that gaol. They beat you with a rubber whip with bits of lead in it. After beating you a bit

> they stop to pour water over you and then they beat you some more. Of the seven comrades, two are from the MPLA committees and they are the worst off because the South Africans say they are teaching the people about the MPLA's policies. There in Namibia, there are many Angolans. Many comrades have died there. Some want to come back. But the UNITA and FNLA say they can only come back after 'liberating Angola'. UNITA has barracks inside the South African army camps. I heard Savimbi was there to fetch money. I heard he uses the Camoes money from colonial times to pay his troops. They say Nzau Puna is in South Africa itself, organizing weapons.

Lucio Lara of the MPLA Political Bureau toured Kuando Kubango in September 1977. At a public rally in the country town of Kuito Kuanavale, Lara said,

> The *tugas* (Portuguese) called Kuando Kubango the world's end, but is not world's end – it is a heroic land. When we face up to our problems, when we stand here looking at our small pioneers, at how they are, words are difficult. Words are useless. I am not going to talk much. But those of us who are here are going to report on Kuando Kubango's problems.

Agostinho Neto had gone to Menongue, the provincial capital, in December 1976, and there had been a concerted effort since to supply food, equipment and farming implements to the province. In Menongue Lara said

> Our people today know what socialism is all about not from books. In Kuando Kubango socialism is being conquered with weapons, with hoes, and tractors, not with words. We are fed up with words, and the whole world must know that here in the wounded province of Kuando Kubango – wounded in the life and death struggle against apartheid – we aren't just shouting down with the South African racists!
>
> Our FAPLA and People's Defence militias, our MPLA, Women's Organization and Pioneers are laying down their lives for the freedom of our people and the freedom of southern Africa.

With Lara were Mariano Puku, the Province Commissioner, and Manuel Pacavira, Minister of Agriculture, both former inmates of the Missombo political prison mounted by PIDE, nearby. 'They built these houses here in Menongue, as part of their forced labour. Although their windows have been smashed by the puppets, we shall rebuild those houses because they were built by our patriots, the prisoners of Missombo in struggle'.

Lara ended, 'We would like to invite these excellencies, the Senghors of Senegal and Boignys of Ivory Coast to come here to Kuando Kubango and dare, in front of our people, our people in struggle, give their support to the puppet traitors.'

On 11 November 1978, Angola's third anniversary of Independence, Neto gave details of joint UNITA-South African operations in southern Angola. Neto accused South Africa of 'wanting to wage a permanent undeclared war against the People's Republic of Angola, a war of hypocrisy and limited violence, designed to exhaust our energy and have us capitulate to its evil aim of dominating Africa.' Neto said SADF troops were in and out of Kunene and Kuando Kubango every day, attacking civilians and villages and supplying logistical air and ground as well as fighting support for UNITA. President Neto revealed that Savimbi had been traced to have been inside Kuando Kubango on 31 October, when the FAPLA troops had closed in. The UNITA Secretary General Nzau Puna had radioed to the SADF Runtu base for a helicopter to evacuate the party, which included South African military personnel and a French citizen of undisclosed identity. The radio message, in English, had said 'Please send chopper to evacuate us at 2100 hours Angolan time on Wednesday 1 November to take 15 including your team and the French friend. Please bring tinned food.' Angolan reconnaissance confirmed that the helicopter arrived and flew into Namibia.

Neto cited prisoners' statements, captured documents and intelligence from the FAPLA, that built up a complete picture of the South African destabilization of Angola and its use of UNITA as spies, bandits and saboteurs. At the time, however, nothing was known about the Bagani base and Buffalo battalion. Captain José Ricardo Belmundo, a black Angolan recruited into the SADF in 1976, provided this information, and gave the most detailed account so far of the training and operations of Pretoria's mixed black and white forces. Testifying in Luanda to an International Commission of Inquiry, in February 1981, he told how in 1973 while in Zaire he had been forced into the FNLA army, as had thousands of other Angolan refugees.*

After the FNLA defeat he had been forced to retreat with the SADF troops who, before reaching the Namibia border, had trained their guns on their black 'allies', disarmed them and then conducted them at gunpoint into Namibia. There they had been recruited into the SADF and made 'South African citizens'. A special battalion, the 32 Battalion, was formed with 9,000 Angolans under white officers. A US army Colonel Carpenter had been instrumental in organizing the force. In September 1976 Belmundo was selected for special training, and proceeded to Dukunduku base near Durban in South Africa, for a commando course. 'We were around 80 altogether, including five Mozambicans, two Zambians, ten Zimbabweans, 32 Angolans and the rest were white South Africans.' He was afterwards sent to Pretoria for an officers' training course that lasted until 1978. From then until the end of 1979, when he deserted, he was constantly on operations in and out of

*The build-up of CIA operations in Angola should be dated to this time when the CIA station in Kinshasa was heavily reinforced and at the same time Zaire police were arresting Angolan nationals and taking them to FNLA training camps.

Angola. Questioned on links between 32 Battalion and UNITA he said,

> We had no contacts with UNITA unless the South African army ordered it. We were a unit of the SADF and there were no UNITA or FNLA in our unit. Our main operational front was Kunene. But sometimes UNITA would request units from our Battalion to help them out of trouble in Kuando Kubango province. They do not have the same skills we do. I personally took part in such bailing out operations of UNITA.

Belmundo said two kinds of action were carried out in Kunene. There were deep reconnaissance and commando raids, when they were fitted out with special equipment and uniforms different from the standard SADF ones 'so if we were caught we should say we were UNITA and nobody could prove we were SADF troops.' The other type of action entailed large scale armoured, ground forces and artillery operations, when they wore regular SADF uniforms with the insignia of Buffalo base, Bagani.

On these raids they had instructions to kill everything that moved, burn and destroy villages and crops, sabotage water supplies and economic installations and lay waste to shops, schools and medical posts. Belmundo reported that he and many other blacks were revolted by their tasks: 'The South Africans think we are stupid and don't feel anything when we are being sent to murder our own people.' But deserting is dangerous: informers are spread through the ranks to detect disaffection, and the borders are heavily patrolled by all-white units. Black troops, unlike whites, are not allowed into the towns on furlough but 'kept in the bush in the bases', and wages were lower for them than for white mercenaries. In spite of all this, however, Belmundo reported, a few had managed to escape.

Trevor Edwards was one of the white mercenaries who left 32 Battalion after serving with it for several months in 1980. He told British television and news media that women and children were frequently wiped out in southern Angola.

> These other kids popped up and started to run . . . some of them were completely naked. They'd taken their clothes off to show they weren't armed. We started shooting. We shot this young girl. She must have been about five. And we shot her father. We shot about nine in all.

He also described torture of Angolan civilians for information:

> Sometimes we take the locals for questioning. It's rough. We just beat them, cut them, burn them. As soon as we've finished with them we kill them. We've got Angolan government soldiers and taken them back to base for proper questioning. Sometimes you have to do it to the children to make the adults talk. There was a 12-year old boy. We wanted to know what was going on. We wanted his mother to talk, so

> we tied him up like a chicken with his wrists up behind his back, strapped to his ankles. Then we played water polo with him, put him into this kind of dam and pushed him about, let him sink. Every so often we took him out. He wouldn't cry. He just wet himself. The mother didn't tell us anything. In the end we just left him in the water and he drowned.

On 32 Battalion's efforts to help UNITA, Edwards said,

> They hang around in the south-east where their tribe is and they can probably defend themselves but they can't take somewhere like Savate. We do it for them, because it improves their bargaining position . . . there were no SWAPO at Savate. It was a base for Angolan government soldiers and we knew that when we went in there.

Edwards had been involved in the SADF during 1980 and its June invasion of Angola, 'Operation Smokeshell'. This had used far more massive force than the 1975 invasion. Three brigades of infantry, armoured columns, three squadrons of Mirage fighter bombers and heavy Buccaneer bombers were deployed. There were almost 400 civilian deaths in southern Angola and 38 FAPLA soldiers were killed. But the Angolans beat off the invasion single handed without Cuban aid. It marked another turning point in the war. From now on, Pretoria had to resort to heavy air attacks to soften up the Angolans and pin down the FAPLA's crack troops deployed in the south.

When the Boer generals launched 'Operation Protea' in July 1981, more than 11,000 SADF ground troops were backed by heavy bombing from the air, which penetrated more than 300 miles north of the border. Over 90 Centurion tanks, 250 armoured cars and Saracen and Ratel armoured personnel carriers were brought in. Extended range shells were used in 120 and 155mm long range fieldguns, acquired from the US-based Space Research Corporation. 'Operation Protea' displaced 160,000 Angolans from Kunene province, in early 1983 still largely occupied by the South African army. Permanent Angolan refugee camps for the people of Kunene had been set up near Lubango with aid from the International Red Cross.

The extent of South Africa's bombing and domination of the skies has made it impossible for the FAPLA ground forces to regain occupied land. Angola has not deployed air power against the invaders, its MiG pilots are too young and inexperienced to operate against the South Africans, and it does not want to ask allies from the socialist countries to engage Pretoria.

Casualties from 1976 were more than 2,000 Angolan civilians killed in direct South African raids, and nearly 3,000 wounded, before the Protea Operation. The numbers of civilians who have been displaced, kidnapped into Namibia, or have died through starvation and lack of medical care in the occupied zones, cannot yet be calculated.

South Africa's seven year war against Angola is continuing with the tacit approval of all major Western powers who continue to call for withdrawal of

Cuba's internationalists from Angola rather than demand the unconditional retreat of the racist South African Defence Force from Angolan soil. The war against Angola has the open political and covert military support of the US administration.

The motive is clear: there must not be socialism in Angola and there must not be concrete material support to SWAPO or the ANC of South Africa. The MPLA has never, not even at the height of the 1975 invasion, concealed its policy of practical support for these movements. As the South African troops moved on Luanda in 1975 Neto and Iko Carreira, the Defence Minister, publicly pledged this assistance.

Among many messages to MPLA's First Congress in December 1977 was one from the South African Communist Party. The message said:

> You were left with so little on which to build. Yet the little you had you did not hoard. You gave comradely shelter to liberation fighters. You did all in your power morally and materially, to strengthen their resolve and capacity to intensify their struggles. And you did this with the full knowledge that you are risking further imperialist subversion and further aggressive blows against your young republic. This, dear comrades, is proletarian internationalism of the highest order. And that is why, amongst ourselves, we often speak of Angola as the Cuba of Africa.

Angola stands where Angolans declare their country belongs: in the Front Line.

Bibliography

The authors have drawn on personal observation and reporting in Angola from 1975 to 1982, and on official sources mainly in Portuguese. Among works on Angola of general interest are the following:

Books and articles

Abshire, D.M. and Samuels, M.A., eds. *Portuguese Africa: a Handbook*, London, 1969

Alves, N., *A dialéctica e a guerrilha*, Luanda, 1976

Alves, N., *Memória da longa resistência popular*, Lisbon, 1976

Andrade, M. de and Ollivier, M., *La guerre en Angola*, Paris, 1971, translated by Marga Holness, *The War in Angola*, Dar-es-Salaam, 1975

Bender, G.J., *Angola Under the Portuguese: the Myth and the Reality*, London, 1978

Bhagavan, M.R., *Angola: Prospects for Socialist Industrialisation*, Uppsala, 1980

Brieux, *Angola An III*, Paris, 1980

Burchett, W., *Southern Africa stands up*, New York, 1978

Burchett, W. and Roebuck, D., *The Whores of War: Mercenaries Today*, Harmondsworth, 1977

Caetano, M., *Depoimento*, Rio de Janeiro, 1974

Castro, A., *O sistema colonial Português em África: meados do século XX*, Lisbon, 1978

Childs, G.M., *Umbundu Kinship and Character*, London, 1949

Chomé, J., *L'ascension de Mobutu*, Paris, 1979

CIDAC, *Política agrícola e participação camponesa*, Lisbon, 1980

Clarence-Smith, W.G., 'Class structure and class struggles in Angola in the 1970s', *Journal of Southern African Studies*, 7 (1980), 109-26

Davidson, B., *In the Eye of the Storm – Angola's People*, London, 1972

Davidson, B., Slovo, J. and Wilkinson, A.R., *Southern Africa: the New Politics of Revolution*, Harmondsworth, 1976

Davis, N. 'The Angola decision of 1975: a personal memoir', *Foreign Affairs*, 57 (Fall 1978), 109-24.

Edwards, A.C., *The Ovimbundu Under Two Sovereignties: a Study of Social*

Control and Social Change among a People of Angola, London, 1962
Gabriel, C., *Angola: le tournant Africain?*, Paris, 1978
García Márquez, G., 'Operation Carlota', translated by Patrick Camiller, *New Left Review*, 101-2 (1977), 123-37
Guerra, H., *Angola: estrutura económica e classes sociais*, Luanda, 1975
Hambly, W.D., *The Ovimbundu of Angola*, Chicago, 1934
Heimer, F-W., ed. *Social Change in Angola*, Munich, 1973
IDOC, *Angola*, Rome, 1975
Ignatyev, O., *Secret Weapon in Africa*, Moscow, 1977
Jika, *Reflexões sobre a luta de libertação nacional*, Luanda, 1976
Kamitatu-Massamba, C., *Zaire: le pouvoir à la portée du peuple*, Paris, 1977
Lemarchand, R., ed. *American Policy in Southern Africa: the Stakes and the Stance*, Washington, 1978
Mandela, N., *The Struggle is My Life*, London, 1978
Marcum, J., *The Angolan Revolution*, vol. 1: *The Anatomy of an Explosion, 1950-1962*, Cambridge, Massachusetts, 1969, vol. 2: *Exile Politics and Guerrilla Warfare*, 1962-1976, Cambridge, Massachusetts, 1978
Marsh, J., *Stop the War Against Angola and Mozambique*, London, 1981
Monteiro, R.L., *A família nos musseques de Luanda*, Luanda, 1973
Morais, J., *Luta de libertação, exercito nacional e revolução*, Luanda, 1978
Movimento Democrático de Angola, *Massacres em Luanda*, Lisbon, 1974
Neto, A., *Sacred Hope*, translated by Marga Holness, Dar-es-Salaam, 1974
Pike, O., *CIA: the Pike Report*, Nottingham, 1977
Schümer, M., *Die Wirtschaft Angolas 1973-1976: Ansätze einer Entwicklungsstrategie der MPLA-Regierung*, Hamburg, 1977
Silva, P., Esteves, F. and Moreira, V., *Angola, comandos especiais contra os Cubanos*, Braga, 1978
Steenkamp, W., *Adeus Angola*, Cape Town, 1976
Stockwell, J., *In Search of Enemies: a CIA story*, New York, 1978
Valdés Vivó, R., *Angola: fin del mito de los mercenarios*, Havana, 1976
Vaz, C., ed. *Angola: rumo à independência: o governo de transição*, Luanda, 1975
Vinicius, M. and Saldanha, M.J., *Jonas Savimbi: um desafio à ditadura comunista em Angola*, Pontão-Avelar?, 1977
Wolfers, M., 'People's Republic of Angola', in Szajkowski, B., ed. *Marxist Governments: a World Survey*, vol. 1, London, 1981
Wolfers, M., ed. *Poems from Angola*, London, 1979

Documents and pamphlets

MPLA publications:

Confiscos e nacionalizações na R.P. de Angola, Luanda, 1978
Documentos-3a reunião plenária do Comité Central do MPLA, Luanda, 1976, or unofficial English translation, *Documents MPLA Central Committee*

plenary 23-29 October 1976, London, 1977
Documentos e teses ao 1 Congresso, Luanda, 1977
Informação do Bureau Político sobre a tentativa de golpe de estado de 27 de Maio de 1977, Luanda, 1977, or English translation in *Information Bulletin* 1:4, July 1977
MPLA Partido do Trabalho: estatutos e programa, Benguela, 1978
O MPLA o Partido: documentos do DEP para o 1 Congresso, Luanda, 1977
Orientações fundamentais para o desinvolvimento económico-social no periodo de 1978/80, Luanda, 1977
Orientações fundamentais para o desinvolvimento económico-social no período de 1981-1985, Luanda, 1981
Relatório do Comité Central ao 1o Congresso do MPLA, Luanda, 1977, or English translation in *MPLA First Congress: Central Committee report and theses on education*, London, 1979
Relatório do Comité Central ao 1o Congresso extraordinario do Partido, Luanda, 1981 or unofficial English translation in *1980 Angola Special Congress: report of the Central Committee of the MPLA-Workers' Party*, London, 1982
1o encontro nacional dos trabalhadores da indústria, Luanda, 1978
Sobre o movimento de rectificação algumas perguntas e respostas, Luanda, 1978

Other publications:

Organização Comunista de Angola, *Teses e resoluções da 1a conferência*, Lisbon ?, 1976
Report on the human casualties and material and other damage resulting from repeated acts of aggression by the racist regime of South Africa against the People's Republic of Angola, United Nations Security Council, S/13473, New York, 1979
United Nations Children Fund, *Country programme profile, Angola*, UNESCO, E/ICEF/P/L.2061, 1981

Newspapers and periodicals

Afrique Asie (Paris)
Angola Information (Luanda)
Boletim de Informação (Luanda)
Diário de Luanda
Expresso (Lisbon)
Financial Times (London)
Granma (Havana)
Guardian (New York)
Jornal de Angola
Morning Star (London)

New York Times
Novembro (Luanda)
People's Power (London)
Tempo (Maputo)
The Guardian (London)
Vitória Certa (Luanda)
West Africa (London)

CONTEMPORARY HISTORY/REVOLUTIONARY STRUGGLES

AQUINO DE BRAGANCA AND IMMANUEL WALLERSTEIN (EDITORS)
The African Liberation Reader: Documents of the National Liberation Movements
Vol I: The Anatomy of Colonialism
Vol II: The National Liberation Movements
Vol III: The Strategy of Liberation
Hb and Pb

EDWIN MADUNAGU
Problems of Socialism:
The Nigerian Challenge
Pb

MAI PALMBERG
The Struggle for Africa
Hb and Pb

CHRIS SEARLE
We're Building the New School!
Diary of a Teacher in Mozambique
Hb at Pb price

MAINA WA KINYATTI
Thunder from the Mountains:
Mau Mau Patriotic Songs
Hb

EDUARDO MONDLANE
The Struggle for Mozambique
Pb

BASIL DAVIDSON
No Fist is Big Enough to Hide the Sky:
The Liberation of Guinea Bissau and Cape Verde: Aspects of the African Revolution
Hb at Pb price

BARUCH HIRSON
Year of Fire, Year of Ash:
The Soweto Revolt – Roots of a Revolution?
Hb and Pb

SWAPO DEPARTMENT OF INFORMATION AND PUBLICITY
To Be Born a Nation:
The Liberation Struggle for Namibia
Pb

PEDER GOUWENIUS
Power to the People:
South Africa in Struggle: A Political History
Pb

HORST DRECHSLER
Let Us Die Fighting:
The Struggle of the Herero and Nama Against German Imperialism (1884–1915)
Hb and Pb

GILLIAN WALT AND ANGELA MELAMED (EDITORS)
Mozambique: Towards a People's Health Service
Pb

ANDRE ASTROW
Zimbabwe: A Revolution that Lost its Way?
Hb and Pb

RENE LEFORT
Ethiopia: An Heretical Revolution?
Hb and Pb

TONY AVIRGAN AND MARTHA HONEY
War in Uganda: The Legacy of Idi Amin
Hb and Pb

LABOUR STUDIES

DIANNE BOLTON
Nationalization: A Road to Socialism?
The Case of Tanzania
Pb

A.T. NZULA, I.I. POTEKHIN, A.Z. ZUSMANOVICH
Forced Labour in Colonial Africa
Hb and Pb

LITERATURE

FAARAX M.J. CAWL
Ignorance is the Enemy of Love
Pb

OTHER TITLES

A. TEMU AND B. SWAI
Historians and Africanist History: A Critique
Hb and Pb

ROBERT ARCHER AND ANTOINE BOUILLON
The South African Game:
Sport and Racism
Hb and Pb

WOMEN

RAQIYA HAJI DUALEH ABDALLA
Sisters in Affliction:
Circumcision and Infibulation of Women in Africa
Hb and Pb

CHRISTINE OBBO
African Women:
Their Struggle for Economic Independence
Pb

MARIA ROSE CUTRUFELLI
Women of Africa:
Roots of Oppression
Hb and Pb

ASMA EL DAREER
Woman, Why do you Weep?
Circumcision and Its Consequences
Hb and Pb

MIRANDA DAVIES (EDITOR)
Third World — Second Sex:
Women's Struggles and National Liberation
Hb and Pb

Zed press titles cover Africa, Asia, Latin America and the Middle East, as well as general issues affecting the Third World's relations with the rest of the world. Our Series embrace: Imperialism, Women, Political Economy, History, Labour, Voices of Struggle, Human Rights and other areas pertinent to the Third World.

You can order Zed titles direct from Zed Press, 57 Caledonian Road, London, N1 9DN, U.K.